# TRADING PAINT

## 101 GREAT NASCAR DEBATES

### JERRY BONKOWSKI

**WILEY**

John Wiley & Sons, Inc.

Published by John Wiley & Sons, Inc., Hoboken, New Jersey
Published simultaneously in Canada

Design by Forty-five Degree Design LLC

"Respecting NASCAR" on pages 292–296 © 2010. Reproduced from Yahoo! Sports with permission from Yahoo! Inc. YAHOO! and the YAHOO! logo are trademarks of YAHOO! Inc.

For general information about our other products and services, please contact our Customer Care Department within the United States at (800) 762-2974, outside the United States at (317) 572-3993 or fax (317) 572-4002.

Wiley also publishes its books in a variety of electronic formats. Some content that appears in print may not be available in electronic books. For more information about Wiley products, visit our web site at www.wiley.com.

*Library of Congress Cataloging-in-Publication Data:*

Bonkowski, Jerry, date.
   Trading paint: 101 great NASCAR debates / Jerry Bonkowski.
     p.  cm.
   Includes index.
   ISBN 978-0-470-27875-8 (pbk.)
   1. NASCAR (Association)—Miscellanea. 2. Stock car racing—United States—Miscellanea. I. Title.
   GV1033.B66  2010
   796.72—dc22

                                   2010020775

Printed in the United States of America

10  9  8  7  6  5  4  3  2

To my wife, Cyndee, who has dedicated her life to me. She has been the foundation I've built my career upon and is the rock I lean on.

To my daughters, Heather and Sarah, and my son, Bradley. You have brought me such great joy and pride as you've developed into fine young adults.

To my late mother, Stella, and her sister, my late aunt Adeline, who never stopped believing in me and always told me I could do whatever I set my mind to.

If it hadn't been for all of them, this book would never have seen the light of day. I'll be forever grateful to each of them.

# CONTENTS

## *GREEN FLAG*
### NASCAR's Best and Underrated

## RED FLAG
### NASCAR's Worst and Overrated

## YELLOW FLAG
## Things to Make You Think

# BLACK FLAG
## Things That Should Be (or Finally Were) Changed

# WHITE FLAG
## The Final Lap

# CHECKERED FLAG
## NASCAR's Future

## VICTORY LANE

# FOREWORD

By Dave Moody

There's only one thing a NASCAR fan enjoys more than stock car racing.

No, it's not beer, though that's a very close second. Looking at pretty girls? Not even close, amazingly enough. What NASCAR fans *really* enjoy is arguing, or as it's known in more genteel society: debating.

Walk into your local watering hole on a midsummer Sunday afternoon, round up a group of NASCAR fans, and ask them to tell you about the greatest stock car driver of all time. You'll hear passionate, top-of-the-lungs endorsements of King Richard Petty, David "The Silver Fox" Pearson and the great Intimidator, Dale Earnhardt. Each case will be backed by a veritable encyclopedia of supporting evidence—some of it legitimate, most of it not—designed simply to "one up" the evidence presented in support of the previous driver. There'll be more finger-pointing, chest-thumping, browbeating, and name-calling than in any three *Jerry Springer* episodes, and you'll experience a level of religious zealotry that your local al-Qaeda recruiter can only dream of.

NASCAR fans will argue about almost anything. They'll debate the merits of modern era racing versus "The Good Old Days," get red in the face over the demise of North Wilkesboro Speedway and burst a freakin' artery over the mortal sin known as the Top Thirty-Five Rule.

They'll come to blows over the relative crew-chiefing merits of Ray Evernham versus Chad Knaus, then overturn the entire verdict and start the argument over again when an old-timer rubs their noses in a healthy dose of Dale Inman.

NASCAR fans will question one another's parentage over the necessity of road course races on the Sprint Cup schedule. They'll sever a lifelong friendship after a disagreement over Cup drivers being allowed to compete in Nationwide Series races, and divorce a spouse before admitting that Richard Brickhouse's 1969 Talladega victory was tarnished in any way.

They'll argue about whether or not it's going to rain. And then when it does, they'll bicker over whether it's a full-fledged shower, or just a little sprinkle.

In the mind of the average NASCAR fan, there is only one possible point of view for every subject. If you don't like the new double-file, "shootout style" restart rule, you're an idiot. Pure and simple.

People who like the Chase for the Sprint Cup should be taken outside and flogged, with no questions asked. You say Richard Petty is campaigning Fords this season? Utter sacrilege, and I'll loosen the teeth of any man who dares to say otherwise. It's one thing to believe Dale Earnhardt Jr. hasn't been the same driver since his daddy died. But just say it out loud and see what happens . . .

Budweiser or Coors, Daytona or Talladega, Ford fan or Chevy man—NASCAR fans will fight about them all. It helps fill the considerable downtime between "Silly Season" and the Daytona 500, not to mention those insufferably long Monday-to-Thursday gaps between races.

We like to fight. Heck, we *need* to fight! It reminds us that we're still alive. So sit down here, right next to me, and tell me what you think of Kyle Busch. We've got plenty of time.

Dave Moody serves as lead turn announcer for Motor Racing Network's live radio broadcasts of NASCAR Sprint Cup, Nationwide and Camping World Truck Series racing, and as host of *Sirius Speedway*, heard weekdays from 3 to 7 p.m. ET, on Sirius NASCAR Radio, Channel 128. You can read more of his opinions each week in *Area Auto Racing News* and on his outstanding blog, www.sirius-speedway.com.

# INTRODUCTION

I couldn't have attended a better first race of the National Association for Stock Car Auto Racing—better known as NASCAR—than the Checker 500 at Phoenix International Raceway on November 6, 1988. It was there that the late Alan Kulwicki won what would be the first of his five career Cup victories, capped off by the spontaneous and celebratory debut of Kulwicki's infamous backward, or "Polish," victory lap.

It would be the first of two Polish Victory Laps that Kulwicki would perform in his life; the other came at the end of 1992, when he clinched the biggest prize in NASCAR, the Winston Cup championship. That was the biggest accomplishment and achievement of Kulwicki's career. It was sad that he was able to enjoy the fruits of his labor as champion for less than five months before he and three others were tragically killed in a plane crash just a few miles from Bristol Motor Speedway. He left us at the far-too-young age of thirty-nine.

With both of us proudly being from a Polish heritage and strong Midwest family roots—he from suburban Milwaukee and myself from the South Side of Chicago—Kulwicki and I became fast friends. He was amazingly smart (the first Cup champion to ever graduate from college), witty, and funny.

The thing I admired most about Kulwicki was the persistence he had even when facing the most difficult odds. Somehow he found a way to do what needed to be done to beat those odds. It is with that in mind that I undertook the challenge of writing *Trading Paint*. I knew it would be a lengthy and difficult task, but it was one that I had to do, the odds be damned.

Covering NASCAR and motorsports in general for *USA Today*, ESPN.com, Yahoo! Sports, and Sirius NASCAR Radio over the past quarter of a century has been, without question, the best part of my professional life. The friendships I've forged, the people I've met, the notoriety I've achieved, and the thrilling races I've attended throughout the years have by far been the most satisfying and the most humbling aspects of my career.

This book, *Trading Paint*, became a natural extension of the column of the same name that I wrote during my four and a half years as national NASCAR columnist for Yahoo! Sports. It was one of Yahoo!'s most popular features and a task that became not only a labor of love but also an interaction with readers that was more like a weekly good-natured debate between friends. You have no idea how much I looked forward to writing each edition of "Trading Paint," more than two hundred over the years.

Love it or hate it, agree with its rules and the way it does things or not, NASCAR is what it is. Although I've covered every major professional and collegiate sport in my career, I've never found a sport whose fans and participants are more zealous and passionate than NASCAR.

One thing NASCAR fans and participants love almost as much as the racing itself is good old-fashioned debating: it starts with "My driver's better than your driver" and goes from there. It was this mind-set that became the genesis for *Trading Paint*, to present 101 of the most popular and pressing questions in NASCAR and stock car racing today and to debate their merits.

Most of this book is meant to reflect modern-day NASCAR, from 1972 to the present. There are some categories, like all-time greatest driver or crew chief, that transcend the more than six decades of the sport, but for the most part I've chosen debates that reflect modern-day fans and their knowledge base of the sport and its history.

You are holding in your hands and preparing to read the result of the largest and most difficult task I've ever had in more than thirty-five years of sportswriting and sportscasting. It was an exercise in enthusiasm and optimism, in frustration and melancholy, and ultimately in patience, persistence, and pride at not only going through the experience but also finally seeing the finished product in my hands. In the end, it was all more than worth it.

As you read through the 101 debates, you may not agree with me on some of the contentions I present. That's fine. I accept that. All I ask is that you keep an open mind and respect me for my opinion as much as I respect you for yours.

This book isn't about whose opinion is right or better, it's about a mutual love for a sport that flows through our brains, our veins, and our hearts. No matter what we do for a living, we all have one very significant thing in common: we're all NASCAR fans, first and foremost. I've shared a great deal of myself in this book, and I thank you for sharing it with me by reading it.

I'll never forget that in celebration of Kulwicki's championship, his favorite song was played at the NASCAR awards banquet: Frank Sinatra's "My Way." I've done this book in the same fashion: my way. I hope you enjoy it!

# GREEN FLAG

## NASCAR's Best and Underrated

# Who Was the Greatest NASCAR Driver Ever?

This debate always gets passionate fans going, with typically mild-mannered individuals turning into raving, obsessed fanatics if someone dares to challenge the superiority of the guy they so proudly call "their" driver. Think of a 140-pound, Woody Allen–looking dweeb who lives and breathes Kasey Kahne suddenly getting a surge of testosterone, puffing out his chest while forgetting common sense, and stupidly trying to take on a hulking, 300-pound redneck who takes great offense if you say anything bad about Dale Earnhardt Jr.

Then watch the punched-out Woody Allen–esque fan suddenly wind up doing a frightening, almost cartoonlike barrel roll through the air like the great Rusty Wallace did more than a few times during his career at places like Talladega Superspeedway.

Mamas, don't let your babies grow up to be cowboys, and make sure you teach 'em never to diss Dale Junior—but I digress.

In more than sixty years of racing, NASCAR has had more than its share of greats, the most notable being The King, Richard Petty, and the equally colorfully nicknamed Intimidator, the late Dale Earnhardt.

Both Petty and Earnhardt share a record that will most likely never be broken in Cup racing, each having won seven championships. Even Jeff Gordon, a guy who is just as talented as Petty and Earnhardt, will probably never make it to seven titles in the years of racing he has remaining. Say what you want about Gordon but if a gifted driver like him can't tie or break the joint Petty-Earnhardt mark, it's doubtful that anyone else will ever do so. Remember, Gordon has now gone eight seasons since his last championship in 2001.

Of the other drivers besides Gordon who are currently active, Jimmie Johnson—who is tied with Gordon, taking home trophies in the last four championships (2006 to 2009)—arguably has the best chance of coming closest to, if not surpassing, the Petty-Earnhardt mark. Johnson is four years younger than Gordon; he turns thirty-five in September 2010 while Gordon will be thirty-nine that August. Since 2002, his first full year in Sprint Cup racing, Johnson has earned 47 wins to Gordon's 24 (through 2009), including 29 in his championship-winning reign (compared to Gordon's 9 wins in those same four seasons).

Some folks can make a case for drivers like David Pearson (105 wins), Bobby Allison and Darrell Waltrip (both with 84 wins), Cale Yarborough (83 wins), and even Gordon (82 wins heading into 2010) as being the best of the best.

(Sorry, and I know their fans will take offense, but guys like Sterling "Swervin'" Marlin and Derrike Cope simply just don't make the cut when picking NASCAR's numero uno.)

For my money, there are really only two drivers who can be considered for the title of NASCAR's best driver ever: Petty and Earnhardt. You can make all the counterarguments you want, but their respective numbers and careers don't lie.

Of Petty's 200 wins, 126 came on tracks that are no longer part of the modern-day NASCAR scene. Most prominent are his 15 wins each, the most at any track he ever raced on, at the now-shut North Wilkesboro Speedway in North Carolina and at the still-active Martinsville Speedway in Virginia. Petty's other great track closed at the end of 2002, but not before. The King earned 11 career wins at North Carolina Speedway, more commonly known as Rockingham or simply. "The Rock."

Petty also was the king of short and intermediate tracks that had much shorter tenures on the NASCAR schedule and are no longer part of the Cup slate: Nashville, Tennessee (9 wins); Maryville, Tennessee, and Greenville, South Carolina (6 wins each); Riverside, California, South Boston, Virginia, and Hickory, North Carolina (5 wins each); and Weaverville and Winston-Salem, North Carolina (4 wins each).

A large reason for Petty's incredible success was that he had the best organization on the Cup level pretty much from 1962 until 1979, when he earned the last of his seven championships. As the saying goes, The King got while the gettin' was good.

Petty retired at the age of fifty-five, having competed in 1,184 Cup and Grand National (the predecessor to Cup) competitions, ending with a winning percentage of 16.9 percent—the fourth highest in NASCAR history and by far the highest percentage of the sport's most successful drivers.

By the time Petty hung up his driver's suit for good at the end of the 1992 season, his retirement was long overdue. He spent the last eight seasons of his illustrious career failing to reach victory lane even once, averaged less than two top-five finishes per year and had just one top-ten season finish (eighth in 1987) in that final eight-year stretch of his thirty-five-year racing career.

Earnhardt, in contrast, competed in fewer than half the races Petty did—676, to be exact. He won 76, which made him fifth on NASCAR's all-time list. His overall winning percentage is 11.2 percent, which may seem paltry at first. But Earnhardt also competed more often—and overall was more successful—on bigger, longer, and faster tracks than Petty did during his career.

The King earned 10 career wins at Daytona International Speedway while Earnhardt had only 3 (including just one Daytona 500 to Petty's 6), but Earnhardt was more successful overall when it came to racing at places acknowledged by most experts as some of the toughest tracks in the sport: Talladega (10 wins to Petty's 2), Atlanta (9 to 6), Bristol (9 to 3) and Darlington (9 to 3).

Earnhardt was killed in February 2001 on the final lap of the season-opening Daytona 500, less than two and a half months before he would have turned fifty years old. Even though many (who were obviously not Earnhardt fans) considered him washed-up at that point, having won his last championship in 1994, let's not forget that Earnhardt still finished second to champ Bobby Labonte in 2000. This unquestionably proved that there was still a lot of high-powered fuel left in Earnhardt's tank—and he definitely still had what it took to be successful at the highest level of stock car racing.

Just prior to his fatal crash, Earnhardt told reporters he planned to race for at least another two or three years while also guiding and shepherding the career of an up-and-coming driver: his son, Dale

Earnhardt Jr. Although the elder Earnhardt would most likely never approach the success he enjoyed during the early part of his career, he might have added another 6 or more wins to his overall total, had it not been for his tragic wreck and resulting death. Given what he did in 2000 (2 wins, 13 top fives, and 24 top tens) he obviously had enough left in him to win an eighth championship, which could have put him above Petty once and for all in most championships.

There's no disputing how good Petty was in his day. But he was the big fish in the little pond, competing with teams that usually were not as well funded or did not have the same type of win-capable equipment that Petty and the fabled blue and white No. 43 STP Dodge-cum-Pontiac had.

Earnhardt, in contrast, didn't earn his fearsome nickname The Intimidator by happenstance or by having bad breath. Just his looming close in a rearview mirror was often enough to strike fear in a competitor, causing that opponent to get nervous and even rattled enough to allow Earnhardt to get by, either by choice or by Earnhardt's weapon of choice: the bumper on his menacingly all-black No. 3 Chevrolet. Earnhardt's bumper wasn't called "the chrome horn" for nothing; either you moved or he'd move you, plain and simple.

What's more, Earnhardt competed in an era when NASCAR had much greater parity and more popularity than in Petty's days. It was tougher for Earnhardt to win races and championships than it was for Petty, which made those wins and championships much more meaningful overall than Petty's.

The bottom line is that Earnhardt was the greatest driver NASCAR has ever seen. He may not have won as many races as Petty or Pearson, Allison, Yarborough, and Waltrip—and eventually he lost his fifth-place title on the all-time wins list to Gordon—but he raced in a much more competitive and pressure-filled era than Petty did.

Don't believe me? In the fourteen full seasons (1979 to 1992) in which they went head-to-head in Cup competition, Earnhardt won his first five Cup championships and 53 races. In that same period, Petty won just one championship and 20 races. 'Nuff said.

## Who Does Richard Petty Think Is the Greatest Driver Ever?

It's not jealousy over all the money Petty's rival, Dale Earnhardt, earned during his career: $42 million to Petty's $8.5 million. It's not Earnhardt's lasting fame, nor is it a case of lingering bitterness that someone actually had the audacity to tie Petty's record for most championships.

Richard Petty insists none of these things play into his pick for the greatest driver ever. According to Petty's assessment, while there's no doubt the late Dale Earnhardt was a great driver, he definitely wasn't the greatest. So who does Petty pick for the best Cup driver of all time (himself not included, of course)? "David Pearson to me was a lot better race car driver than Earnhardt," Petty said. "That's my first pick."

Although a distant second to Petty on NASCAR's all-time wins list with 105 wins compared to Petty's 200 triumphs, Pearson was the man . . . or perhaps we should call him "The King's Man."

"Pearson could run any kind of racetrack and win any time—on a road course, short track, dirt track, superspeedway—effortlessly," Petty said. "He was just a pure, natural deal with no emotions or any of that stuff.

"Pearson was a whole lot like Earnhardt in that he'd figure out a way to beat you. He was a little smarter than Earnhardt. Earnhardt drove hard to make his deal work better, while Pearson drove hard and also thought hard. So if he couldn't outrun you physically, mentally he'd work on your mind. He was just really good."

Another thing that worked against Pearson is the fact that he was, for most of his career, essentially a part-time driver, often running just half of a yearly season schedule, or even fewer races than that. In fact, he competed "full-time" in just three seasons—and even those weren't full seasons, with Pearson missing either two or three races over the course of the year.

What's more, Pearson had an incredible 18.3 percent winning percentage, winning 105 of his 574 career starts. Equally amazing, he totaled 301 top-five finishes (including his wins) in that 574-race skein, meaning he finished in the top five in over 52 percent of his starts.

Had Pearson not been a part-time driver, there's no question his career victory tally would have been greater—and Petty's total likely would not have been as high. Ditto for championships: if Pearson had run more often, he probably would have added to his three career Cup titles, most likely at Petty's expense.

Pearson, whose overall win total included outstanding individual seasons of 16, 15, 11 (for two seasons), and 10 wins over the course of his career, might have closed the gap on Petty in total wins if he had reached the Cup level a bit earlier. Petty made his debut at NASCAR's highest level at age twenty, while Pearson didn't appear on the scene until he was twenty-five.

By comparison, Earnhardt, who didn't go full-time at the Cup level until age twenty-eight, won just 76 races in his career, which ended tragically when he was killed on the final lap of the 2001 season-opening Daytona 500, a race that had vexed him for so many years before he finally won his first (and only) Daytona in 1998.

"You had [Cale] Yarborough that won 80-some races, [Bobby] Allison won 80-some races, [David] Pearson won a hundred-some races, that's your core right there, and I raced against them all," Petty said. "That was before Earnhardt came in and won his 70-some races."

Had Earnhardt started at age twenty as Petty did, who knows how many more wins he could have added to his career total. Still, that doesn't make Petty want to change his assessment of Earnhardt.

"He was of a different era," Petty said. "So you can't compare eras versus eras. I can't really compare Earnhardt with those guys [Pearson, Allison, Yarborough, and so on] because they didn't run together. They came at different times under different circumstances."

While Petty and Earnhardt did go head-to-head for fourteen full seasons, one must remember that Petty had already logged nineteen full seasons (plus two part-time campaigns at the beginning of his career) on the Cup circuit before Earnhardt got his first full-time ride in 1979. In a sense, when Earnhardt took that first ride, one man was beginning the downward road in his career, while the other was just beginning his ride upward.

The fact that Pearson took No. 1 on Petty's personal best list doesn't mean Earnhardt automatically took No. 2. "You have to figure that I ran against a bunch of good people, Yarborough, Allison, all those guys," Petty explained. "Those guys were unreal because the equipment they drove and the circumstances they were under were extremely difficult compared to the later crowds that came through.

"If you look at that crowd and put all the wins together, those guys were the ones that had all the wins and were running each other at the same time. They didn't come in there one and out."

Petty refuses to say where he'd ultimately put Earnhardt on his own list of best drivers. Part of the reason for that, in a sense, was Earnhardt was born too late to be considered among the best of the best.

Still, Petty would have loved to have gone mano a mano with The Intimidator when both were in their racing primes. "Earnhardt would have been pretty good," Petty said. "He was old-school enough to manhandle race cars and be able to drive in that era. A lot of guys could have never driven in that era because of the [lack of] power steering and the way the cars are downforced. We didn't have any of that kind of stuff.

"Earnhardt was just a natural driver. What he did, he didn't have to work at. He was just absorbed with just having fun, doing the deal. There's a lot of good drivers out there, but there's very few racers.

"Guys like Pearson, Allison, and Yarborough were racers. They weren't just only good drivers, they were racers because they won races and knew how to win races—and Earnhardt was one of those."

Petty-speak translated: Earnhardt was a good racer—just not quite as good as Pearson or Petty himself.

## Who Are the Most Beloved NASCAR Drivers of All Time?

This question is as loaded as you're going to find. The answer to it can come from several directions, including fans, fellow drivers, and the media. One man's favorite driver is another's most hated. To make such a selection even more difficult, there are sixty-plus years of drivers who have come and gone through the Grand National Cup Series.

So many drivers will be covered in this book that it would be somewhat redundant to go into great detail here, so I'll simply list my five most loved drivers, taking into account many different elements, such as judging criteria, fan base, rivalries between drivers, and how the media perceives certain drivers. By comparison, my list of most hated drivers is in the Red Flag section. Ironically, three drivers made *both* lists, which just goes to show how fickle popularity or hatred in NASCAR can be.

Here are my picks:

1. **Richard Petty.** It's hard to find anyone who doesn't love The King; there may be some who hate him for dominating the racing scene, having won so many races (200) and championships (7). Even now, nearly twenty years after he retired as a driver, Petty still commands the greatest amount of respect from fans, current drivers, and just about everyone else in the NASCAR Nation. The soft-spoken seventy-three-year-old Southern gentleman is the greatest living ambassador for the sport, a role he will hopefully be able to continue in for many more years.

2. **Dale Earnhardt Sr.** As much as the fans of other drivers (most notably Jeff Gordon's fans) hated him, no other driver of his era, other than Petty, commanded the type of respect that Earnhardt received. He was The Intimidator both on and off the racetrack, making drivers fearful of what he'd do behind the wheel, as well as the driver who wielded the most influence with NASCAR chairman Bill France Jr. When Petty began to slow down, literally and figuratively, in the waning years of his racing career, it was on Earnhardt's back and persona that NASCAR built its future, using the mustachioed man in black as a symbol that attracted millions of new fans and helped to take stock-car racing from a primarily Southeast-based sport to one that stretched from Loudon (New Hampshire) to Los Angeles.

3. **Dale Earnhardt Jr.** Junior has proven the old saying that the apple doesn't fall far from the tree. He's been NASCAR's most popular driver for the last seven years and will likely continue

in that role for several more years. Junior not only picked up countless fans who used to cheer for his late father after Dale Sr.'s tragic death at Daytona in 2001, he also gained his own fan base of millions worldwide. Is it any wonder that his Junior Nation is arguably one of the largest fan bases in all professional sports? Even though he hasn't had the kind of on-track success that his late father enjoyed, there's no question that Junior shares almost the same iconic position in the sport that Dale Sr. did.

4. **Jeff Gordon.** The all-American-boy antithesis of the late Dale Earnhardt Sr., Gordon was Mr. Clean in the white hat to Earnhardt's man-in-black persona. If you were not an Earnhardt fan, you typically cheered for his chief rival, which was Gordon. And even though he hasn't won a championship since 2001, Gordon is still arguably the second most popular driver in the sport, after Dale Jr.

5. **Darrell Waltrip.** Once one of the most hated drivers in the sport, Waltrip has become one of the most beloved characters due to his presence on Fox TV and SpeedTV telecasts. His "Boogity, boogity, boogity, let's go racin', boys" call when the green flag drops has become almost legendary, a true trademark for the former three-time-champion-turned-broadcaster. With an aw-shucks, down-home personality, Waltrip has endeared himself to countless viewers and fans with his homespun tales of NASCAR days gone by as well as his unique take on racing today. He is quite a departure from what he once was considered to be.

# Who Was the Best Crew Chief Ever in NASCAR?

Chad Knaus, Ray Evernham, Robbie Loomis, Andy Petree, Kirk Shelmerdine, Gary Nelson, Tim Brewer, Jeff Hammond, Smokey Yunick, Greg Zipadelli, Harry Hyde, Bud Moore—some of these guys

were good, some were great, but who was the best crew chief to ever
sit atop a Cup pit box?

a. Knaus
b. Shelmerdine
c. Evernham
d. None of the above

The answer, without equivocation, is *d*. The man who falls into that
category is not on the list of choices because so many fans and media
members seem to have forgotten about him and the accomplishments
he achieved during his stellar career. No one, absolutely no one, even
comes close to the kind of superiority he displayed in car preparation,
pit strategy, and plain old-fashioned savviness that he deserves his own
special place in NASCAR history.

Evernham? From the last race of 1992 through the 1999 season,
he led Jeff Gordon to 47 career wins and three Cup championships
in four years (1995, 1997–1998). He was even voted the greatest crew
chief of all time in a 2006 vote of NASCAR media members.

Shelmerdine? He led the late Dale Earnhardt Sr. to four of his
seven career championships—in a six-year period, no less (1986–1987
and 1990–1991), as well as 46 wins. But is he the best crew chief?

Knaus? Coming into 2010, he had led Jimmie Johnson to a record
four consecutive Sprint Cup championships and nearly 50 race wins.
Surely, Knaus is the greatest then, right?

None of them come close to the best. The best crew chief has credentials that no one can match. Don't believe me? How about these
two very key statistics:

- Eight, yes, *eight*, NASCAR Grand National Winston Cup championships to his credit, including all seven of Richard Petty's
  championships (1964, 1967, 1971, 1972, 1974, 1975, and 1979)
  and the first of two Cup titles by Terry Labonte (1984). No other
  crew chief has ever won more than four championships.
- Leading Petty to 192 of his 200 career wins and Labonte to 4
  other trips to victory lane. By comparison, Evernham led Gordon
  to just 47 wins, Shelmerdine directed Earnhardt to 46 wins, and

by the end of 2009, Knaus had shepherded Johnson to victory lane 47 times from atop the pit box (or from home when he was under suspension for various rule infractions).

Old-time stock-car racing fans still revere the name of Dale Inman. Even today, they speak with reverence at how Inman was without peer atop the pit box. Unfortunately, because most of his success was more than three decades ago, the fans who have come into the sport since then were deprived of the pleasure and joy of watching Inman at work. And because he has always been a relatively low-key, quiet sort who was not wont to toot his own horn, Inman has (through no fault of his own) rarely received the recognition he so richly deserved, particularly among modern-day fans and media.

King Richard was forty-two years old when he won his seventh title, but many thought that he still had enough left in his gas tank, so to speak, to win another one or two Cup championships. I firmly believe that had he not "retired" shortly after Petty's last Cup title in 1979—and then gotten so antsy almost immediately after deciding to take it easy that he subsequently joined Hendrick Motorsports—that Inman would indeed have led Petty to at least one or two more Cup championships. Don't believe me?

Once Inman left the Petty Enterprises fold—he did return as a consultant in 1986 (but never again as a crew chief), a role he still holds today—Richard Petty would go on to win just 8 more races in the next five seasons (1980–1984), but he had a big fat 0 in the wins column in the final eight seasons of his racing career (1985–1992). Coincidence? Without Inman calling the signals, I think not.

## Who Is the Most Underrated Crew Chief in NASCAR Today?

Let's face it, being a crew chief at the level of the Sprint Cup Series is not exactly a ringing endorsement for job security. Go down the list of crew chiefs today, and you'll find few who have been in their positions (or with the same driver) for more than three or four years.

Being a crew chief in NASCAR is much like being a manager in major league baseball. When things go right, you get all the praise. But when things go wrong and continue to spiral downward, you're typically the first to be fired.

Given the transitory nature of the job, choosing the most underrated crew chief is difficult. Some crew chiefs bounce from team to team throughout their careers, and few of them stand out because it seems as though they're just getting warmed up when suddenly they're on to another team.

When I first started writing this book, I settled on two choices for the most underrated crew chief. My second choice, Robbie Reiser of Roush Fenway Racing, was promoted to its general manager after 2007, overseeing all five Cup teams within the organization (until the number of teams was reduced to four by NASCAR mandate in 2010). Unfortunately, that promotion also ended a ten-year tenure for Reiser as Matt Kenseth's crew chief—a relationship that stretched back to the early to mid-1990s. First they raced against each other, then they paired up to race late models back in their native Wisconsin, with Kenseth behind the wheel and Reiser atop the pit box.

Reiser and Kenseth formed a potent team that was one of the most consistent operations in Cup racing, ultimately leading to their winning the final Winston Cup championship in 2003. As much as I admire and respect Reiser, and even if he were still atop Kenseth's pit box, he'd still be just the runner-up for my choice of most underrated crew chief.

The top honor goes to Greg Zipadelli of the No. 20 Home Depot Toyota team. For ten years, Zippy wasn't just driver Tony Stewart's crew chief, he was so much more: advisor, best friend, father figure, father confessor, counselor, guiding light, voice of reason, and containment specialist (of Stewart's often volatile temper), among other things.

Besides that, he's a master tactician and strategist on race day. Stewart's talent is unquestioned, but it's unlikely that he'd have won Cup championships in 2002 and 2005 if Zippy hadn't been making the calls.

"He's like the brother I never had," Stewart said of Zipadelli, after winning his second Cup title. "He understands me but also can put me in my place when I need it. I can't see myself with anyone else as my crew chief."

Unfortunately, the pairing ended after 2008, when Stewart became half owner and driver for the renamed Stewart Haas Racing team. While Zipadelli had the option to follow Stewart, he chose to remain at Joe Gibbs Racing out of loyalty to team owner Joe Gibbs and team president J. D. Gibbs.

At the same time, Zipadelli took on just as daunting a task as trying to keep Stewart in line: he became crew chief for a much-hyped rookie driver, Joey Logano. Even though Logano failed to make the Chase for the Sprint Cup in 2009, the pairing with Zippy promises to deliver great dividends in the coming years.

From an individualistic standpoint, Zipadelli's best trait is the one thing Stewart lacked early in his Cup career: patience. Stewart has gotten less volatile as he's aged, but Zipadelli has still always been there to calm him down, reason with him, and put the driver in his place when necessary. It's the same now with Logano, only Zipadelli is also more of a mentor than he ever had to be with the headstrong Stewart.

Not one for the limelight, Zipadelli gladly let Stewart take the spotlight during their time together. He prefers to be in the background—the brains behind the operation, so to speak.

With that eschewing of attention, Zipadelli and Reiser have never really gotten the recognition they so truly deserve from the fans or the media. When their drivers did something big, like win a race or a championship, they'd quickly credit Zippy and Robbie in victory lane or in postrace press conferences. That's their time to shine. But as soon as the crowds of fans or reporters thinned out, so did the attention and the credit.

That's where it ended. That's why I picked them as the first and second most underrated crew chiefs in modern-day NASCAR, even if Reiser has moved on to other responsibilities.

There's one group of people who will always recognize Zipadelli and Reiser and give them the credit they so richly deserve: their peers. Go through the Cup garage and poll the crew chiefs and the team members on who are the best crew chiefs in the business, and Zippy's and Reiser's names will typically be the first mentioned—as well as the guy I nominate for the most overrated crew chief (in the Red Flag section).

## What Was the Most Important Race in NASCAR History?

Picking the best or the worst race in NASCAR history is an exercise in futility, at best. While the question comes from a genuine desire for an objective response, the result is unfortunately far more subjective in nature. It's like trying to pick the winning number in Powerball: there are fifty-four numbers that have equal potential to be the winner. What distinguishes the outcome is the fact that only one number can ultimately be drawn. Trying to pick the best or the worst race is like saying that chardonnay is a better or worse wine than burgundy, chablis, or zinfandel. It's a matter of the beholder's taste.

For every event you pick as the all-time number one race in the sport's history, there are thousands, if not millions, of dissenting voices from fans, the media, drivers, crew chiefs, team owners, and the like. That's why I've intentionally stayed away from having a "best race ever" debate in this book (although I do have a "worst race ever" debate in the Red Flag section for what you will see are fairly obvious reasons). Had I included a best race, the debate that would result from it would rage endlessly, and I'd be no closer to a resolution than when I started.

However, there is one debate that can be brought forth and one that few would challenge: the most *important* race in NASCAR history. I've reached this conclusion not from how a particular race was won or lost, who did the winning or losing, or who won or lost a championship in it as a result.

I looked at each of the nearly twenty-three hundred races that have gone into the Cup history book, from the first sanctioned race by NASCAR on June 19, 1949, through Jimmie Johnson's clinching his fourth consecutive championship in 2009. No one race stands out more in how it helped to shape the history, growth, and future of NASCAR than the twenty-first running of the Daytona 500 on February 18, 1979. It shows how significant just one event could be. Actually the second race of the season, preceded more than a month earlier by the official 1979 season opener on the road course at Riverside, California, the Daytona 500 was the biggest gamble NASCAR had ever undertaken: live, wire-to-wire coverage on national television of the Great American Race.

NASCAR had been featured on TV highlights and newsreel clips and had even been interspersed in pretaped segments in programs like ABC's *Wide World of Sports* over the years, but a race had never been aired live and complete from green flag to checkered flag. It all started with what many call NASCAR's "perfect storm." Had it not been for a meteorological calamity of sorts, who knows if NASCAR would have ever had another chance to strut its stuff in such a significant way.

On the night before the 1979 Daytona 500, a major icy snowstorm blanketed, and literally shut down, much of the northern half of the United States, reaching even as far south as the Carolinas. It forced millions to stay home, and many of them found little else to do but to watch TV. Because there were only three major TV networks at the time (certainly not the hundreds of cable TV stations in business today), the viewers' picks were limited. As more and more folks flipped through the trio of channels, they saw auto racing live from Daytona, a combination that immediately held the interest of millions of first-time stock car racing viewers.

CBS took a major gamble in televising the race, which almost turned to failure when rain inundated Daytona the night before and the early morning hours of race day. Still, NASCAR founder "Big Bill" France and his son, "Little Bill" Jr., were determined to get the race going, knowing perhaps more than anyone alive on the planet that day what a successful race, live on network television, would mean to the future of the sport.

When Daytona's clouds parted and the racetrack dried out, weather-marooned fans in much of the rest of the country saw one hell of a race that culminated with a last-lap crash in the third turn between the two leaders at the time (Donnie Allison and Cale Yarborough), followed by the resulting surprise of NASCAR legend Richard Petty suddenly finding himself in the lead after he had already conceded first and second place to Allison and Yarborough moments earlier, as the final lap had begun. It would be the sixth and arguably the biggest of Petty's seven career Daytona 500 victories.

Then, shortly after Petty crossed the finish line, there was what has become known in NASCAR annals simply as "the Fight," when Yarborough and Allison (who received some last-second backup from his brother Bobby) scrapped in the infield after wrecking and knocking each other not only out of any chance of reaching victory lane but, more important, completely out of the race itself. They were scored fourth and fifth in the final race standings.

When the drama finally ended, a new tradition had been born that day. NASCAR was a huge hit in the TV ratings, and it was then that stock-car racing began to grow into the multibillion-dollar enterprise that it is today. The event laid the groundwork for the current megabillion-dollar, eight-year TV contract shared by ESPN, ABC, Fox, and Turner that expires in 2014.

"I think it made a lot of fans for the sport," Yarborough said in an interview several years later. "It was one of the biggest things that ever happened to the sport. It got people's attention."

That it did—and NASCAR has been getting people's attention ever since. The story of that race, if you're interested in learning more about it, is exquisitely chronicled in *The Great American Gamble: How the 1979 Daytona 500 Gave Birth to a NASCAR Nation* by veteran NASCAR writer Joe Menzer.

# What Two NASCAR Records Will Never Be Broken?

Statistics and records are the lifeblood of any sport, from professional to the lowest amateur ranks. It's not always how you do, but what you do. You may have the greatest talent in the world, but your performance will always be measured in numbers.

The same holds true in motorsports. You can be from the United States, Japan, or Spain, yet no matter what language you speak, two measures are part of a universal language and are first and foremost in every racer's mind: speed and elapsed time. The faster and quicker you are, the better you are, plain and simple.

Although winning is the goal each time a driver straps himself into a stock car, there's another mark that every driver hopes to ultimately make: to break a record and make it his own.

Ah, records. The more you own, the more successful you're considered against your peers and the best of the best. As NASCAR progresses through its second fifty years, more records will obviously fall. It's just part of a sport's evolution. After all, as the old saying goes, records are meant to be broken.

But while almost everything else is fair game, two of NASCAR's records are pretty much out of reach, one more so than the other. It would take a driver of perhaps the most exceptional talent ever to even attempt to come close—and he'd still likely fall short, far short.

One reason is age. Drivers today are not driving as long or in as many races as their predecessors in the golden age of NASCAR racing, roughly from the late 1970s until the mid-1990s. Richard Petty didn't retire until he was fifty-five, but Jeff Gordon will be lucky if he's still in Sprint Cup competition by the time he's fifty in 2021.

Another reason some records are seemingly unbreakable is a simple numbers game: in the "good old days," some drivers competed in forty, fifty, or more races a year. By comparison, today's NASCAR limits the Sprint Cup season to thirty-six races.

Look through NASCAR's record books, and you'll see that these two are all but untouchable.

1. **Most career wins.** Richard Petty's incredible mark of 200 career wins is so far out of reach that it's in a class of its own—perhaps the only record in all sports that will never be broken. Even Babe Ruth's major league baseball home run record of 714, once considered the most unbreakable of any record, has since been shattered by both Barry Bonds and Hank Aaron.

But Petty's mark will forever stand the test of time. It doesn't make a difference who a driver is or how good he is, there's little likelihood that he could win 100 races in his career, let alone 200 like Petty.

The only driver who has come even remotely close to Petty's record is the Silver Fox, David Pearson, who is second on NASCAR's all-time wins list, with a mere 105 victories. Of course, if Pearson would have been more than a part-time driver in his career, he might have closed the gap somewhat on Petty, but even 95 more wins is more than any other driver has ever accomplished. (Darrell Waltrip and Bobby Allison are behind Petty and Pearson with a distant 84 wins apiece.)

Think about it: it's a simple mathematical question. If a driver were to earn 10 wins in every thirty-six-race season, it would take him twenty seasons to tie Petty's mark. Even if Jimmie Johnson, who won 10 races in 2007 en route to his second consecutive Nextel Cup championship, continued at that pace for the rest of his career, he'd have to go nearly sixteen more seasons to break Petty's record—and that wouldn't happen until Johnson was fifty years old. Simply put: It ain't happening.

2. **Most career championships.** This one is, at best, a "maybe" record to be broken—and a long-shot maybe, at that.

Richard Petty and the late Dale Earnhardt Sr. earned seven championships each in their careers, either in the Winston Cup or its predecessor, the Grand National Series. Only twenty-eight drivers have won Cup championships in NASCAR's sixty-year history. Some obviously won more than others, such as Petty and Earnhardt. Other greats, like Rusty Wallace, Bill Elliott, Dale Jarrett, and the late Alan Kulwicki, earned just one title each in their careers.

There are currently only two drivers that have even an outside chance of challenging the mark Petty and Earnhardt share. First is four-time champ Jeff Gordon. Of course, if you're a Gordon fan, you'd beg to differ, arguing that if it wasn't for the newfangled Chase for the Cup format, Gordon would have ran away with his fifth and sixth championships in 2004 (the first season of the

Chase) and 2007. Unfortunately, what he might have won is not the same as what he did win.

Second, and tied with Gordon, is Gordon's Hendrick Motorsports teammate Jimmie Johnson, who has won the last four Cup championships (2006–2009). After Gordon and Johnson, Tony Stewart is the only active driver who has won multiple championships, in 2002 and 2005. With Stewart approaching forty years old, it's unlikely he will win more than *maybe* two more championships, thus equaling the current mark shared by Gordon and Johnson.

So even though almost every record has a chance of being broken someday by somebody, it's doubtful that we'll see an eight-time champion in our lifetimes—if ever. After all, it's likely easier to capture the first four championships than the second four titles. Gordon is living proof of that.

# Who Does Richard Petty See as a Potential Challenge to His Career Wins and Championships Records?

Richard Petty is a realist, not a braggart. The man they call The King knows all too well that if any record in motorsports—make that *any* professional sport—will be safe in perpetuity, it's his record for career wins (200) in the Grand National/Winston Cup competition. No driver is even close to Petty's mark—and it's likely no driver ever will be.

Among active competitors, Jeff Gordon is the closest to achieving those heights—but I'm using "closest" in very loose terms. Gordon, a four-time Cup champion, still needs about 120 more wins just to tie Petty, a near-impossible task given the parity and extreme competition in NASCAR's Sprint Cup Series today.

"As far as the 200 wins, it's kind of improbable," Petty says not boastfully but matter-of-factly. One needn't look any further than mathematics and logistics to verify his assertion.

"They run 36 races a year, and . . . winning 10 races a year is going to take you a pretty good while," Petty said, trying to put an optimistic spin on the matter.

But then, much as he did in many of his 200 career wins, Petty effectively and bluntly closes the door on the competition. "They're not going to win 20 or 30 races a year, they're not even going to win 10 races a year for 20 years," said Petty, who once won 27 races in one season (1967) and 21 four years later.

Believe it or not, hunger may be another quality separating Petty from today's racers. Even if a budding superstar who could potentially win 10 races or more per year emerges fifty years from now, the money-is-everything attitude that has permeated the sport in recent years will likely prevent today's drivers from having the same kind of thirty-five-year racing tenure Petty had as an active driver at NASCAR's highest level.

And it wasn't just an appetite for success. Petty was legitimately hungry: the pride and joy of Randleman, North Carolina, was forced to race as much as he did—sometimes three or four times a week—to put food on the table and pay the bills.

Consider that Petty earned a grand total of just over $8.5 million in his three-and-a-half decade career, an average of about $244,000 per year. By comparison, today's drivers are spoiled. They earn a lot more money than Petty ever did. For example, Jimmie Johnson earned over $60 million for his four back-to-back championships from 2006 to 2009.

Petty insists that today's drivers don't have the same burning desire in their stomach. "The big deal is the guys are not going to stay in here very long," he says. "The good ones are going to come in, they're going to make so much money and they're just going to say, 'Forget it, we're out of here.'

"I don't see any of the drivers having the longevity of the crowd I came through with, the [Bobby] Allisons, [David] Pearsons and [Cale] Yarboroughs. I don't see any of that longevity coming in the future."

Petty does grant one concession: he wouldn't be surprised to see some driver, such as Gordon, tie and potentially even surpass the record seven Grand National/Winston Cup championships he shares with the late Dale Earnhardt. "The seven championships is a possibility because Earnhardt got to that," Petty said.

But there are no ifs, ands, or buts that Petty's 200-win mark will live on in infinity.

Surprisingly, Petty doesn't have the slightest twinge of regret that no one will likely make a formal challenge to best his best. "I couldn't care less," he said. "I done my thing in my time and what anybody else does beyond that—there was no records when I was doing it, or there were records but nobody paid any attention to them—it's really immaterial.

"They didn't pay anything for the records, so the records don't really mean anything from that standpoint. They probably would pay for somebody to break 'em, but they didn't pay me for setting 'em."

## Who Are Currently the Best Team Owners?

Picking the best team owners is perhaps one of the easiest tasks there is in NASCAR. Just look for the guys with the most money, sponsors, and championships.

But there's more to ranking who's the best and who isn't. There are intangibles like character, fieriness in competition, intelligence, the right people in key positions, and, in some cases, the best and most creative cheater.

There's an old adage in NASCAR: "If ya ain't cheatin', ya ain't tryin'." From the first organized races in the late 1940s on the sandy shores of Daytona Beach, Florida, the sport has had a long history of guys bending the rules, pushing the envelope, working in the gray area, or exploiting the rule book.

Some teams don't look at cheating as cheating. They look at it as a unique way to beat the competition, kind of a "Get them first before they get us" mentality. Yet at the same time, no other organized professional sport so often turns a blind eye to—if not unofficially endorses—teams that don't necessarily play fair and square. But if you look at the makeup of some current and former NASCAR officials, you get a better understanding of why such blatant rule bending, if not outright rule breaking, is tolerated.

For example, Gary Nelson, NASCAR's former director of research and development, was one of the best at the game. A former two-time Daytona 500 winning crew chief, Nelson was always looking for an edge—any edge, be it right or wrong—over the next guy.

His most famous stunt was while serving as crew chief for Darrell Waltrip. Because Cup cars at the time were weighed before a race but never after, Nelson figured out that a car would run better if it became lighter. So he placed several pounds of buckshot in a secret compartment in Waltrip's car. During parade laps, Waltrip would release the buckshot, which flowed out in a trickle so as not to be readily detected. Voilà—the car became lighter and more maneuverable, and more often than not, Waltrip would jump straight to the front of the race, or near it, in short order.

Current NASCAR vice president Robin Pemberton is another good example of someone who was an "innovator," having been penalized several times during his previous career as a crew chief for drivers such as Mark Martin (whose illegal carburetor spacing plate ultimately cost him the championship in 1990) and Rusty Wallace. However, since assuming the role of head cop in NASCAR—enforcing rules, catching and punishing rule breakers, and trying to clean up the sport to a more tolerable level than its former Wild West, everything-goes days—Pemberton has nailed some of the sport's top teams whose hands got caught in the cookie jar.

Pemberton has penalized Chad Knaus, Jimmie Johnson's crew chief, several times. Likewise, Michael Waltrip Racing was heavily penalized for a still unknown (or perhaps NASCAR doesn't want to reveal it) substance that appeared to be like jet fuel, found in the motor of Waltrip's car during Speedweeks in Daytona Beach in 2007.

Others who have been punished by Judge Pemberton include Steve Letarte (Jeff Gordon's crew chief), Robbie Reiser (Matt Kenseth's former crew chief), Tony Eury Jr. (Dale Earnhardt Jr.'s former crew chief), Todd Berrier (Kevin Harvick's former crew chief), Bob Osborne (Carl Edwards's crew chief), and Kenny Francis (Kasey Kahne's crew chief).

It's difficult to pick the best team owners, because as much as I don't want to use being "creative"—aka cheating—as a basis, it is still an element for some of the success the owners have had over the years. So as much as I'm known for being a harsh critic of cheating and of those who practice that "art," I have to play it straight when giving my picks for the best team owners in the sport. In so doing, I have ranked them using a variety of grading tools, including championships won, total race wins, strategy, initiative, quality of personnel, available budget (and sponsorship), and yes, even creativity of cheating.

And while I'm sure some readers may bring up guys like Junior Johnson, who not only won 50 races as a driver but also had another 132 wins as a team owner, or Richard Petty, who had 200 wins as a team owner (or partly shared them in his earlier years with father Lee Petty), I'm focusing solely on current owners.

Here goes with Cup racing's A-list:

1. **Rick Hendrick, Hendrick Motorsports (HMS).** Nine Cup championships (four by Jeff Gordon, four by Jimmie Johnson, and one by Terry Labonte) and nearly 190 career Cup-level wins entering the 2010 season. Without question, HMS is the standard by which all other teams are measured in today's Cup-level racing. With a driver lineup including Gordon, Johnson, Dale Earnhardt Jr., and Mark Martin, HMS is a veritable Murderers' Row of NASCAR.

2. **Joe and J. D. Gibbs, Joe Gibbs Racing.** Three Cup championships (two by Tony Stewart, one by Bobby Labonte) and more than 75 career Cup-level wins. With a driver lineup including Kyle Busch, Denny Hamlin, and superstar-in-the making Joey Logano, Joe Gibbs Racing has probably the best chance of any team owners of toppling the Hendrick regime in the coming years.

3. **Jack Roush and John Henry, Roush Fenway Racing.** Two Cup championships (one each by Matt Kenseth and Kurt Busch) and more than 115 career Cup-level wins. Roush Racing (which was renamed Roush Fenway Racing in 2007) was once considered the sad sack of Cup racing for coming so close to winning a Cup

championship only to come up short again and again (four run-ners-up and six third-place finishes between 1988, when the team started, and 2002). But that ignominious streak finally came to an end when Kenseth won the final Winston Cup title in 2003 and Busch won the first Nextel Cup championship the following year. Its five-driver lineup (the lone remaining structure of its size) of Kenseth, Carl Edwards, Greg Biffle, Jamie McMurray, and promising youngster David Ragan was cut to four teams for 2010 to meet a NASCAR mandate, with McMurray ultimately being the odd man out.

4. **Richard Childress, Richard Childress Racing (RCR).** Six Cup championships (all by the late Dale Earnhardt Sr.) and nearly 90 career Cup-level wins coming into 2010. This was once the most feared organization in the sport, thanks to Earnhardt's reputation as The Intimidator and his incredible win record of 76 career victories on the Cup scene (67 while driving for Childress). But when Earnhardt was killed on the final lap of the 2001 Daytona 500, RCR went into a major and understandable depression, both on and off the racetrack. It wasn't until Childress returned to more hands-on control in 2006 that the organization's three Cup teams began to show marked improvement. With a lineup of Kevin Harvick, Jeff Burton, and youngster Clint Bowyer, RCR looked to be in good shape for many years to come, particu-larly when those three drivers finished fourth, fifth, and sixth in the 2008 Chase. Unfortunately, 2009 was a totally different story, which included the addition of Casey Mears in the long-sought fourth RCR team. Things went into a major tailspin when no RCR driver made the Chase and Harvick announced late in the season that he likely would be leaving the organization after his contract expires after 2010.

5. TIE: **Chip Ganassi and Teresa Earnhardt, Earnhardt Ganassi Racing (formerly Dale Earnhardt Inc.), and Roger Penske, Penske Racing.** Not exactly A-list material, per se, but both organizations are almost always threatening to pull off a strong run. Very similar in several ways, including never having won a Cup championship, both have Daytona 500 victories (EGR/DEI

with Michael Waltrip in 2001 and 2003, Dale Earnhardt Jr. in 2004, and Jamie McMurray in 2010; Penske with Ryan Newman in 2008). Penske has more career Cup-level wins, more than 60, than EGR/DEI, which has nearly 25. However, EGR/DEI, which began racing on the Cup level in 1996 (first as DEI, then merging with Chip Ganassi Racing before the 2009 season), did not earn its first Cup victory until 2000 with Steve Park; Penske, which originally formed its Cup team in 1972 (and then re-formed in 1980 after a two-year hiatus), earned 36 of its wins prior to 2000. Also, both organizations have never come close to their roots. EGR/DEI has never approached the success that late founder Dale Earnhardt Sr. had with Richard Childress Racing, and Roger Penske has continually been frustrated at not being able to achieve a success similar to what he has had in the open-wheel racing world (11 championships as well as 15 Indianapolis 500 victories).

# Who Were the Five Most Important Individuals in NASCAR's Modern-Day Development?

When it comes to NASCAR's development into the multibillion-dollar monolithic enterprise that it has become, it might be easier to list those who made little or no contribution than those who helped build it. There are just so many names, faces, and talents that helped to shape the sport, from its roots on the beaches of Daytona in the late 1940s to the thirty-six-race, twenty-two-track national and even international enterprise it is today.

The sport was built on the backs of talented drivers and crew chiefs, who provided the excitement, while NASCAR officials and track owners provided the organized competition and the venues. And let's not forget one of the most important aspects of NASCAR's development into a multibillion-dollar enterprise: the infusion of hundreds of corporate sponsors and "partners" who provided necessary funding to keep both competitors and the sanctioning body fiscally alive and vibrant.

Trying to take the hundreds, if not thousands, of key individuals who helped to build NASCAR to what it is today and whittle them down to just five is an exercise in futility. No matter whom I pick, someone is going to find exception with at least one of my five picks, if not more.

I have chosen the five individuals who have played the biggest part in advancing the sport, making it more than just racing—making it a riveting, exciting spectacle and elevating its top players, particularly the drivers into modern-day heroes and even folk legends.

In order of importance and overall significance, here's my list of the top five individuals who made NASCAR what it is today:

1. **Bill France Jr.** "Big Bill" France Sr. may have conceived and founded NASCAR, but it was "Little Bill" France Jr. who took the sport and sanctioning body to unprecedented heights. In his thirty-one-year reign as NASCAR chairman, the man almost everyone called "Bill Jr." brought far-reaching changes to the sport, including the first live telecast of the Daytona 500 in 1979 (which served as a precursor to the multibillion-dollar TV package of today), the expansion of the schedule to thirty-six races, the construction of numerous new racetracks, and the purchase of existing facilities. Perhaps most important, he attracted tens of billions of dollars in corporate sponsorship support to both the sanctioning body and the teams, not only assuring their survival and prosperity but also consistently reinvesting capital for further growth and to attract millions of new fans. More than anyone else, Bill Jr. made NASCAR the place to be for drivers, team members, owners, and, most important, fans. He passed away in 2007, but his legacy will always be part of the sport, and his influence will continue to be felt for decades to come.

2. **Richard Petty.** The man known as The King was the ideal prototype for NASCAR's growth: a lean, soft-spoken, true Southern gentleman who let his performance on a racetrack do the majority of his talking for him. Petty became an icon in the sport because of what he represented in his role-model persona: he came from a strong family; lived his life by strong morals, ethics, and beliefs; raced cleanly (or at least more so

than most of his competitors); always made sure he gave plenty of time and of himself to his fans; and could drive the wheels off a race car better than anyone else, ultimately winding up with 200 career Cup-level wins, a record that will most likely never be broken. Petty blazed a trail for the likes of Dale Earnhardt, Darrell Waltrip, Cale Yarborough, David Pearson, Jeff Gordon, and so many others. And even though his team fell on hard times after he retired, his presence ranks almost as high as that of Bill France Jr., with a legacy that will also be felt for many years to come.

3. **Dale Earnhardt Sr.** The man in black, the cursed Snidely Whiplash of NASCAR, didn't earn his infamous nickname, The Intimidator, for being a nice guy. He earned it by being the most ferocious and feared competitor on any racetrack on which he wheeled a race car. Earnhardt was both loved and hated by millions of fans. Those who loved him were usually drawn by his win-at-all-costs driving style. Those who hated him usually did so because he kicked the asses of so many of their favorite drivers. But Earnhardt was an icon in other ways, too. Women loved him because he symbolized what they wanted most in a man, and men admired him because he was the prototypical man's man, the kind of guy most other men aspired to be. His popularity was so immense that when he died tragically in a last-lap crash in the 2001 Daytona 500, the subsequent mourning rivaled the grief after the death of Elvis Presley. While many wondered if NASCAR could survive such a major blow as Earnhardt's death, not only did he leave a legacy that helped the sport to continue to grow to unprecedented heights, his impact will continue to be felt as much as France's and Petty's for a long time. Perhaps the most telling aspect of Earnhardt's legacy is that now, nearly a decade after his death, he remains one of NASCAR's most popular figures. His fans just don't want to let go of his memory, which is one of the reasons for the thriving business of Earnhardt-related souvenirs and memorabilia that continues to be a multimillion-dollar cash cow for his widow, Teresa Earnhardt.

4. **T. Wayne Robertson.** As director of sports marketing for the R. J. Reynolds Tobacco Company (RJR), Robertson followed in the footsteps of his mentor, the late Ralph Seagraves, in using NASCAR as a vehicle for one of the greatest product and promotional enterprises that the business and the sports worlds have ever known. From the time that RJR entered the sport in 1972 and became the title rights sponsor for NASCAR's premier series (formerly known as the Grand National Series), Winston Cup racing became synonymous with NASCAR, and vice versa. It was impossible to tell where one ended and the other began, they were so closely linked.

When federal government edicts in the late 1960s and the early 1970s limited tobacco advertising, Seagraves and Robertson came up with the ingenious idea to market the Winston brand of cigarettes not so much through advertising but just by name and brand recognition. Because the name "Winston" was so heavily plastered around race venues, race fans, particularly those who smoked, were understandably drawn to the brand; many believed that if the company was good enough to sponsor their favorite sport, then the company's product was good enough for them to smoke. The partnership lasted through 2003, when RJR was finally forced to withdraw its multimillion-dollar sponsorship due to heightened federal government pressure and restrictions. Nextel (now Sprint) replaced Winston as the title rights holder for the Cup Series in 2004, but to this day there are many die-hard fans—and even competitors—who occasionally slip up and refer to the series as the Winston Cup Series.

Robertson was selected as one of the most powerful men in all sports several times during his career, and for good reason: he created an empire that would most likely never have been toppled if not for the government lawsuits. Robertson was tragically killed, along with five friends, in a boating accident in January 1998, just eight months before his mentor Seagraves also passed away. Some say that RJR would still be sponsoring the series today—perhaps in another fashion or with a nontobacco product of the RJR family—if Robertson had not been killed. I am inclined to agree.

5. **Rick Hendrick.** Since the time he started his first Cup team in 1984, Rick Hendrick has become one of the most prolific and successful team owners in Cup history. Heading into 2010 and throughout a span of more than twenty-five years, the drivers who have carried the Hendrick Motorsports banner have amassed nearly 190 wins (a collective average of nearly 7.2 wins per season) and nine Cup titles, including four each by Jeff Gordon and Jimmie Johnson (the other was by Terry Labonte). Even though Hendrick has stoically supported his teams and employees when they were found to be in blatant violation of NASCAR rules (for instance, Chad Knaus's numerous suspensions for cheating), there's no discounting the fact that Hendrick has not just set the bar for other teams and owners, he's raised it into a whole other zip code. No other owner currently even comes close. And when it comes to former owners, the closest comparison would be Junior Johnson, whose drivers won 132 races (including 13 by Johnson) and six championships for him. While Johnson won 50 races as a driver, he never won a championship behind the wheel. Hendrick and his operation, which employs a staggering five-hundred-plus employees, has set, holds, and will likely continue to hold the top standard against which all owners and teams will be measured for many, many years.

## What's Right with the Chase for the Sprint Cup?

Other than the so-called Car of Tomorrow, no other "innovation" during NASCAR chairman Brian France's tenure has created more controversy than the Chase for the Sprint Cup.

The Chase was originally designed to increase the emphasis on winning and to eliminate championship runs like the one in 2003 that saw eventual champ Matt Kenseth take the Winston Cup title despite earning just 1 win during the course of the entire thirty-six-race season.

France assumed his position as NASCAR's chairman in October 2003, replacing his retiring father, Bill France Jr. He wanted to create a system that drew lots of attention in NASCAR's direction, both with the fans and the media. It took nearly three months of discussion and going through countless "what if" scenarios, but France finally found a formula that he thought would work. He introduced it to the media in his first State of NASCAR preseason address in January 2004.

Although there was considerable consternation among the fans and the media during the first twenty-six races (dubbed the "regular season") about how the subsequent ten-race Chase would fare, it ended far better than anything France could have predicted or expected. For more on the events of that first year, read number 3 in the list on page 36.

As the Chase has evolved in its first six years, there has been a steady decline and erosion of the effectiveness and parity of the system. En route to four consecutive championships, Jimmie Johnson proved with his performance that drivers in essence had to have 10 nearly perfect races during the Chase to have any chance of winning the championship. One or more faltering steps early in the Chase, and a driver's chances to bounce back were all but eliminated.

A perfect example of this was in 2008, when Kyle Busch dominated the first twenty-six races, only to struggle in the first three Chase races (finishing 34th, 43rd, and 28th, respectively), which quickly made him a nonentity the rest of the way. He ultimately finished a disappointing 10th in the final standings.

I admit that I wasn't a big fan when France announced the Chase, but it quickly grew on me, especially with the way the first season played out. However, as each subsequent Chase has played out, I find myself, like so many others, questioning whether the Chase still remains a viable format. Has it already outlived its usefulness just six years into its run? So let's cut to the chase (no pun intended): Has the Chase for the Sprint Cup—known as the Chase for the Nextel Cup in its first four incarnations—proved to be good or bad for the sport and for NASCAR as the sport's overseer?

Here's how I see what's right with the Chase (I cover what's wrong with the Chase in the Red Flag section):

1. Faced with near-stifling competition from other sports, NASCAR needs a unique playoff system of its own to build excitement and to help it stand out from the more popular professional football season, the college football season, major league baseball's play-offs, and the World Series, along with the start of the basketball and hockey seasons. The Chase helps to create a buzz and a vibe for the sport at the time of year it needs it the most.

2. As the Chase has evolved, it has created two unique periods of excitement: first, during what has unofficially become known as the "Race to the Chase" (the seven races or so leading into the Chase, typically starting with the Brickyard 400 and continuing through the final Chase-qualifying race in Richmond, Virginia, in early September, where drivers on the bubble are faced with a make-or-break situation to qualify for the Chase), and then again during the actual ten-race Chase itself.

3. Although the last few Chases have not exactly created that level of excitement, many Chase supporters still hearken back to the way the first Chase to be contested played out in 2004. The championship was not decided until the final lap of the final race of the Chase, with Kurt Busch ultimately beating Jimmie Johnson by a razor-thin 8-point margin, the smallest championship-winning spread in the sport's history. Hollywood could not have written a better script if it had tried. Subsequent Chases have been judged against that inaugural edition, fair or not, and it still serves as the prime example of what all Chase battles should strive to be like.

4. The system is fair, for the most part—even if it means that some of the sport's best or most popular drivers sometimes miss out on the fun. For example, Jeff Gordon and Dale Earnhardt Jr. both missed the 2005 Chase due to poor performance during the first twenty-six races. And 2005 Chase champ Tony Stewart failed to qualify to defend his title in the 2006 Chase, ultimately settling for eleventh place, the highest a driver could finish if he didn't make the so-called playoffs. NASCAR subsequently expanded

the Chase field to twelve drivers in 2007 (with some critics saying that it was done to placate the stars who just barely missed making the top ten, like Earnhardt, Gordon, and Stewart), but the current twelve-driver field seems to have brought the sport a happy medium. However, there continues to be talk among the teams and the fans to potentially expand the Chase field once more, to fourteen or fifteen entrants. France has thus far resisted this move, and I commend him for doing so. Otherwise, you might as well open the Chase to everyone, thus negating the purpose for the format in the first place.

5. The Chase has helped to eliminate runaway championship drives. With the points reset that is done heading into the Chase, the drivers who have built huge leads during the twenty-six-race regular season—much like Jeff Gordon did in 2007—suddenly find themselves back at square one, ready to go back to battling for everything they can get. Some think this isn't fair, that a driver who has excelled in the first twenty-six races should not capriciously have the fruits of his hard work taken away when the Chase begins. But if there was no reset, how exciting would it be to see a driver build a lead of 500 or more points as the season wears on to a conclusion? The Chase was designed in part to keep things close—or at least closer than under the former system—and regardless of what Jimmie Johnson did between 2006 and 2009, it has still managed to stick pretty close to its original intent.

## What Are the Best Racetracks in NASCAR?

For more than twenty years, people have constantly asked me what I think are the best and worst racetracks in NASCAR. Generally, those questions come from newer fans who want to maximize the enjoyment and experience of attending their first Cup race in person. Going to your first race in person is almost like losing one's virginity: you want your first time to be memorable and an experience you'll never forget.

Obviously, watching a race at a track and on TV are two entirely different experiences. You might have more comfort watching at home or at a bar, but there's nothing like the workout that your senses get live and in person:

**The sights:** the wonderful world of colors that permeates the entire experience, including more than forty multihued cars; the appealing or sometimes gaudy-colored uniforms of the team members who are working the pits or standing in unison for the national anthem; awe-inspiring airplane flyovers; watching the cars take the green flag; holding your breath when a car crashes only to exhale a sigh of relief when the driver emerges from the wreck unscathed; the fan in front of or alongside you, potentially a new friend, even if you cheer for rival drivers.

**The sounds:** race car engines roaring to life; the (sometimes off-key) national anthem; the cheers and jeers of as many as a hundred thousand fans or more; my favorite at-track sound, "Gentlemen, Start Your Engines!" Life doesn't get any better than that.

**The smells:** rubber burning off tires as the cars make yet another lap around the track; the exhaust fumes from the motors; the beer your neighbor just spilled all over you; acrid cigar or cigarette (both legal and illegal) smoke in the stands; the variety of food, ranging from the normal fare of hot dogs and hamburgers to more exotic offerings like sushi and Wolfgang Puck entrées.

You can see why having a great experience is so important when you attend your first Cup race in person. Anything less than a wonderful day will be cloaked somewhat in disappointment. But picking the best and worst racetracks on the NASCAR circuit isn't just for first-timers or newbies. Longtime fans who don't venture far from their closest or favorite track also want to know where they should or shouldn't go if an opportunity arises to expand their Cup horizons.

Picking the best of twenty-two tracks is a rather subjective exercise. The tracks I think are the best might not be on your list, and that's fine. That's the beauty of NASCAR: being able to agree and disagree. But with twenty-five years of writing about NASCAR and other forms of motorsports, I've heard from and talked with enough fans, drivers, and team members to have a pretty good read on the pulse of the best tracks in the business.

So, without further ado, here are the five best tracks on the NASCAR circuit (conversely, the five worst tracks are in the Red Flag section):

1. **Bristol Motor Speedway** (.533-mile oval, 160,000 capacity). This legendary East Tennessee track is NASCAR's mecca, a place that offers an almost religious pilgrimage for fans who want to pay homage to some of the sport's greats who once raced or continue to race there. Nowhere else on earth can you squeeze so many race fans into such a small space. But that's the beauty of Bristol, with its close and often furious racing. It's one of the favorite tracks for many drivers, and it has some of the best sight lines for fans of any venue in all sports facilities. Just as spectacular is the noise factor: with the stands rising up to the clouds, the sounds that reverberate during a race make you feel like you're in the middle of a hive full of angry bees. Bristol is so popular that many fans actually put their season tickets in their wills to pass on to the next generation. There used to be a waiting list of more than fifty thousand for season tickets for both Cup races every year. The track has since refined its process to a yearly lottery in which the fans send in postcards for blind draws, and that lottery still draws more than ten thousand entrants who are seeking a chance to purchase four season ducats. Say what you want about fabled places like Daytona and Indianapolis, but when it comes to the hottest ticket in NASCAR, Bristol is it. If you had to pick which of the two yearly races to attend, the nod goes to the summer Saturday night race, which enhances the Bristol experience all the more with tens of thousands of cameras flashing away at any given time in almost strobe light–like fashion. If you attend only one race in your lifetime, Bristol is the place.

2. **Daytona International Speedway** (2.5-mile oval, 200,000-plus capacity). This track takes on an atmosphere unique in stock-car racing during February's two-week Speedweeks session, which leads up to the legendary and season-opening Daytona 500.

It's an experience comparable to spending the month of May at Indianapolis in preparation for the Indianapolis 500. This is where the all-time best enjoyed some of their greatest moments in stock-car history. It's no wonder that everyone in the sport refers to the Daytona 500 as NASCAR's Super Bowl; it's the biggest and greatest race. If you go there, another must-see is the Daytona 500 Experience, a museumlike exhibit in front of the speedway. Besides, you can't beat the frequent seventy- to eighty-degree weather in the middle of winter.

3. **Indianapolis Motor Speedway** (2.5-mile oval, 300,000-plus capacity). For the first eighty-three years since it opened in 1911, the most legendary racetrack in the world only featured Indy-style, open-wheel racing with its marquee event, the Indianapolis 500, otherwise known as the Greatest Spectacle in Racing. In 1994, the track opened its doors to NASCAR for the first time for the Brickyard 400. In a decade and a half since, that event has become the second largest and second richest event in stock-car racing, after the Daytona 500. Visiting this track is like going to Bristol, a pilgrimage of sorts in which the fans not only watch a great race but also immerse themselves in some of the greatest moments in motorsports at the Indianapolis Motor Speedway Hall of Fame and Museum, located in the track's infield. If you're a diehard race fan, be prepared to spend several hours in the museum, which has one of the most reasonable admission prices in all of sports: three dollars for adults and one dollar for kids six to fifteen years old.

4. **Texas Motor Speedway** (1.5-mile oval, 160,000-plus capacity). Even though this is one of the seven "cookie cutter" tracks that dominate the Cup schedule, a race here is more than just another 1.5-mile event. It's a spectacle, with some of the biggest crowds, biggest driver paydays, and best racing action you'll find anywhere. It definitely lives up to its state's motto: it does things bigger and better in Texas. The fan who attends a race here winds up being as much of a winner as the guy who ultimately takes the checkered flag.

5. TIE: **Phoenix International Raceway** (1.0-mile oval, 85,000 capacity) and **Las Vegas Motor Speedway** (1.5-mile oval, 150,000

capacity). Where else could you watch a race while sitting on the side of a mountain (just watch out for the occasional wayward snake that might slither through the underbrush) with a spectacular view of the track below? The aesthetics of the Phoenix track are unlike any other track on the Cup circuit. Although attendance could stand to be increased, the 1-mile flat track is a cozy venue for watching NASCAR's biggest stars. And more often than not, the racing is among the tightest and closest side-by-side competition you'll find anywhere. But you also can't ignore its neighbor three hundred miles to the north in Las Vegas. With the reconfiguration of the track prior to 2007, and with higher banking and the fan-friendly Neon Garage in the middle of the infield, the Las Vegas track joins its sister track in Texas as one of the showplaces of the Cup circuit. And like Phoenix, Las Vegas has its own aesthetics to boast about: Nellis Air Force Base is right across the street, giving race fans some spectacular air shows for free.

HONORABLE MENTION: **Darlington Raceway**, the second oldest track on the circuit, built in 1950—the fabled Lady in Black (a reference to its original black asphalt) is a must-see for diehard Cup fans • **New Hampshire Motor Speedway** may be in the middle of nowhere, but you'd be hard-pressed to find better side-by-side racing • **Talladega Superspeedway** is so large (2.66-miles around) that you could fit a small country in its massive infield • **Infineon Raceway** is arguably one of the most picturesque road courses in all of racing.

# What Is the Best Track for Ingress and Egress?

Getting to and from every racetrack on the Sprint Cup circuit is like the old navy saying "It's not just a job, it's an adventure."

For many fans, it takes longer to get into—and even longer to get out of—a racetrack than to watch the entire race itself. More often than not, the way to get to a track quickly is not necessarily the easiest or the most convenient route. Rather, it's the road less traveled, otherwise known as a shortcut.

Take my word for it: NASCAR officials are the kings at finding previously undiscovered ways to get to a track quickly. You may have to do a bit of dirt-road driving, but would you rather be stuck in traffic for a couple of hours or be in your seat less than forty-five minutes after leaving home or your hotel?

Here are the five best tracks for ingress and egress (I'd throw in my patented shortcuts for many of these tracks, but then, if I give my secrets away, I'll be back to fighting traffic in another venue):

1. **Kansas Speedway.** I can't lavish enough praise on the Kansas Highway Patrol and Kansas City police for making it so easy to get into and out of this place, which is nestled in the juncture of I-435 and I-70. It's rare that you are sitting in line for more than twenty to thirty minutes, if even that. And if you take some streets that parallel the track, you can just breeze right into the parking lot. This place gets an A-plus from me.

2. **Phoenix International Raceway.** As I mentioned earlier, this track is on the side of a mountain. The key is *not* to take I-10. Avoid it at all costs. And if you're coming from Phoenix, remember the following parallel roads (they'll get you to the track *much* faster): Broadway Road, Buckeye Road, Lower Buckeye Road, and Van Buren Street.

3. **Homestead-Miami Speedway.** Even though this track is about thirty miles from downtown Miami, a quick hop on the Florida Turnpike can get you here fairly quickly. The key, though, is to get off before everyone else does. Remember exit 9, and follow the signs for coming in the back way, along the outskirts of Homestead Air Force Base. You can thank me later.

4. **Michigan International Speedway.** This is the biggest surprise of all. Five years ago, I would have picked this as one of the five worst tracks for ingress and egress. But the job that track president Roger Curtis has done the last couple of years in conjunction with the Michigan State Police and local county and municipal police departments has been nothing short of spectacular. You used to sit in traffic two to three hours coming into

or leaving this track, but now you can typically be on your way within an hour or so after the race ends. You may have a few miles of bumper-to-bumper traffic, but it clears up quite quickly, compared to other locales. A bit of advice if you're heading to the track on race day: even though ingress has improved, you should still leave early. The worst time for traffic backups is between two and three hours before the green flag. One other tip: Invest in a good local map (or GPS) and plot out some of the back roads that are in the area. You may rarely even hit your brakes because the track comes into view so suddenly.

5. **New Hampshire Motor Speedway.** If you don't mind getting your car dirty, there are lots of back roads and dirt roads that can help you to avoid roughly 90 percent of race day traffic (that's right, I said 90 percent). Don't come in from the south on Route 106. Take I-93 to exit 20 (Tilton Road, also known as Route 140). Take Tilton east until you hit Route 106 southbound. You may be going a few extra miles out of your way, but trust me, you'll get to the track much faster than the cars that are creeping and crawling several miles from the south.

HONORABLE MENTION: **Chicagoland Speedway**—circle around and come in from the south, and you'll have very little stress on race day, but the postrace egress can be rough, especially if the police send you in the opposite direction from where you want to go and then you have to continue for a couple of miles before you can turn around • **Atlanta Motor Speedway**, if you take the back roads instead of Route 19/41, which runs right by the track.

Of course, as attendance has continued to plummet, race day traffic has continued to improve, but that's a story for another day.

## What Are the Best Cities in NASCAR?

I can't count the number of e-mails I have received over the years from fans asking the same question: if there are only a couple of cities that a diehard NASCAR fan should visit, which ones would they be?

We've already covered the best NASCAR tracks, but what about the best cities or metropolitan areas that surround some of those tracks? Which are the best at supporting the sport and the sanctioning body? Which offer the most entertainment or activities away from the racetrack?

The answers to these questions are pretty easy. There's no need to give a top-ten or even a top-five list. There are really only two cities that best encapsulate the NASCAR experience. You might be surprised at my choices, but after a decade on the NASCAR beat, twenty-five years in motorsports coverage, and thirty-five years overall in sportswriting, I cannot find any other locales that rival these two.

First stop, **Charlotte, North Carolina.** (You thought I'd probably say Daytona Beach, Florida, didn't you?) There's no other city that compares in the U.S. motorsports community, not even the king of the open-wheel world, Indianapolis, Indiana. Often referred to as "Daytona North," Charlotte and its environs (Mooresville, Lake Norman, Concord, Kannapolis, and others) are home to the largest concentration of racing teams around. Virtually every Sprint Cup and most Nationwide and Camping World Truck series teams call this area home.

The center of everything is Charlotte Motor Speedway (known until the end of 2009 as Lowe's Motor Speedway), the so-called Beast of the Southeast, one of the best racetracks out there. Everything seems to branch off from the track like the tentacles of an octopus, including places where fans can get a true grasp on not only the history but also the present and the future of stock car racing.

There are more than a dozen museums dedicated to motorsports (primarily NASCAR), so a diehard race fan can immerse him- or herself for more than a week in NASCAR culture and still not see everything. There's the North Carolina Motorsports Museum in Mooresville, the Hendrick Motorsports Museum in Concord, the Richard Childress Museum in Welcome, the Dale Earnhardt Museum just outside Mooresville, and many others.

NASCAR opened its long-awaited and celebrated Hall of Fame and Museum in May 2010, which will take the sport to even greater levels of attention, notoriety, and popularity.

But museums aren't everything. Many teams offer tours of their shops to race fans. Among the top ones are Joe Gibbs Racing, Hendrick Motorsports, Penske Racing, Michael Waltrip Racing, and Dale Earnhardt Inc. Even if you're not a fan of a particular team, if it offers a tour, take it. It'll be an experience you'll never forget.

Next on the diehard's destination list is **Daytona Beach, Florida**. Before the hiatus to Charlotte by most teams in the 1980s and 1990s, Daytona Beach used to be *the* place to be for a lot of NASCAR teams. And even though Charlotte has overtaken it as the top destination for NASCAR fans, how can you ignore NASCAR's birthplace? Not only does it offer the legendary Daytona International Speedway, it also has the adjoining Daytona 500 Experience (formerly Daytona USA), an interactive museum that traces the history of the Great American Race. If you're in town on race weekends, you can also visit the fan zone, which allows fans to watch race teams as they do their work; this provides great opportunities for autograph hunting. But wait, there's more.

What helps Daytona stand out from other areas is that besides enjoying the race-related activities, you can escape a long, cold winter by traveling to the beaches that sit just a few miles east of the house that "Big Bill" France built. There's also the world's most popular family vacation destination, Walt Disney World, just outside Orlando, about an hour's drive away.

If you're a baseball fan, there's plenty of major league baseball spring training action within a few hours' drive in February and March, as well as a whole slew of minor league action during the summer.

Then there are a couple of honorable mentions. Talladega Superspeedway in **Talladega, Alabama**, is arguably the best place to party in the sport today—and certainly one of the wildest places on God's green earth on race weekends. Although Daytona used to be the king of drunkenness and debauchery, it's given way to Talladega, which is as close to a modern-day Sodom and Gomorrah as you'll find anywhere. Often fueled by alcohol, the fans make the 'Dega infield and the surrounding campgrounds look more like Mardi Gras in New Orleans. Beads have become quite popular in and around Talladega, precious rewards for female fans to show off their sometimes far-too-ample charms.

Finally, if you've seen Charlotte and/or Daytona, sooner or later you have to trek several hundred miles north to **Indianapolis, Indiana.** It's a miniature version of Charlotte, and it's home to other forms of motorsports—not just open-wheel teams in the Indy Racing League but also an increasing number of National Hot Rod Association drag racing teams. Just like their stock car counterparts in Charlotte, several of these teams offer tours of their respective shops, and there are numerous opportunities for fans to purchase souvenirs of their favorite teams or drivers.

# What Were NASCAR's Five Biggest Comebacks?

Nothing deserves more respect or appreciation, in my opinion, than overcoming incredible odds to end up with a major success or prize. When a NASCAR driver rallies from what would seem to be insurmountable odds to achieve success, he earns this kind of respect, which is rarely attained. Ever since NASCAR's "modern era" began in 1972, it has had some really incredible comebacks by drivers.

Here are the top five (actually six, because my fifth pick ended in a tie) comebacks, in countdown style, that I think have been the most significant and incredible rallies that the sport has ever seen:

5. TIE: **Richard Petty, 1979,** and **Terry Labonte, 1996.** They don't call Petty The King for nothing. In the same year that he earned perhaps the most memorable of his seven Daytona 500 victories, Petty ended the season in as much of a flourish as he began it with. Down 229 points with eleven races left, he put on perhaps his greatest championship-winning effort ever. It was quite fitting, indeed, for it would wind up being Petty's seventh and final Cup championship, as well, and would end up being the second closest finish in Winston Cup history (after Kulwicki's 1992 run and prior to Nextel/Sprint coming into the sport in 2004), defeating Darrell Waltrip by a mere 11 points.

Labonte overcame a 111-point deficit with four races left to overtake Jeff Gordon and go on to win his second career Cup championship, ultimately defeating Gordon by 37 points. Had it not been for Labonte's remarkable comeback, we'd be talking about Gordon's *five* career Cup championships today.

4. **Darrell Waltrip, 1985.** Even though he had a tendency of making things look easy, Waltrip's third and last championship was far from easy. He trailed Bill Elliott by 206 points with eight races left—a hard enough margin to overcome. But not only did he do just that, once Waltrip caught Elliott, he went on to win the whole dang title by 101 points, to boot.

3. **Jimmie Johnson, 2006.** October 8, 2006, is a day that—to borrow from the late president Franklin D. Roosevelt—will live in NASCAR infamy. The UAW-Ford 500 had just finished at Talladega Superspeedway, and young Johnson had finished a disappointing 24th, dropping him to 8th place and 156 points out of 1st with six races left to go (after disappointing finishes of 39th, 13th, and 14th in the first three races of the Chase). "I thought it was over for us at that point," Johnson recalled. "I figured we were done, we were out of it. I told Chad [Knaus, the crew chief] that we might as well start working on things for next year." But Knaus wasn't as willing to throw in the towel as his driver was. He assured Johnson that the team could still come back—and indeed, that's what they did. Two years after finishing second to Kurt Busch by a mere 8 points, Johnson would win the first of what would become four consecutive Cup championships. Was Johnson's "we were done" claim merely a bluff, so that other teams would discount his chances in the remaining half a dozen Chase races? If they did, then the bluff was obviously successful, because Johnson went on a hell of a tear from that point on, finishing first or second in five of the remaining six races and ultimately winning the championship by 56 points over runner-up Matt Kenseth. Johnson's feat just added to the legacy and the lore of a season that began with a win in the Daytona 500 (without Knaus, who was suspended prior to the race for improper adjustments to Johnson's race car) and another restrictor-plate win at Talladega in

April, and finally one of the biggest wins of Johnson's career came in August when he captured the Allstate 400 at the Brickyard at the fabled Indianapolis Motor Speedway.

2. **Darrell Waltrip, 1981.** Waltrip always had a flair for the dramatic as a driver, and that was never more apparent than in the way he won all three of his Cup titles between 1981 and 1985: he had to rally back in the standings each time to become champion. But it was his first title that stands out the most. Many decidedly Waltrip fans still consider his 1981 comeback as the greatest in the sport, rallying from a 341-point deficit in the final seventeen races to win his first Cup title. How he did it was sheer Waltrip magic: he earned fourteen top-five and three other top-ten finishes in those final seventeen races. Most notable was an astounding fourteen-race streak down the stretch in which Waltrip finished no lower than third place in each event, with 8 wins, 5 second-place finishes, and 1 third-place showing. He would ultimately defeat Bobby Allison, who at midseason looked like the man to beat, by 53 points.

1. **Alan Kulwicki, 1992.** What the Greenfield, Wisconsin, native achieved in 1992 was to many (including myself) the greatest comeback NASCAR has ever seen. Kulwicki rebounded from a 278-point deficit with just six races left to ultimately win that season's championship by a mere 10 points over the favored Bill Elliott. That an underdog like Kulwicki, who owned and raced for his own single-car team—and even did much of the grunt work like working on shock absorbers and springs—could bounce back from such a huge deficit and wind up winning at the end is a ready-made script for Hollywood. Ironically, back in 2003, NASCAR's media relations department came up with a list of the top-ten championship comebacks of all time and ranked Kulwicki only in third place. But if you look at his stats, compared to those of others who also were considered among the sport's greatest comeback honors, what Kulwicki did—and the short period in which he did it—would win, hands down. For the record, Kulwicki needed and got an average of 48 points

more per race in the final six events before the season was over. Also, he won the title, even though the final running order in the season finale at that point had Elliott winning the race and Kulwicki finishing second. The difference was in the number of laps that each driver led in that race: Elliott led 102, but Kulwicki led 103. In addition, this particular race will be remembered for two key points in NASCAR history: it was Richard Petty's last (finished 35th of forty-one drivers) and Jeff Gordon's first (finished 31st).

# Who Are the Most Underrated Drivers in NASCAR Today?

It's easy to cite the biggest names in NASCAR. After all, they're the ones who have earned multiple championships or have the biggest followings. But what about the guys who do well yet rarely get the attention they deserve? Is it because they're not as flashy or successful as guys like Dale Earnhardt Jr., Jimmie Johnson, or Tony Stewart? Do they not covet or like the spotlight? Do they do their job in yeoman fashion, worried more about doing their best than counting wins or top-five finishes?

That's why I've always thought it best to gauge an underrated driver by his overall record compared to his notoriety and popularity. Let his performance speak for him, even if he doesn't necessarily get the attention he often so truly deserves.

For example, Jeff Gordon would never be considered underrated, given that he's won four championships and more than 80 races in his Cup career. At the same time, just because a guy has won a Cup championship shouldn't exclude him from being tagged as "underrated." You'll see a perfect example of this in a moment.

Much of the input I received for the selections to this question came from fans I heard from in recent years. So if you're going to blame anyone, blame them—not me. Only kidding! It just so happens that I agree with these top three picks:

1. **Mark Martin.** He should wear a cape with a *U* on his chest, signifying the most underrated driver in modern-day NASCAR racing. Even though Martin is one of the most respected drivers in the garage, serving as an example to his peers of a good character, a clean life, and one of the most competitive racers, he'll forever be known for never having won a Cup championship. He gets respect, but there is little acknowledgement of his accomplishments. He's been a runner-up in the final season five times, but no other driver has gotten as little attention as Martin has, compared to drivers like the late Dale Earnhardt Sr., Jeff Gordon, and Tony Stewart. He deserves so much better.

2. **Matt Kenseth.** Kenseth is the "perfect example" of an underrated past champion that I mentioned earlier. Although his performance has slipped in the last two years—he missed the Chase for the Sprint Cup for the first time in his career in 2009, leaving Johnson as the only driver to have qualified for all of the first six Chases—Kenseth is still one of the most consistent drivers on the circuit when he's on top of his game. That consistency is so legendary that when Kenseth won the final Winston Cup championship in 2003, he did it primarily through consistency and not by wins. The fact that Kenseth had just 1 win that season en route to the title prompted NASCAR chairman Brian France to devise and implement the Chase for the Nextel (now Sprint) Cup the following year. France sought to give more weight to winning, because the way Kenseth won the title was, for all intents and purposes, boring. That's not a knock against him; he merely did the best collectively of all the drivers, even if he was more about top-five finishes than wins.

3. **Jeff Burton.** If Mark Martin is the elder statesman of NASCAR (not by age but by demeanor, attitude, leadership, character, and overall talent), then Burton could be mini-Mark. Like Martin, Burton is an eloquent and deep-thinking speaker (one of the

reasons he's always in demand by reporters), has been the main influence in resurrecting Richard Childress Racing, lives a clean life (has never been involved in any scandals), is a mentor to young drivers (like teammate Clint Bowyer), and has an almost prophetlike outlook on the sport and the world today. He's engaging to speak with on everything from getting through a turn to politics and solutions to the world's problems—which would explain why he's nicknamed The Senator in the garage area. Oh, yeah, and the South Boston, Virginia, native is one heck of a race-car driver. Unfortunately, as with his former teammate Martin, it just doesn't seem to be in the cards that Burton will ever win a Cup championship or get more of the attention he so deserves.

HONORABLE MENTION: **Ryan Newman**, **Greg Biffle**, and **Kevin Harvick** are all examples of the proverbial "he's much better than his overall record indicates" label.

As a postscript, some of you might wonder why I haven't included drivers like Clint Bowyer, Denny Hamlin, Carl Edwards, and Kyle Busch in this category. The reason is simple: these are budding superstars in the sport and still have long careers ahead of them. Check back with me in about ten years, and I bet none of them will be underrated by then.

# When Jeff Gordon Retires, What Will Be His Legacy with NASCAR?

For nearly two decades, Jeff Gordon has been the most successful driver in Cup racing. Ever since he ran his first race in the 1992 season finale—in what many consider one of the most significant changing of the guards in the sport: Richard Petty's last career Cup start and Gordon's first—the driver of the No. 24 Chevrolet has gone on to become one of the greatest stars in the sport's history.

Among some of Gordon's most notable accomplishments: four Winston Cup championships (1995, 1997, 1998, and 2001); more than 80 wins in NASCAR's top division; at least 1 win at every current track on the circuit except for Homestead-Miami Speedway; more than 260 top-five and 350 top-ten finishes in fewer than 600 career starts; more than 20,000 leads in 165,000 laps; nearly 70 career poles; and more than 215,000 miles logged in a Cup race car.

Gordon came to NASCAR after an outstanding career in sprint cars, midgets, and other open-wheel racing, primarily under the auspices of the United States Auto Club. And while he quickly developed a large and loyal fan base, he was met with significant resistance from many longtime NASCAR diehards. For one thing, Gordon was a California native, although he spent much of his formative racing years in Indiana, the hotbed hub of sprint and midget racing. Gordon was therefore looked at by many Southern race fans as an outsider—a Yankee by some, a slick Californian by others.

Ironically, that perception only became compounded by the fact that Gordon became an almost immediate winner. Paired with crew chief Ray Evernham, he blazed through the Cup ranks, particularly from 1995 through 1999, when he notched three of his four Cup titles and won 47 races, including 13 in 1998 and 10 each in 1996 and 1997. Gordon's fourth title came in 2001, with Evernham prodigy Robbie Loomis at the helm as crew chief. (Evernham had moved on to form his own team and help Dodge return to the sport in 2001.)

With that kind of success, it is easy to see why Gordon might be the subject of hatred from non-Gordon fans. He was taking wins and championships away from other fans' drivers, most notably guys like the late Dale Earnhardt, Darrell Waltrip, Dale Jarrett, Terry and Bobby Labonte, Rusty Wallace, Ricky Rudd, and Mark Martin.

Martin is an especially poignant example, for he finished second to Earnhardt in 1994, fourth to Gordon in 1995, third to Gordon in 1997, and second to Gordon in 1998. Martin fans could make a strong case that if "Wonderboy" (as Gordon was derisively called by some non-fans) hadn't come along, Martin might very well have been able to earn at least one career Cup championship.

During his most successful seasons, Gordon was both cheered and booed. He became the subject of abject criticism and derisiveness. One well-known comedian, Tim Wilson, even recorded a song that became semilegendary among non-Gordon fans, called "Jeff Gordon's Gay!" That song and others of the same ilk were funny—even Gordon has good-naturedly laughed at them numerous times over the years—but only one thing is important: Gordon has been one of the biggest positives the sport has ever seen.

He exuded a clean-cut, all-American-boy image. When first wife, Brooke, filed for divorce, even non-Gordon fans came to Jeff's defense, essentially vilifying the former Miss Winston for doing her man—and their man, the way they saw it—wrong.

Gordon has been a perfect example of strong values, a tough but fair competitor, and a clean racer (most of the time). He has never had any off-track incidents that brought him or the sport any ill repute—something that can't be said of many other athletes in other professional sports. He's practically been the prototype of professionalism and classiness. Unfortunately, many other athletes have chosen to go in another direction.

As Gordon begins to close in on the end of his long and successful Cup career, something else needs to be pointed out about him. Had it not been for NASCAR's implementation of things like the Chase for the Sprint Cup or the Car of Tomorrow, Gordon would most likely have enjoyed even greater success, even during the waning years of his career.

For example, if the old format had stayed in place and the Chase had never come to be, Gordon would probably have won one to three more Cup championships from 2004 to 2009 (particularly in 2004, as well as 2006 and 2007). Unfortunately, Hendrick Motorsports teammate Jimmie Johnson wound up taking away three of Gordon's best chances from 2006 to 2009. And had it not been for the extreme difficulty of adapting to the Car of Tomorrow in 2008, Gordon might have added significantly to his total career wins.

In fact, I believe that Gordon would have had six championships and would have been closing in on 100 career Cup wins by now had it not been for the Chase, the Car of Tomorrow, and, of course, the success of his prodigy, Johnson.

Gordon came onto the NASCAR scene just as its biggest hero, Richard Petty, was calling it a career. Cut from a similar mold as gentleman Richard, Gordon brought class, fierce but clean competitiveness, and an example of how clean living and hard work can lead to success—just as Petty displayed during his nearly-four-decade racing career.

Gordon became Earnhardt's archnemesis and rival—much as Earnhardt had been to Petty during the final fourteen years of The King's Cup career—and when he eventually leaves NASCAR, it will be a much better organization for having had him in its ranks.

When he does ultimately retire from NASCAR—which given Gordon's new-found second wind to keep racing for several more years could be anywhere between 2015 and 2021—Gordon will likely be a unanimous first-ballot inductee for the NASCAR Hall of Fame in much the same fashion as Petty and Earnhardt, the two biggest names in NASCAR history that preceded him. That's true greatness right there—and Gordon certainly deserves to be in that category, if not a category of his own.

# Which Drivers Made the Biggest Leap to Stardom by Jumping to Another Team That Led Them to Greatness?

If at first you don't succeed, change teams. That has been the formula for many Cup champions since 1972. It is becoming increasingly rare for a driver to remain with the same team and the owner who first brought him either to the Cup level or into the sport as a whole, and several drivers have left one team to achieve the kind of success they always hoped for with another.

In many cases (such as the late Dale Earnhardt's), the jump to another team did pay off beyond a driver's wildest dreams. But there were also some bittersweet end results (such as Rusty Wallace's).

The top two reasons why a driver jumps from one team to another are the opportunity to earn significantly more money and the opportunity to potentially earn more wins and championships. Other reasons include wanting to leave a team that doesn't have enough resources to be competitive (and most likely never will), following a sponsor the driver is readily identified with to a new team (such as when Dale Jarrett followed United Parcel Service from Robert Yates Racing to Michael Waltrip Racing in 2007), or simply wanting a different type of pace with another team (such as when Bobby Labonte left Joe Gibbs Racing after the 2005 season to join Petty Enterprises and, more important, to be able to spend more time with his family).

Even valid active contracts don't stop drivers from jumping to another team. After 2005, just a year removed from winning his first Cup championship with Roush Racing (now Roush Fenway Racing), Kurt Busch was given a less than amicable release from his existing contract to sign with Penske Racing, replacing Wallace, who retired after his "Rusty's Last Call" (a takeoff on Wallace's primary sponsor, Miller Beer) farewell tour at the end of that campaign.

Ditto for Jamie McMurray, who essentially replaced Busch at Roush Racing for 2006. McMurray also had an existing contract with Chip Ganassi Racing with Felix Sabates, but after lengthy haranguing he eventually won his release as well, thus paving the way for him to sign and race for multicar team owner Jack Roush.

Unfortunately, McMurray's tenure with Roush lasted just four seasons, for after 2009, Roush was forced to release McMurray and disband the No. 26 Ford team to comply with a NASCAR mandate that limited team owners to operating no more than four Sprint Cup teams at any one time. Roush had five teams and had to divest himself of one by the end of 2009. Unfortunately, McMurray and his team were the odd men out.

Although I wanted to choose five drivers here, I wound up choosing seven. I was probably more torn about this choice than any other I've made in this book, but I decided that the other two drivers deserved at least an honorable mention.

So let's look at the top five drivers (with two others close behind) who went from "standing at the altar" with one team to achieving a success afterward that they could only dream about:

HONORABLE MENTION: Awesome **Bill Elliott from Dawsonville, Georgia,** wasn't very awesome at the beginning of his Cup career, when he was driving for Elliott Racing, which was owned by his father, George. In sixty-five starts for the family business, Bill managed just a pair of top-five finishes. It wasn't until he moved to Melling Racing (owned by Harry Melling) in 1982 that Elliott began to carve his path to racing history. During his ten-year tenure with Melling, Elliott earned 34 of his 44 career Cup wins, as well as his lone Cup championship in 1988. When Elliott moved to Junior Johnson's team in 1992, he earned 6 wins in three years, but he never came close to approaching what he achieved during his glory days with Melling. ▪ After two years with Cliff Stewart, **Rusty Wallace** decided to move to Raymond Beadle's team in 1986. Beadle had achieved success in drag racing with his infamous Blue Max Funny Car and had decided to try his hand at NASCAR Cup team ownership. It took the duo just three years to earn the Cup championship in 1988 (they also would earn 18 wins together). Here's where the melancholy enters: Wallace parted ways with Beadle and joined Roger Penske's organization in 1991. He'd go on to win 37 races there, becoming one of NASCAR's most beloved and popular drivers in the process, but unfortunately he was never able to earn another Cup championship. It's the same with Wallace's successor at Penske, Kurt Busch. He won the Cup title in 2004 and 14 races overall for Roush Racing, moved to Penske in 2006 to replace the retiring Wallace, but has yet to repeat his championship achievement with Roush Racing.

5. **Dale Jarrett.** Early in his career, Jarrett drove for Eric Friedlander's team, split duties in the same season driving for teams owned by Cale Yarborough and Hoss Ellington, and eventually drove for the Wood Brothers (winning his first Cup race in 1991). He then moved up the ladder a bit higher by joining

Joe Gibbs Racing in 1992, where he stayed for three seasons and won 2 races. Finally, in 1995, Jarrett found a home at Yates Racing, and the rest is history. In the next twelve years in the Yates camp, Jarrett would win 29 of his 32 career wins, including the 1999 Cup championship.

4. **Cale Yarborough.** Yarborough was an interesting case. He drove for a number of different team owners during the first fourteen years of his career, but only on a part-time basis. He finally moved up to full-time in 1973 for team owner Richard Howard, where he stayed for a year and a half before moving to Junior Johnson's camp. It was there that Yarborough would have the greatest success of his career, not only earning 45 of his 83 career Cup wins but also becoming the first driver in NASCAR history to win three consecutive Cup championships (1976–1978). Once he left Johnson's team after 1980, Yarborough essentially came full circle. He would race for another nine seasons, but only on a part-time basis, much like the way he started in the sport.

3. **Darrell Waltrip.** The kid from Owensboro, Kentucky, came into the sport doing things his own way, racing primarily for his self-supported team early in his career. Waltrip enjoyed limited success driving for himself until he moved to the DiGard team near the end of 1975. He stayed there through 1980, earning 26 wins, a total he nearly equaled in his first two seasons (12 wins apiece in 1981 and 1982) with Junior Johnson. It was under Johnson's tutelage that Waltrip became one of the greatest drivers in the sport, not only earning more than half (43) of his 84 career wins in Cup racing but also capturing all three of his career championships (1981, 1982, and 1985).

2. **Jeff Gordon.** Everyone knows that Gordon won all four of his Cup championships and more than 80 career wins driving for Hendrick Motorsports. But here's one of the best bar bets in the sport: who did Gordon actually race for when he first came into NASCAR? No, it was *not* Rick Hendrick. Gordon actually came into the sport with Bill Davis Racing. Yep, it's true; you can look it up. In fact, Gordon wound up finishing fourth in the then Busch Series standings in 1992, winning 3 races as well, before he made his Cup debut

for Hendrick in the season finale at Atlanta that same year. The rest, as they say, is history.

1. **Dale Earnhardt.** It's hard to believe that one of the greatest drivers in NASCAR history couldn't get anyone to believe in his talent and ability early in his career. Earnhardt finally got his big break when a new hotshot team owner from California, Rod Osterlund, took Humpy Wheeler's advice and hired Earnhardt for his first full-time ride in Cup racing in 1979. Everyone knows that Earnhardt won seven career Cup championships, tying him with Richard Petty. And most average NASCAR fans may believe that all seven of those titles were earned while racing for Richard Childress Racing. Wrong. Guess again. Earnhardt actually only won six titles with Childress. The first of his seven Cup championships came in 1980 while racing for Osterlund. Almost as quickly as he came into the sport, Osterlund was gone by halfway through 1981, selling his operation when funds became scarce. Earnhardt finished the season racing first for Jim Stacy and then Childress, but he moved to Bud Moore's team in 1982. He stayed there for two years before moving permanently to Childress's operation in 1984 and earning 67 of his 76 career Cup wins.

# What Are the Five Biggest Off-Track Developments to Change NASCAR in the Last Twenty-five Years?

I talk a lot about the so-called Car of Tomorrow in this book. It and NASCAR's commendable push to optimize safety for drivers have been two of the most significant developments to change the sport in the last two and a half decades.

But there have also been several off-track developments in the last twenty-five years that have helped to take stock car racing from just a simple sport, based primarily in the Southeast, to a major league, national enterprise. I'm talking about things that have helped drivers more from a business, time-management, and comfort standpoint than the newest engine-chassis setup or lightning-fast tires.

There have certainly been other changes that have helped drivers to worry more about racing and less about nonracing details, but here are what I think are the five most significant changes that the nonracing aspect of the sport has seen:

5.  **The Internet.** Many race fans arguably now receive the majority of news about races or their favorite driver from Web sites such as ESPN.com, NASCAR.com, Yahoo.com, and Jayski.com. The online explosion has revolutionized the way we get our information and how quickly we get that information (we know about breaking news almost as soon as it has happened). It has opened a whole new universe in which race fans can share their thoughts and cheer their favorite drivers through social networking sites like Twitter and Facebook.

    There's also a side of things that is not as well publicized, but I predict it will become much more important in the next few years: driver-owned Web sites. Instead of having a fan-run site, as many celebrities do, a driver typically contracts an outside firm to host and develop his site. In turn, the driver often shares information about himself or a particular race as well as his thoughts on subjects that he might not share with the mainstream media (TV, radio, newspapers, magazines).

    We've seen it far more frequently in football, baseball, and basketball: an athlete will give his side of a story only to his personal site, keeping mainstream media in the dark and out of the loop.

    This trend is not lost on NASCAR drivers, and I predict that in the next few years you're going to see even more drivers utilize their own sites to get their message across. They'll still have to fulfill certain mainstream media obligations, but the less a driver can say to those outlets, the more he can say on his own site.

    One other area that is virtually brand-new is NASCAR's experiment with so-called citizen journalists (fans who maintain general-interest racing sites and receive full access as "real" reporters). Because so many mainstream media outlets have drastically cut, if not totally eliminated, their motorsports coverage—primarily NASCAR coverage, and particularly in newspapers—the sanctioning body hopes that the citizen journalists will fill a coverage void. Time will tell.

4. **Private airplanes.** When you travel cross-country several times a year for races or sponsor-related appearances, or you need to get somewhere more expeditiously than by commercial airline, your travel choices become somewhat limited. That's why most Sprint Cup drivers have gone the route of either owning or leasing private airplanes. They're not held to airline schedules, they can typically fly into smaller and less populated (that is, less busy) airports, and they don't have to hassle with long security checkpoint lines.

"Having your own private airplane saves you an incredible amount of time and hassle," Sprint Cup driver Carl Edwards said. "When you want to go, you just take off and go. No matter where we're racing in the U.S., we can typically be back home within four, five hours. You can race during the day and be back in your own bed later that night. It's just so, so convenient."

Some drivers have even gone as far as to take flying lessons and earn pilot licenses from the Federal Aviation Administration so they can fly themselves to and from races. Some drivers who are also pilots are Mark Martin, Matt Kenseth, Jeff Burton, Greg Biffle, Jamie McMurray, and Camping World Truck Series driver Mike Skinner.

Edwards also became a pilot, partly out of design and partly out of necessity. As a teen, Edwards had visions of becoming a fighter pilot in the military. If it hadn't been for his prowess behind the wheel of a race car, he just might have fulfilled that dream. Besides, when you compete in close to seventy Sprint Cup and Nationwide series events per year, not to mention doing numerous sponsorship appearances and TV commercial shoots, hopping into your own airplane becomes as routine as climbing into a race car.

3. **Driver-endorsed or driver-licensed memorabilia.** What drivers earn from race winnings can be chump change compared to the

multimillions of dollars they earn from other sources throughout their careers.

The trend toward big memorabilia cash began in the 1990s, when diecast cars—fully detailed and exact duplicates of the cars that drivers drove in actual races—came into prominence, thanks to companies like Action Performance, Team Caliber, and Racing Champions.

The industry became so lucrative that in 2005, NASCAR's International Speedway Corporation and its rival, Speedway Motorsports, merged with Action Performance and Team Caliber to create a new company called Motorsports Authentics.

While diecasts remain popular, other driver-branded and licensed merchandise has also taken off, particularly T-shirts, jackets, caps, seat cushions, pennants and flags, bumper stickers for fans' personal cars, and even driver-sanctioned credit cards.

When Dale Earnhardt Jr. decided to leave Dale Earnhardt Inc. for Hendrick Motorsports after the 2007 season, having the best equipment and organization was only part of the reason. Both Junior and team owner Rick Hendrick realized the huge financial windfall that Earnhardt's move would bring to both the driver and his new home, particularly since new primary sponsors (including the National Guard and Amp Energy Drink) were replacing Earnhardt's former sponsor, Budweiser, which had been the biggest memorabilia vendor in the business (thanks to Earnhardt). Who can forget the sea of red shirts, baseball caps, and jackets that followed Earnhardt from one venue to another? This trend has now been replaced by the green, white, and blue colors of Amp and/or the National Guard.

2. **Driver-team public relations person.** As NASCAR became more popular, the drivers needed someone to oversee their media efforts, coordinate fan club and newsletter notes about them, schedule appearances, and, in general, point them in the right direction, making sure they're where they're supposed to be to do what they're supposed to do.

A PR person's biggest role remains dealing with the media, and it has taken an ironic twist in the last decade. As drivers and the sport have increased in popularity, media availability has actually decreased; many PR directors are severely limiting media access to "their" drivers, as they like to call them. Particularly with some of the biggest teams in the sport, PR directors often even go so far as to offer driver availability only to those reporters who have favored status with the team or the driver or who usually write only positive stories or broadcast positive reports about the driver.

On the one hand, PR directors are a blessing for the drivers and the teams. On the other hand, they are also somewhat of a curse. That's why there's so much turnover in the industry; some individuals are almost like journeymen, jumping from one driver or team to another every year or two.

Of course, the drivers sometimes play a hand in that. I know of one very popular Sprint Cup driver (I won't mention his name because I don't want to embarrass him) who fired his PR person because he forgot to bring the driver's sunglasses to a fan event at which the driver was appearing.

1. **Business managers or agents.** NASCAR has not seen the often overbearing presence of agents that is seen in other pro sports—particularly football, baseball, and basketball. However, they're out there, and they're getting significantly more important with each passing year and every contract, endorsement, and invest-ment deal that they complete for the drivers they represent, further maximizing each driver's name, reputation, and "brand."

The biggest agent and firm in NASCAR is Cary Agajanian and his Motorsports Management International (MMI). Agajanian, one of several sons of legendary West Coast motorsports pro-moter J. C. Agajanian, has been involved in racing his entire life, including race promotion, track management, and team owner-ship. But Agajanian has made one of his biggest marks on the sport by representing drivers, helping them to earn substantial amounts of money and then save and protect their earnings. His client roster includes Tony Stewart, Kyle Busch, Kasey Kahne, David Reutimann, Jamie McMurray, Bill Elliott, and Denny Hamlin.

In a sense, Agajanian is part father, part advocate, part watch-dog, and part handyman in the way he oversees his drivers' careers. Not only does he do the standard thing that sports agents typically do—negotiate contracts with team owners—he also takes care of things like investments, taxes, sponsorships and personal endorsements, insurance policies, and anything else that needs to be watched over.

In a business that can be cutthroat, Agajanian has one of the kindest hearts in it. He's spent countless hours helping up-and-coming drivers, even giving advice or direction for free. In fact, not many people know it, but Agajanian played one of the biggest roles in Jeff Gordon's development—and pretty much gratis because Gordon and his stepfather, John Bickford, had no money to pay for Agajanian's services at the time.

But don't call Agajanian or his employees "agents." "We're very, very careful not to call ourselves agents, because we're not," Agajanian said in an interview with *NASCAR Scene* magazine in June 2005. "We really are managers. There's a difference, too. We do some similar things to what an agent does, but our company is called a management company, and there's a purpose for that. We're not out trying to find jobs for people. That's not what we do. We want to make sure that the life of the professional race driver is managed properly, his business and all aspects of his business life. That's why we call ourselves managers."

Another significant representative of drivers is Birmingham (suburban Detroit), Michigan, attorney Alan R. Miller, who has represented a number of drivers in NASCAR, as well as the Indy Racing League, including Kyle Busch (before he jumped to MMI) and Indy 500 multiwinner Helio Castroneves.

## What Are the Best NASCAR Movies of All Time?

For the most part, the phrase "best NASCAR movies" is a perfect example of an oxymoron. For as much as Hollywood has tried to bring the serious drama of stock car racing to the big screen, it more often than not has turned portrayals of the sport into cartoonish and comedic spoofs. That's not to say that those laughable louts are all bad, but it doesn't exactly put the sport in the best light when it's being made fun of so often—whether or not it's good-natured mockery.

When *Sports Illustrated* came up with its list of the top fifty sports films of all time in 2003, only one race-car driving movie made the list, and it wasn't even a NASCAR movie: the 1966 racing classic *Grand Prix*, which starred James Garner as a Formula One driver. Oh, the indignity—not one NASCAR flick on the list. But then, given how Hollywood really doesn't take NASCAR all that seriously, such a choice is not surprising.

I'd love to see a NASCAR-themed movie that would be a combination of three of the greatest sports movies of all-time: *Bull Durham*, *Slapshot*, and *Rocky*. It's unlikely we'll ever see anything like that, unfortunately.

My picks for the best NASCAR movies are a cross-section of decent drama and seemingly unnecessary, over-the-top comedic caricatures of the sport and its people. In making my picks, I've tried not to take things too seriously while maintaining a semblance of respect and dignity for the portrayals that came the closest to showing moviegoers the real inside story of NASCAR life:

1. *The Last American Hero* (1973). Not to be confused with the TV show of the early 1980s, *The Greatest American Hero*, this flick is blessed with a great story line (based on the life of the legendary Junior Johnson), great inspiration (based on a 1964 *Esquire* magazine story by Tom Wolfe), and great acting by the likes of Jeff Bridges, the late Ned Beatty, and even Gary Busey (five years before his breakout portrayal of Buddy Holly and before all his personal problems occurred). This is about as close as you're going to get to a real-life story about NASCAR's early days, tales about moonshine running, and how stock car racing evolved. Even though it's been nearly forty years since this movie hit the big screen, a DVD or a videocassette of this is a must-have for the true NASCAR fan.

2. *Greased Lightning* (1977). The true story of the late Wendell Scott, the first black driver to be a regular in NASCAR's Grand

National (predecessor to the Winston Cup, Nextel Cup, and now Sprint Cup) Series. Richard Pryor plays it straight in this drama and gives one of the best performances of his acting career. Scott's career was one of fighting prejudice, injustice, and adversity, and Pryor pulls off his portrayal of Scott with uncanny believability and aplomb.

3. *Days of Thunder* (1990). I can't win with this pick. NASCAR purists hate this movie, but those who like it think it should be ranked first instead of third. Actually, I was going to rank it fourth, but there's no way it could rank below *Talladega Nights*. Tom Cruise and Nicole Kidman star, along with great supporting performances from Randy Quaid as Tim Daland (a character that is loosely based on Rick Hendrick) and Robert Duvall, who especially stands out as Harry Hogge, Cole Trickle's (Cruise's) crew chief. Although some of the scenes are overplayed, especially Trickle's ongoing conflict with chief rivals Rowdy Burns (Michael Rooker) and Russ Wheeler (Cary Elwes), the good and the bad times on and off the track are very close to what we see in real-life NASCAR, with everything from pathos to comedy. My first two picks are equally close to being real-life portrayals, but this one is a bit more relevant to modern-day NASCAR, even if it is—hard to believe—twenty years old now.

4. *Talladega Nights: The Ballad of Ricky Bobby* (2007). I have to admit that I loved this movie when it first came out; I even picked it ahead of *Days of Thunder* as a favorite at one point. But time has mellowed my feeling somewhat. It's hysterically funny, but when it comes to reality, it's *way* off base. Ironically, it's that off-base story line that actually made this movie such a fan favorite, with Rick Bobby (Will Ferrell) matching wits and accelerator pedals with archrival Jean Girard (Sacha Baron Cohen), a gay ex–Formula One driver who has come to the United States to be the best in stock car racing, Bobby's providence. If you are feeling down or want a good example of outlandish NASCAR-related story lines, this is the movie for you. But please, don't make the mistake that many did when this movie was first released and think that this really is true-life NASCAR. Even though the sanctioning body

gave its full cooperation and support to making this film, the story line couldn't be further from the truth.

5. ***NASCAR 3D: The IMAX Experience* (2004).** I really debated whether to include this film, because it's a documentary rather than a drama. But given that it really shows NASCAR in its truest form, there really is no excuse not to include it as one of the best portrayals of the sport and its participants. Although you can pick this up on DVD at most video stores, the *only* way to experience the full fury and action is at a real IMAX theater (this movie is one of the highest-grossing IMAX productions ever made). The sounds, the visuals, and the story line are the closest you'll come to NASCAR, short of climbing behind the wheel of a Cup car yourself.

HONORABLE MENTION: ***Cars* (2006):** It really pains me to include *Cars* in this category, but facts are facts: this animated story, based on NASCAR but without any direct references to the sanctioning body (for example, cars race for the Piston Cup championship rather than the Nextel/Sprint Cup title in real life), has become one of the most popular racing movies of all-time, especially for kids. Think of a touching racing version of *Toy Story* and *A Bug's Life*, and you'll get the idea of *Cars*, complete with race action and even an underlying love story. Frankly, it's only in this type of format that you would probably ever have both Paul Newman (voice of the retired Doc Hudson) and Larry the Cable Guy (voice of Mater, the tow truck). As much as I hate to admit it, this is also a must-have for NASCAR fans ▪ ***3: The Dale Earnhardt Story* (2004):** A made-for-TV movie produced by ESPN, *3* is an outstanding depiction of the life of the late Dale Earnhardt. Underrated actor Barry Pepper gives one of his best career performances (his portrayal of baseball legend Roger Maris in "*61*\*" was slightly better) as The Intimidator, particularly in the later, most successful stages of Earnhardt's career. If you want to know the real story of Earnhardt's development from childhood to becoming one of NASCAR's greatest drivers, pick this one up.

Postscript: As we went to press with this book, rumors were swirling of sequels in the works for *Talladega Nights*, *Cars*, and even *Days of Thunder* (let me guess, Cruise tries to win one last championship before he hangs up his firesuit for good). That's just what we need: even worse follow-ups to the originals.

# What Were the Best Tracks That Are No Longer Used by NASCAR?

A week rarely goes by when I don't receive at least one e-mail from old-time NASCAR fans who are lamenting that some of their favorite tracks have gone by the wayside due to "progress"—in other words, because they aren't making enough money. Most of the e-mails say the same thing:

"I loved The Rock. NASCAR should never have closed it."

"It's a shame what's happened to North Wilkesboro. They should never have closed it."

"I sure miss Ontario and Riverside out in California. They really had some good races there."

NASCAR's Sprint Cup currently races on twenty-two different race-tracks, from Loudon, New Hampshire, to Fontana, California. There are thirty-nine races each season: thirty-six regular season events, the Budweiser Shootout and the split-field Gatorade Twin 150 (which are part of Speedweeks, leading up to the season-opening Daytona 500), and the Sprint All-Star Race in May.

But NASCAR's most popular series has also played at 146 other venues over the years; some that are still in existence, but many others have been torn down, taking lore, legend, and history with them—again, all in the name of "progress."

Of those 146 tracks, 6 stand out as the ones that fans lament and miss the most:

1. **North Carolina Speedway, Rockingham, North Carolina.** Without question, North Carolina Speedway is the track that fans miss most today. The Rock, as it was fondly called for the forty years it hosted Cup events (1965–2004), is also the track

most recently jettisoned from the Cup schedule. Unfortunately, although many fans say they loved The Rock and considered it their favorite racetrack, these fond feelings did not necessarily translate into ticket sales. When you have a capacity of 60,000 and you consistently fail to sell out the place—and attract fewer than 50,000 for the final Cup race there on February 22, 2004— it is easy to see why a supposed fan favorite just could not be sustained. One bright note, though: former racer Andy Hillenberg bought The Rock in 2007 and has attracted both the Automobile Racing Club of America and the United Speed Alliance Racing Hooters ProCup for events at The Rock, and he hopes to further expand its slate with other racing series. I don't know about you, but I'd love to see a Camping World Trucks or Nationwide series race back at Rockingham. We can only hope.

2. **North Wilkesboro Speedway, North Wilkesboro, North Carolina.** When New Hampshire International Speedway owner Bob Bahre and Speedway Motorsports chairman Bruton Smith needed additional race dates for their respective facilities, they combined efforts to purchase North Wilkesboro Speedway. They closed the 40,000-seat venue in 1996. One of NASCAR's original tracks, it opened in 1947. Efforts to reopen the track since it was shut have failed. The track was sold to a developer in 2007 for the dirt-cheap price of $12 million, but nothing has changed since then. At best, the site is most likely on life support. At worst, don't be surprised to see a shopping mall or an office park eventually built upon its hallowed land.

3. **Hickory Motor Speedway, Newton, North Carolina.** Just forty-three miles from North Wilkesboro sits Hickory Motor Speedway, which hosted Cup events from 1953 until 1971 and then opened its doors to the Busch Series from 1982 to 1998. But unlike its neighboring track, it has remained in operation as a venue for sportsman racers on the weekends since NASCAR pulled out. Opened in 1951, the 13,200-seat facility—which ultimately was its downfall because it could not expand any further and NASCAR was moving into much larger venues—continues to be popular among fans of exciting grassroots short-track

racing. As a result the track continues to call itself the "Birthplace of the NASCAR Stars."

4. **Ontario Motor Speedway, Ontario, California.** This is one of the greatest yet short-lived tracks in racing history. Designed to be similar to the Indianapolis Motor Speedway (it even had a circle of bricks from Indy in its victory lane), it ultimately wound up being slightly faster, and it had the best of both worlds with a 2.5-mile oval and an infield road course. Unfortunately, NASCAR ran just nine races there before the track went bankrupt, allegedly due to mismanagement, and was eventually torn down (just eleven years after it opened), giving way to commercial development and housing. Ironically, California Speedway, a 2-mile high-speed facility, opened in 1997, just two miles away from the former Ontario site, and hosted its first NASCAR event in 2001. (It now hosts two races each season in the renamed Auto Club Speedway of Southern California.)

5. **Riverside International Raceway, Riverside, California.** One of NASCAR's most unique tracks, this 2.6-mile road course hosted stock-car racing from 1958 to 1988, before the value of its land became worth more than the racing action there (a direction in which Pocono Raceway may soon go, as well). If you ever find yourself at Moreno Valley Mall at Towngate and listen really close, you might still hear the sounds of the cars of the late Dale Earnhardt or Richard Petty in the distance. "The House That Dan Gurney Built" (a reference to one of the most versatile, prolific racers ever in motorsports history) deserved a much better fate than it received. Only memories remain, but ah, what memories they were.

HONORABLE MENTION: **Bowman-Gray Speedway, Winston-Salem, North Carolina.** Although this track hasn't seen major-league NASCAR action since 1971 (having started in 1958), Bowman-Gray holds a special place in NASCAR lore for its unique makeup. How many other racetracks do you know that have a football field in the infield (home to the Winston-Salem State University football team)? What's more, it continues unabated as NASCAR's longest-running weekly racetrack, hosting a variety of sportsman events from spring to fall. To think that this 17,000-seat facility was once one of the biggest and most successful tracks on the Grand National circuit shows just how far NASCAR has come since then and how much it has grown. Still, Bowman-Gray will always hold a place in the hearts of die-hard race fans. If you've been there, you know what I'm talking about. If not, and you consider yourself a true race fan, do what you can to someday make a trek here.

# Who Are the Five Most Underrated Front-Office People in NASCAR?

In NASCAR, team owners typically get all the glory (or criticism), pay the bills, and hire and fire the drivers and the crew chiefs. What else would you expect from the guy whose name is on the front door, like a Rick Hendrick, a Richard Childress, a Jack Roush, or a Joe Gibbs?

But one man is not an island unto himself, and owners are known for hiring some of the smartest minds to help them run things. More often than not, you hear very little from them publicly or in the media, but they are undoubtedly among the most powerful individuals in the sport.

I've looked at all Sprint Cup organizations, as well as within NASCAR, the sanctioning body for those individuals who have meant so much to their respective teams and organizations. Here are my picks for the five most underrated front-office guys in NASCAR (in no particular order):

- **Geoff Smith, President, Roush Fenway Racing.** Smith has one of the toughest jobs in the sport: Jack Roush's right-hand man. While Roush is out and about running a multimillion-dollar performance company in Michigan, flying his fleet of airplanes and playing owner of four Sprint Cup teams on weekends, it's Smith who is the glue that holds everything together. Think of it in these terms: if Roush Fenway Racing were a suburb, Roush would be the part-time village president or mayor while Smith would be the full-time village or town manager or administrator. When things have to get done, Smith is typically the guy who lays the groundwork. He has Jack sign off on it, and then he seals the deal.

- **Marshall Carlson, Executive Vice President and General Manager, Hendrick Motorsports.** Carlton is one of the friendliest guys in the sport, but don't let his smiling face fool you. He's also one of the most intelligent negotiators and administrators around. Of course, it doesn't hurt that he's Rick Hendrick's son-in-law and the likely heir if and when Hendrick retires. Hendrick was grooming his son, Ricky, to eventually replace him, but that possibility ended tragically in 2004 when Ricky was among the ten victims who perished in the crash of a Hendrick team airplane into a mountainside near Martinsville, Virginia. Carlson runs the day-to-day operations at Hendrick Motorsports and played a major role in bringing Dale Earnhardt Jr. and Mark Martin into the Hendrick fold.

- **Kerry Tharp, Senior Director of Communications, NASCAR Front Office.** A veteran of sports public relations, including more than twenty years as sports information and assistant athletic director at the University of South Carolina, Tharp has done a tremendous job since joining NASCAR in 2006. Based out of the sport's Research and Development Center in North Carolina, Tharp is all business, but with a personable side, much like his boss, longtime NASCAR official Jim Hunter. If and when Hunter, who is approaching seventy years old, decides to retire, Tharp is a perfect replacement.

- **Jay Frye, Vice President and General Manager, Red Bull Racing.** A long-time administrator in the sport who continually flies under the radar of recognition, Frye has worked for several organizations in an executive role, including MB2 Motorsports, the short-lived Ginn Racing, and currently Red Bull Racing. Frye is one of the most organized individuals in the business, has great chutzpah, and is the type that would give you the shirt off his back—provided it had a Red Bull logo. If and when NASCAR officials like Mike Helton, John Darby, and Robin Pemberton retire, Frye is a strong candidate to move up the ladder into a high-ranking administrative role within the sanctioning body.

- **Ty Norris, Vice President and General Manager, Michael Waltrip Racing.** Norris is the quintessential underrated executive. Though not known much in fan circles, he's one of the most respected executives in the business. Norris was invaluable in the formation and development of Dale Earnhardt Inc., taking the company of the late Dale Earnhardt and his widow, Teresa, from a small-time operation to one of the most efficiently run major teams in the business. Norris was also a key factor in the planning and construction of DEI's "Garage Mahal," the modern, multimillion-dollar headquarters of the organization, which is now called Earnhardt Ganassi Racing. Norris has done wonders at the helm of Michael Waltrip Racing, not only in building the team with its namesake owner but also as one of the best in the business at attracting and retaining sponsors. He also helped his current boss develop Waltrip World, an interactive combination museum and shop tour in suburban Charlotte. Like Frye, Norris would be a strong candidate to one day move up to NASCAR's corporate headquarters.

HONORABLE MENTION: **Eddie Jarvis, Tony Stewart's business manager, Stewart Haas Racing.** While guys like Frye and Norris fly under the radar, Eddie Jarvis is downright stealthlike invisible. And that's the way he likes it. A former motor coach driver, Jarvis endeared himself so much to Stewart that he eventually became his business manager. In addition, Jarvis is one of the most respected and trusted individuals in the garage, a person whom numerous drivers on competing teams actively reach out to, confide in, or seek advice from, knowing he won't betray them. In a sport in which it's often hard to find anyone you can trust fully, Jarvis has proven over the years to be one of the exceptions.

# Whose Rookie Season Gave Us the Best Hint of What Was to Come?

NASCAR used to have one of the most convoluted systems for choosing each season's Rookie of the Year. From 1958 until 1973, a bunch of NASCAR officials would get together and simply pick the person they thought was the top newcomer in the sport. There was no true points system, per se, which contributed to some controversial decisions and choices.

Unfortunately, they goofed a time or two, particularly in 1973, when Lennie Pond was chosen over a promising young racer from Kentucky by the name of Darrell Waltrip. As a result of that last straw of a faux pas, the entire Rookie of the Year system was overhauled for the 1974 season, a points system was implemented, and, with a few tweaks over the years, has remained fairly constant since.

I like the system for the most part, but I do have a problem with how NASCAR allows a young driver to have up to seven starts per season and still retain his rookie status. Although it's not common, some drivers over the years have run up to seven races in *more than one* season and have still been considered "rookies."

Then there are the veteran race car drivers, particularly those who came to NASCAR from other series, like the Indy Racing League, who were considered "rookies" when they reached the Sprint Cup level. That's a misnomer if I ever heard one. But so be it; those are the stipulations NASCAR has in place, and we have to live with them.

Since 1974, a number of young drivers have come into the sport and either went on to become stars or faded away almost as quickly as they came. But whose rookie season gave us the best hint of what was (or was not) to come? I am including the Rookie of the Year only from 1974 to 2007, because it takes at least two years for a rookie to really get on the path to success in NASCAR.

In order, from fifth to first, here's my list of the top five rookies (and the year they won their respective titles) in the modern era who would go on to greatness:

5. TIE: **Alan Kulwicki (1986), Davey Allison (1987), and Kyle Busch (2005).** Kulwicki and Allison never reached their full potential as drivers because they died (about three months apart) in 1993 in tragic flying incidents. Kulwicki perished with three others when their small plane crashed on its final approach to the airport in Johnson City, Tennessee. Allison was killed in a parking lot of Talladega Superspeedway while practicing landings in a brand-new helicopter he had just purchased. (Legendary driver Red Farmer was also in the chopper and was severely injured but survived.) Kyle Busch, the younger Busch brother, is one of the most prolific, exciting, and controversial figures in the sport, and he just turned twenty-five! If what he's accomplished thus far is any indication of what's to come, Busch could become one of the greatest drivers the sport has ever known; he's already got a great start in that direction.

4. **Rusty Wallace (1984).** Wallace came out of the St. Louis area, having first raced for a team owned by his father, as well as being the first of three brothers (with Kenny and Mike) who would eventually go racing in Sprint Cup competition. After earning Rookie of the Year honors, it would take Wallace five more seasons before he would win his first and only Cup championship. Although he failed to win any more titles, he did go on to win 55 career Cup races, which is a lot by anyone's measuring stick.

3. **Tony Stewart (1999).** Stewart came to NASCAR after a brief but superlative career in Indy cars, preceded by a lengthy stint of numerous wins and several championships in sprint-car and midget-car racing. It took Stewart just four years to win a Cup title, a feat he repeated three years later. He is closing in on 40 career wins on the Cup circuit.

2. **Jeff Gordon (1993).** Like Stewart, Gordon built his racing foundation in sprint and midget cars. He quickly became one of the Sprint Cup's most prolific winners and champions, earning his

first title in his third season of full-time competition (1995), followed by three other titles, in 1997, 1998, and 2001. He also has won more than 80 Cup races and may hit 90 before he retires.

1. **Dale Earnhardt (1979).** No modern-day rookie can match what the late Intimidator did in his career. It took Earnhardt just two seasons, including his rookie campaign, before he won his first championship (1980). He went on to win six others, tying Richard Petty for most Cup titles earned (seven). Earnhardt also won 76 career Cup races. Had he not tragically perished in the 2001 Daytona 500 at the far too young age of forty-nine, Earnhardt might have gone on to win at least one more championship and several more races. After all, he finished second in 2000 to champion Bobby Labonte and won 5 races in the two previous seasons before his untimely death.

# What Are the Best Tracks for Tailgating and Partying?

For many fans, attending a Sprint Cup race in person is number one in their hearts and minds, followed closely by tailgating and partying. It's no secret that NASCAR fans love to party. And as wild as today's crowds may seem, they're actually tame compared to the race crowds from the late 1960s until around the mid-1990s. For many during that era, going to a NASCAR race was a celebration of speed and drunken debauchery. Women showing their breasts, couples having public sex, and the almost obligatory drunken brawls were practically stalwarts of the NASCAR crowd during that period.

As NASCAR made a conscious move to become more family-friendly, some of that craziness has been greatly reduced—but not completely reduced. Go to places like Daytona, Talladega, and Michigan, and you can still see a lot of skin and more.

The men at 'Tona and 'Dega like to shower the women who obligingly bare their breasts with Mardi Gras–like beads, a prized commodity and great symbol of bragging rights. If you see a woman walking around a track with a whole slew of multicolored beads, there are only two ways she got them: she bought them, or she flashed to a number of appreciative men.

Talladega is known not only for that proclivity but also for some of the most memorable fights among the fans, in the stands, the parking lots, or the campgrounds. It's no wonder there is such a huge police presence at each of Talladega's two annual races, including police officers who look into virtually every car leaving the track to see if they can spot open containers or drunk drivers.

If you haven't been to any or many NASCAR races and want to see humanity at its most basic animalistic core, here's a primer of the best tracks at which to tailgate and party—and oh yeah, to eventually see a race:

5. **Michigan International Speedway.** Some folks like to call Michigan International Speedway the Talladega of the north because of the pervasive party atmosphere. The Midwest ethic includes lots of tailgating, camping, and drinking. If you didn't know any better, you'd say the crowd was tailgating before a football game, because the vibe is almost the same. Situated in south-central Michigan, in the picturesque Irish Hills area, this track is almost a perfect venue for partying and racing. Numerous lakes—and lake house rentals—wind up being either the start or the end of each day's partying going to or returning from the track. Of special note: If you leave the racetrack and go west on Route 12, be prepared to enter a flashing zone, where race fans line both sides of the two-lane road, waving signs or chanting the phrase "Show us your boobs." I've seen sixty-year-old grandmothers take off their tops, much to the delight of the audience.

4. **Texas Motor Speedway.** This is one of the few tracks on the circuit that lets folks who are camping or in RVs arrive a week before the race. What does that tell you? Plenty of party time! Texas Motor Speedway also arguably has the best tailgate cooking around. I've spent many hours walking around through parking

lots where I've watched folks cooking everything from full pigs to monstrous Texas steaks to alligator meat. Oh yeah, and don't forget the Texas chili. But be forewarned: Bring a gallon of ice cold water with you, just in case, because Texans love to spice up their chili with things like jalapeños and wasabi. Talk about hot—you can easily wind up with a five-alarm fire in your mouth and gut if you're not careful. (I've actually seen people be taken to the hospital as a result.) If you smell something good, ask for a sample—and ask if it's hot. Folks are very friendly and always love to make new friends.

3. **Bristol Motor Speedway.** Virtually a carbon copy of Texas, only in a much smaller geographic footprint. Parking lots and campgrounds are situated very close to the racetrack. Over the years, Bristol has become much more of a family-friendly track, so if you're looking for excessive skin display, fall-down drunkenness, and downright debauchery, you've come to the wrong place. A few instances pop up here and there, but for the most part, the partying and tailgating here is rather sedate.

2. **Daytona International Speedway.** This place used to be the king of partyin', drinkin', flashin', and tailgatin'. But as the track has gone through a number of capital improvement programs, including new race garages, the creation of a very popular fan zone, and the like, mischief in the infield has been ratcheted way down. Still, it has its moments. Be especially careful if you're walking around the RV lots and campgrounds: I was brushed by a car a few years back while walking alongside the main access road through the middle of the infield. Had I been two inches more to my left, I might not be writing this now. It was an elderly gentleman—I'm not sure if he was under the influence or just couldn't see (but how can anyone miss a 275-pound behemoth like me, anyway?). I'll never forget how his car brushed my buttocks and my left arm. Meanwhile, the driver kept on going as if nothing had happened.

1. **Talladega Superspeedway.** Even though the track has cleaned up its act, most notably in the infield, it is still a modern-day Sodom and Gomorrah. The best party action is in the surrounding

campgrounds. Partying typically starts on Thursday and continues 24/7 until Monday, the day after the race. One thing to be prepared for, especially if you're bringing your family, is that lots of skin gets displayed in the campgrounds. The parking lots are a bit tamer, and the infield is a crapshoot. Parts of it are G-rated while others are close to X-rated. As an aside, in terms of places and foods, Talladega was the first place I sampled alligator. And yes, it tasted like chicken.

# What Were the Greatest Daytona 500 Races?

In another chapter of this book, I'll discuss NASCAR's one-hit wonders. Because the nature of a one-hit wonder is doing something so big at a major event that it stands out above everything else, naturally a win in the Daytona 500 would take precedence.

But what about the greatest Daytona 500 races of all—not the one-time wonders, but the races that shaped or defined the sport's biggest contest? Even though it kicks off the season rather than ending it, the Daytona 500 has assumed the persona of NASCAR's version of the Super Bowl: the sport's biggest race with the biggest payday and the most prestige.

Granted, I should cover all sixty-plus editions of the Daytona 500. But because the majority of this book is based upon NASCAR's modern era (1972 to the present), I'm focusing on the five races that made the most impact on the sport's development and are responsible for its ascension to the second most popular spectator sport in the United States.

Here's my list of the five most important modern-era Daytona 500s:

5. **2004.** Three years after his father perished on the final lap of the 2001 Daytona 500, Dale Earnhardt Jr. broke through to win his first—and only, as of this writing—Daytona 500. It took

his father twenty years to win his only 500 title, but Junior did so in just his fifth start. Not only did it show that Junior could do it, it further helped to cement his reputation as NASCAR's most popular driver, a title that would continue to grow with each passing year. According to some accounts, the cheers for Junior were the loudest ever heard for any driver in Daytona's history.

4. **1988.** Bobby Allison showed that even at the age of fifty, father still knows best, for he held off a hard late-race surge by his son Davey to win by two car lengths. It would be one of the few times that father and son would finish right behind each other.

3. **1976.** In one of the greatest battles of their long rivalry, Richard Petty and David Pearson were bound and determined to beat the other to the finish line. Somehow, you just knew something would happen before the checkered flag, and it did: both drivers made contact coming out of turn four, spinning into the front-stretch grass. It was a battle of restarts at that point. Pearson was able to fire his engine and, even with a crippled race car, drove past Petty, who could not get refired in time. Pearson returned to the track and crossed the finish line at a speed estimated to be just 20 miles per hour. It would be Pearson's first and only career triumph in the Great American Race.

2. **1998.** After nineteen previous misses, including losing just two turns from the finish line in 1990 due to a blown tire, Dale Earnhardt finally conquered Daytona, winning in his twentieth start. Earnhardt would amass more than 30 career wins in several different racing series at the legendary 2.5-mile super-speedway, but only once would he be able to claim the title of Daytona 500 champion. It was a triumph not just for Earnhardt but for NASCAR as well, for it was one of the few times that something like this has ever happened: crews from all forty-three teams came out onto the pit road to congratulate Earnhardt on unquestionably the biggest and most satisfying win of his Cup career. It's such a tragedy that he was taken from us three years later.

1.  **1979.** I've already mentioned this as the most important race in NASCAR history and thus in Daytona 500 lore as well. Leaders Donnie Allison and Cale Yarborough got together on the backstretch, sliding into the infield near turn four (and eventually getting into a fistfight after exiting their cars). A shocked Richard Petty slid on past to claim the win, taking the victory by one car length over Darrell Waltrip, with A. J. Foyt finishing third. Not only was it a wild finish, it was the first flag-to-flag live national TV broadcast of a NASCAR race to a mostly captive audience housebound by a blizzard.

# What Are NASCAR's Best Rules?

Why does it always seem that there are more bad things than good things in this world? Elsewhere in this book (the Red Flag section), I mention the worst rules in NASCAR. There are so many bad rules, in my opinion, that I had to resort to creating a top-ten list just to squeeze them all in.

That's not the case with NASCAR's best rules (fortunately or unfortunately, depending on your viewpoint). There are just five rules that are the best overall elements of the sport, making it stand out and be better for everyone. Here are my choices for the five best rules in NASCAR today:

5.  **Pit road speed limits.** Even though there are still mishaps on pit road, the situation today is *much* better than in the past. Who can forget when Ricky Rudd accidentally ran into Mike Rich, the right-rear-tire changer for Bill Elliott, at Atlanta in 1990? Rich, tragically, was killed in the mishap, due partly to the fact that there was no pit road speed limit in effect at the time. Later, two of Rudd's crew members were struck by Ward Burton's car after a pit road collision with Casey Atwood sent Burton's car into Rudd's pit at Homestead, Florida, in the

2001 season finale. That incident eventually led NASCAR to mandate all over-the-wall crew members to wear heavy-duty helmets in addition to already mandated firesuits. Drivers and fans sometimes complain that pit road speeds are too slow, but I'd rather have slow speeds than funerals and paralyzed crew members.

4. **Freezing the field when a caution flag flies.** It used to be that a "gentlemen's agreement" existed between drivers that when a yellow caution was thrown, they wouldn't try to advance their positions. Unfortunately, NASCAR is steeped in a tradition of bootleggers and cheaters, which means that the gentlemen's agreement often went out the window. But when Casey Mears almost broadsided Dale Jarrett's crippled car in 2003 at New Hampshire in an attempt to gain as many positions as possible before taking the yellow caution flag at the start-finish line, NASCAR had seen enough. It implemented a new rule that immediately froze the entire race field at the time the caution flag was thrown. That way, no one could unfairly or sneakily advance his position any longer—and potentially risk the safety of the other drivers on the track. Electronic devices implanted in the race cars and at several points around the racetrack helped to keep everything on the up-and-up. Since its implementation, the system has worked so well that many have wondered why it took NASCAR so long to bring it to fruition. NASCAR is known for its speed on the racetrack but not in the boardroom.

3. **Double-file restart.** Even though this rule was only recently implemented (in 2009), it has earned its weight in gold very quickly. It's hard to find anyone who doesn't like it, other than maybe the field fillers, who rarely get a chance to race up front except in restarts off cautions that preceded the implementation of the double-file restart. Now the leader has the choice of taking either the inside or the outside lane on a restart, the driver running second at the time is then given the other line, and all cars on the lead lap fall in behind in their respective positions at the time of the restart (in other words, the first driver is next

to the second, the third is next to the fourth, the fifth is next to the sixth, and so on). This is yet another example of folks wondering aloud to NASCAR, "What the heck took you so long?"

2. **Green-white checker finish.** I have mixed emotions about this rule. On the one hand, it helps to ensure that a race finishes under green-flag conditions (though it doesn't always work that way). On the other hand, it's an artificially created way to bunch up the field for a two-lap shoot-out to the checkered flag. It certainly injects drama and excitement into the race's finish, but should a race outcome really be decided in just a two-lap battle? I'd be much more in agreement with a five-lap shoot-out, but a two-lap green-white checker is better than nothing, I guess. And if it breeds drama and excitement, even though it was created artificially, that's still a good thing for the sport and the fans.

1. **Mandatory use of head-and-neck-restraint devices.** After Dale Earnhardt was killed at Daytona International Speedway in February 2001, NASCAR moved quickly to require that all drivers wear head-and-neck-restraint devices. It became mandatory in October 2001, roughly eight months after Earnhardt's death, which might have been prevented if he had been wearing one. Earnhardt died from basilar skull fracture; his neck essentially snapped from the trauma and the impact of the crash. An emphasis was also placed on the installation of steel and foam energy reduction barriers at racetracks to cut down on the impact of crashes into retaining walls, but that was a process that took several years to complete at all NASCAR tracks. The head-and-neck devices were much easier and quicker to implement. Although most drivers quickly adhered to the new rule—in fact, some actually started wearing the devices even before NASCAR made them mandatory—there were some holdouts, most notably Tony Stewart. The Indiana native claimed that he suffered from extreme claustrophobia and that the restraint device would impede his ability to drive a race car. Stewart refused to wear the device, but NASCAR had the last word on it, telling Stewart to either wear it or not race. Needless to say, he's worn one in every race since.

# Who Is the Best NASCAR Driver to Never Win a Points-Paying Cup Race?

Thanks to Jeff Turner of McLeansboro, Illinois, for this particular question. It's a great one, Jeff, although I admit I was kind of stumped by it at first. How can you gauge a driver who is the "best" to never win a points race? If he's a good driver, wouldn't you expect him to have lots of wins? But after giving it more thought, I realized that it is actually a good and legitimate question.

Before answering the question, let me preface it with a caveat: Just because a driver has never won a Cup race doesn't make him a bad driver—or a good driver, for that matter. But given how many drivers have come and gone in the Cup Series in the last six decades and have never won a race, you have to draw some type of qualifier to distinguish which drivers are eligible for this category.

To me, that qualifier is success—that is, wins and championships—in other series, most notably the Nationwide/Busch Series and the Camping World/Craftsman Truck Series. A driver may have been a dud, victorywise, in the Cup Series, but he could be a true stud in the other two racing leagues.

Here are some of the main requirements that I used to determine my pick for number one:

- He had to have at least 150 career starts in the Cup Series. So if you're thinking about guys like Mike Bliss, David Green, or Jason Leffler, who are stalwarts in either the Nationwide or the Trucks series, they're eliminated because none have even reached 100 career Cup starts.
- He had to have had marked success in either the Nationwide/ Busch Series or the Camping World/Craftsman Truck Series, with a minimum of 100 career starts in one of those series, as well.
- He's been called upon numerous times in his career as a fill-in driver on the Cup side to replace another driver for reasons of

illness or injury, he served as an interim replacement after a
driver was released, or he was hired to simply "shake down"
a car to see if a poor performance was due to the car itself or the
regular driver.

I'm going to list my top five picks from fifth to first, starting with
three honorable mentions. Because some, if not all, raced in 2009 during the preparation of this book, I've rounded off some of their career
numbers, such as starts and total races, to reflect this.

HONORABLE MENTION: **Kevin Lepage:** 201 career Cup starts;
   more than 250 Nationwide Series starts (including 2 wins)
   ▪ **Dave Blaney:** more than 320 career Cup starts; more than
   115 career Nationwide starts (including 1 win) ▪ **Mike Wallace:**
   188 career Cup starts; more than 330 career Nationwide
   starts (including four wins); more than 110 career Trucks starts
   (including 4 wins).

5. **Jeff Green:** 265 career Cup starts; more than 260 career
   Nationwide starts (including 16 wins); winner of the Busch (now
   Nationwide) Series championship in 2000 and runner-up in 1999
   and 2001.

4. **Kenny Wallace:** more than 340 career Cup starts; more than 450
   career Nationwide starts (including 9 wins); runner-up in the
   Busch Series in 1991.

3. **Todd Bodine:** more than 230 career Cup starts; more than
   320 career Nationwide starts (including 15 wins); runner-up
   in 1997 and third in 1990 and 1992 in the Busch Series; more
   than 135 career Camping World starts (with more than 15 wins);
   won the Trucks championship in 2006.

2. **Ted Musgrave:** 305 career Cup starts (but none since 2003);
   191 career Camping World Truck Series starts (including
   17 wins); winner of the 2005 Camping World Truck Series championship, runner-up in 2001, and third place in 2002, 2003, and
   2004. Even though Musgrave was forced to the sidelines in 2009
   due to a lack of sponsorship, he still maintained his active status
   as a driver per NASCAR licensing. That's why I've included him

here, particularly since it's difficult to ignore the kind of numbers and accomplishments Musgrave has posted in his career.

1. **Mike Skinner:** more than 260 career Cup starts, including being the late Dale Earnhardt's teammate at Richard Childress Racing from 1996 to 2001; more than 200 career Truck Series starts with nearly 30 wins; winner of the Truck championship in 1995 and close runner-up in 2007. It seems that whenever a Cup owner needs a short-term replacement driver or someone to shake down a car, Skinner is typically at the top of the list. In recent years, he's driven for Red Bull Racing, Michael Waltrip Racing, Bill Davis Racing, and Tommy Baldwin Racing, among others. Given his achievements over the years, even if they don't include a Cup win, it's not surprising that Skinner is such a man in demand on the Cup side.

# NASCAR's
# Worst and
# Overrated

# Who Are the Most Overrated Drivers in NASCAR Today?

NASCAR's best drivers are gauged by numerous criteria, the biggest one being championships. Race wins are also notable, but that's a double-edged sword. Racking up a number of wins shows that a driver has what it takes to succeed under pressure and to outdo his peers.

At the same time, a driver can have all the wins in the world, but without at least one championship under his belt, he'll always be "a bridesmaid and never the bride." Being popular with the fans, generating millions in souvenir sales, being a great commercial spokesman for his sponsors, and being media-friendly are nice attributes to have, but without *champion* permanently attached to his name, a driver may be good, but he isn't great.

I know the following two picks for most overrated drivers will generate a great deal of controversy, particularly if you're a fan of one of these drivers. But try to have an open mind when I give my reasons for their being overrated. Maybe then you'll see what I see: good, not great, and certainly not in the same class as those who are indeed great.

1. **Dale Earnhardt Jr.** He's been the most popular driver in the sport for the past seven years. His Junior Nation far exceeds any other driver's fan posse. He's the son of one of the sport's greatest drivers. But the man they call Junior is without question the most overrated and overexposed driver in the sport today. He may have won a couple of Busch Series championships in the 1990s, but the competition he faced and the equipment his competitors had was, for the most part, second-rate. It's no wonder he did so well, with the best equipment and some of the best minds in

the business toiling away at Dale Earnhardt Inc. (DEI). Junior has 18 Cup wins in his nine-season career (through 2009), but how many of those were on restrictor-plate tracks (7) when DEI was the undisputed king of plate racing? It's been said that when DEI dominated, they could have put a chimp in the driver's seat and it would have won.

Junior is a great ambassador for the sport, not to mention its figurehead (a role I'm not sure he totally embraces). But what has he done on the racetrack of late? How many Cup championships has he earned? None. How many seasons has he been a legitimate contender for the championship in the final weeks of the season yet fallen short? One (2003). Although the Junior Nation's voices drown out many of Earnhardt's detractors, there is a substantial silent minority that perceives him as a guy who came into the sport with a silver spoon in his mouth and who didn't pay his dues as much as up-by-their-own-bootstraps guys like Tony Stewart, Kyle and Kurt Busch, Denny Hamlin, and Jeff Gordon. Instead, when Junior came to the Cup level in 2000, he inherited one of the biggest racing operations (DEI), one of the biggest sponsors (Budweiser), and eventually the legacy of his father, who died in 2001.

The problem with Junior, as I see it, is that he has spent far too much time building himself up as a brand and an icon in the sport—in other words, worrying more about money than about becoming a truly good race car driver. Unfortunately, the Junior Nation just can't understand that he'll never be a seven-time champion like his father; in fact, I'll be shocked if he ever wins more than one Cup title in his career. He talks a good game about being determined and committed to his craft, but he just has too many off-track pursuits, including far too many commercials; owns (and visits far too often) a popular downtown Charlotte nightspot; and hangs around with too many rock stars to ever convince us he'll be a great driver. If his name was anything but Earnhardt, he'd be just another fair-to-good driver, period. But, I admit, being Dale Jr. can't be easy. He has so many demands on his time, being pulled in several directions. Let him win even half the number of titles his father did, and maybe we can talk about him being one of the sport's greats. For now, he's just a pretty face with a pretty car and has some good ability and talent. Junior's a good driver, but he's not a great one—and most likely never will be.

2. **Kasey Kahne.** The Enumclaw, Washington, native seems to be as popular in the sport for his looks as for driving talent. Wait, scratch that; Kahne is *more* popular for his looks than his ability behind the wheel, judging from the award-winning success of the series of Allstate commercials he was featured in from 2006 through 2009. You know the ones, where the hot-to-trot thirty- to forty-year-old women will do anything to get the impish-looking Kahne's attention, even if it means crashing into something that results in chaos and havoc. Sure, Kahne makes the ladies swoon, even though he barely looks a day over sixteen (he actually turned thirty in 2010) and is probably carded in every bar he goes to, even though he's sponsored by Budweiser. Prior to coming to the Cup Series, Kahne was part of a high-dollar and highly publicized tug-of-war between Ford and Dodge (team owner Ray Evernham and Dodge ultimately won), but it's pretty obvious that he's not going to live up to the prediction that he'll be a multichampionship winner by the age of thirty. Still, there's the cuteness and popularity factor that he, his handlers, and his fans can't deny. If NASCAR were smart, it would start a *Tiger Beat*–like magazine featuring Kahne, with two editions: one for teenage girls and the other to appease the Allstate women. It would make millions. But what about his driving? He led the series with 6 wins and finished 8th in the Chase for the Nextel Cup in 2006, his career single-season best. But Kahne is one of the most pronounced hot-and-cold drivers in the sport. When he's on, he's on. When he's off—which is more often than not—he's *way* off. If Kahne looked more like, say, Jimmy Spencer, he wouldn't be nearly as popular—but he would still be overrated.

# Which of Today's Drivers Have Been the Biggest Flops?

Picking the flops, careerwise, was tough for me because I'm friends with so many of today's drivers. Criticizing them is not something I take lightly.

That's why I hope that those I list here will understand my rationale for picking them and won't hold any animosity toward me. I'm willing to bet that at least some of them may even agree with me—that they were tabbed "can't miss," but for one reason or another they have never lived up to all the hype.

Here are my top-ten drivers who started out as "can't miss" but have become "never was":

1. **Elliott Sadler.** He has carried the title of "the next big superstar" throughout his career. And after more than ten years of his being on the Cup level, we're still waiting for him to live up to that reputation. Sadler has gone from the Wood Brothers to Robert Yates Racing to Gillett Evernham Motorsports to Richard Petty Motorsports; he has had major sponsors like Ford/Motorcraft, Dodge, M&Ms, and Best Buy on the side of his car; and he's won just 3 races, and his best season finish is ninth (the only top-ten finish of his career). The sad thing is that he's really a great guy and one of my favorites. I just hope he doesn't punch me the next time he sees me.

2. **Casey Mears.** Rick Hendrick kept *him* instead of Kyle Busch to make room for Dale Earnhardt Jr. in the Hendrick Motorsports stable! What was Hendrick thinking? When your uncle (Rick Mears) is one of only three drivers to win the Indianapolis 500 four times, and your father was one of the best off-road racers in the world, some of those great racing genes should rub off on you. Unfortunately, stardom for this Mears in NASCAR is a

never-will-be proposition. He's a great guy but an average racer at best. Maybe he should have stayed in open-wheel racing.

3. **Reed Sorenson.** This Georgia native has been more like the pits than a peach. Part of the reason is Sorenson himself. He's far too low-key for his own good. Even in rare moments of success, he has appeared in TV interviews as if he were just coming back from a funeral. He's a great sportsman driver, but he'll never have what it takes to be a big success in the Sprint Cup. Even driving Richard Petty's legendary No. 43 did absolutely nothing for him, other than to get him released at the end of 2009.

4. **Jamie McMurray.** After winning in only his second career Cup start (filling in for the injured Sterling Marlin), McMurray has seemed to be afraid of success. There really is no explanation for why he hasn't succeeded. He had the equipment and the funding at Roush Fenway Racing (after not having much of either at his prior stop, Chip Ganassi Racing), but he just didn't have the talent to match. And when Roush had to cut down from five to four teams, McMurray was the logical driver in the stable to be let go. It's hard to justify keeping someone like him if he doesn't produce the results. That being said, Jamie's win in the 2010 Daytona 500 could be a sign that he is finally beginning to showcase the talent he does have, and I might have to eat my words here. Only time will tell, I guess.

5. **J. J. Yeley.** He came to Joe Gibbs Racing with Tony Stewart's highest recommendation, but he was never able to succeed at the normal high level expected of Gibbs's drivers, so he was eventually cast aside for Kyle Busch. If you were in Joe Gibbs's position and a talent like Busch became available, wouldn't you do the same thing?

6. **David Stremme.** He's had great opportunities with both Chip Ganassi and Roger Penske, but when it came down to crunch time, Stremme just wasn't able to cut it, unlike his fellow South Bend, Indiana, neighbor, Ryan Newman. It's too bad, because Stremme is really a great guy.

7. **Robby Gordon.** He should have stayed in open-wheel or off-road racing. That seems to be where he is in his element and

does his best as a racer, which cannot be said about his extremely mediocre Cup career.

8. **Jeremy Mayfield.** This Kentucky native is a nice guy, but after being fired from three teams (Penske, Evernham, and Bill Davis), plus his indefinite suspension from racing in May 2009 after he was accused by NASCAR of using illegal drugs, any chance of him ever making it big has been over for many years.

9. **Michael Waltrip.** He has been forever burdened by his older and much more successful brother, Darrell. Michael is a great guy, a great commercial pitchman, a great ambassador for the sport, a great father, and funny and personable, but he has been and always will be an average driver, at best. I wish him well in his switch to part-time driving status in 2010, but I don't expect any miracles now that he'll no longer have to worry about the pressure of the points standings.

10. **John Andretti.** I hate to include John in this category, because I really like him as a friend. Unfortunately, much like Mears, John was never able to live up to the family name in stock car racing. And, like Mears and Gordon, if he had it to do it all over again, he might have been better off staying in open-wheel racing.

## Who Is the Most Overrated Crew Chief in NASCAR Today?

Chad Knaus is a great tactician, strategist, and motivator, but above all else, he's also a cheat. How many times has he been caught by NASCAR bending, if not outright blatantly breaking, the rules? How many suspensions has he received? How many hundreds of thousands of dollars in fines has he had to pay for "being creative," "pushing the envelope," or "working in the gray area," all of which have been Knaus's retorts when he has been caught with his hand in the proverbial cookie jar?

He even has his underlings following in his footsteps—like Steve Letarte, who replaced Robbie Loomis as Jeff Gordon's crew chief in the fall of 2005 and has already been penalized for infractions, including a six-race suspension in 2007 (along with Knaus).

You can argue that Knaus has led Jimmie Johnson to four Nextel and Sprint Cup championships in a row. But do you honestly think that Jimmie would have won all those titles if Knaus had been banned from working or communicating with the team for a year? Even when he was on suspension for past violations, he showed up at the shop during the week and kept in nearly constant contact with his designated backup, Darian Grubb, on race weekends. Grubb was atop the pit box, but it was Knaus who was still calling the shots remotely.

The fact that Rick Hendrick constantly backs and supports an employee every time he is found to be in blatant violation doesn't say much for the kind of team owner he is—in spite of the common belief that Hendrick is one of the most aboveboard and well-respected men in the sport. If Hendrick put honesty and integrity ahead of the winning-at-all-costs philosophy that dominates his multicar organization, Knaus would have been long gone from NASCAR, perhaps back to his roots in sportsman racing in his native Rockford, Illinois.

But Hendrick isn't solely to blame. If NASCAR really wanted to make a statement, instead of merely slapping Knaus's wrist every time he does wrong, it would put some meat into the penalties for blatant cheating.

The next time Knaus—or any other crew chief, for that matter—is caught intentionally breaking the rules, the punishment should fit the crime. How about a one-year suspension without pay or a million-dollar fine? If NASCAR had the guts to be this forceful, I guarantee you that a sport that has for too long advocated an "if you ain't cheatin', you ain't tryin'" philosophy would attain greater heights of credibility and respect from fans than it ever has.

It would also probably draw more media attention and more new fans to the sport, rather than alienating millions of fans and others who have left the sport because they got fed up with shenanigans like Knaus's. There is a lot of credence to Tony Stewart's belief that NASCAR is akin to World Wrestling Entertainment on wheels—with predetermined story lines and sometimes, as much as I hate to say it, predetermined outcomes.

# Who Are the Most Hated Drivers
# of Modern Time?

We talked about the most beloved drivers in the Green Flag section. Now it's time for the antithesis, the most hated drivers in the sport. *Hated* may be a tough word to swallow, but I call 'em as I see 'em. And if a driver is a constant lightning rod for criticism or bad feelings from fans, the media, and even their peers in the garage, then how else would you describe him?

Here are my top-five hated drivers of modern time:

1. **Dale Earnhardt.** For all the reasons he was beloved, the late Earnhardt was also NASCAR's most hated driver. Possessing what many perceived as an almost Snidely Whiplash persona, he was criticized by countless non-fans for his dirty racing style (Earnhardt called it simply being aggressive), in which he knocked aside any driver who happened to be in his way and wouldn't move. Yet even if he was hated on the track, only the most callous, heartless individuals didn't feel sad when he was so tragically killed. There were only a few; the sport doesn't need "fans" like that.

2. **Jeff Gordon.** Derisively nicknamed "Wonder Boy" by many of his non-fans—how much do you want to bet that most of those were fans of the senior and junior Earnhardt?—Gordon remains one of the most booed drivers in Sprint Cup today, particularly during driver introductions. But he takes it in stride: "Cheer for me or boo me, as long as they're making noise is what's most important to me, that the fans are so involved and so fervent in their love for the sport," Gordon said. "It wouldn't be much fun if they were all robots that cheered for only one guy or cheered for everybody."

3. **Darrell Waltrip.** Waltrip will be the first to admit that he was a bad guy earlier in his career and reveled in the role. It was quite a phenomenon to watch him battle Earnhardt for the unofficial

title of most hated man in NASCAR. But as he matured, Waltrip began a transformation into a beloved, humor-filled caricature of his old self, realizing that being a good guy trumps being a badass any day.

4. **Kurt Busch.** Speaking of transformations, Busch has come a full 180 degrees in the last few years. But four years ago, Busch was a horse of a far different color. In fact, the February 2006 edition of *GQ* magazine named him the third most hated athlete in the United States, behind baseball's Barry Bonds and football's Terrell Owens. That's some pretty high—uh, I mean low—company. At the time, the "honor" was deserved, given Busch's temper and sky-high ego at times. In particular, there was his unfortunate episode with a deputy sheriff outside Phoenix late in 2005, which prompted Roush Racing to suspend and then wash its hands of him. But once Kurt moved to Penske Racing—and after Roush Racing president Geoff Smith publicly embarrassed Busch by saying that the organization would no longer make excuses for him—Busch became a completely new man. Drivers who used to hate and despise him are now some of his best friends, on and off the track. Getting married and moving to Penske have certainly made the former bad boy mature into an outstanding driver and representative of the sport.

5. **Kyle Busch.** After older brother Kurt dropped the baton of most hated man in NASCAR, younger brother Kyle unintentionally picked it up, inheriting the role to the point where he revels in being Sprint Cup's number one villain. But he also takes such a dubious distinction in stride; he essentially tries to shake up the sport and bring more attention to it. If he has to act the role of bad boy to get people talking, he'll gladly do it. Actually, however, the younger Busch brother is not all that bad of a guy. In 2008, when no one else stepped up to the plate, Kyle donated more than $100,000 to longtime Nationwide Series driver Sam Ard, who had fallen on hard times financially and physically. Yes, a heart does beat deep within Kyle's body—and there's a lot of good in it, villain or not.

# Who Are the Worst Team Owners and Organizations?

The less we say about these owners and their organizations, the better. Some of them have fallen on hard times, others have had more ups and downs than a roller coaster, and some just flat-out stink.

I've changed the format a bit here because there are significant reasons that some of these organizations trail the rest of the pack.

### The Teams That Time Passed By

1. **Richard Petty, Petty Enterprises/Richard Petty Motorsports.** The Petty clan dominated Cup racing from the 1950s through the first half of the 1980s, first with family patriarch Lee Petty, then with son Richard Petty (who also became a great driver), and then with his son, Kyle Petty. Unfortunately, the team has been on a downward spiral for more than twenty years. It hasn't won a championship, or even come close, since Richard's final crown in 1979. Until Kasey Kahne hit victory lane twice in 2009, thanks to the off-season merger with Gillett Motorsports, Petty Enterprises—rechristened Richard Petty Motorsports after the merger—had not won a Cup race since 1999 (John Andretti), and it didn't have a higher individual-driver finish in the last ten years than 17th place (Andretti, 1999) until Kahne finished 10th of the twelve drivers in the 2009 Chase for the Sprint Cup. Some of the reasons for the lack of success over the last two decades are a stubborn resistance to change, much fewer resources than competitors, and an ambivalence or apathy that as long as they made the races, that was good enough.

2. **Glen and Leonard Wood and Children Eddie, Len, and Kim, Wood Brothers Racing.** Like the Pettys, the Woods have one of the most legendary organizations in the sport, with 97 career wins spanning a period of more than fifty years of NASCAR

racing. Unfortunately, the oldest continually operating Cup-level team has never claimed a championship. Even with the second generation now at the helm, WBR has become almost a carbon copy of Petty Enterprises in terms of why this team has struggled so much throughout the years; its lack of resources and general melancholy permeate the organization to this very day.

### Roller-Coaster Riding

1.  **Chip Ganassi, Chip Ganassi Racing, with Felix Sabates Racing and Earnhardt Ganassi Racing.** Much like Roger Penske, fellow open-wheel impresario Floyd "Chip" Ganassi has never been able to successfully transfer the success he had in the open-wheel world (five championships, 3 Indianapolis 500 victories) to NASCAR. Since purchasing the controlling interest in Felix Sabates Racing (Sabates has remained a minority investor in Ganassi), from 2000 through 2008, Chip Ganassi Racing managed to rack up just 6 victories and only 1 top-ten finish (Sterling Marlin, third in 2001). Things started looking better in 2009, when the company merged with Dale Earnhardt Inc., forming Earnhardt Ganassi Racing. Juan Pablo Montoya had an outstanding year and made the Chase for the Sprint Cup for the first time, ultimately finishing 8th in the final standings. Prior to the merger, Ganassi had arguably the most underperforming organization in the sport. It had everything it needed to perform better, but, inexplicably, it continued to struggle. Let's hope that what Montoya showed in 2009 carries over to 2010 and beyond. As a postscript, Jamie McMurray returned to the organization for 2010 and kicked off the new season with an emotional win in the season-opening Daytona 500. Could that perhaps be another harbinger of better things to come for EGR? We'll see.

2.  **Dietrich Mateschitz, Red Bull Racing.** Mateschitz entered Cup racing in 2007 with a new Toyota program. The jury is still out on this two-car operation with drivers Brian Vickers and former open-wheel star Scott Speed (who wasn't very speedy during his first full Cup season in 2009). Granted, Vickers made the 2009 Chase after narrowly missing it in 2008, but

misfortune in the first playoff races relegated him to the back of the pack, never to rebound. He ultimately finished last in the twelve-driver Chase field. Unfortunately, and much too often, Red Bull Racing can be up one week and struggle unmercifully the following week. Its two young drivers are promising, and it has plenty of resources and money. What it needs most of all is consistency, perhaps the hardest commodity to come by on the Cup level.

3. **Robby Gordon, Robby Gordon Racing.** When Gordon left Richard Childress Racing after 2005—some say he left voluntarily; others say he was forced out in favor of up-and-coming youngster Clint Bowyer—Gordon said he was fulfilling a lifetime dream of owning his own full-time Cup team. Unfortunately, he has struggled to the point where he's considered by many as the unluckiest driver in the series. If bad luck is going to find anyone, it's going to be the guy they call "the other Gordon" or the "anti-Jeff [Gordon]." Gordon has gone from Chevrolet to Ford to Dodge to Toyota in his first four seasons as his own boss. If Toyota doesn't wind up being the ticket, what's next for Gordon, a Kia?

4. **Doug Yates, Yates Racing.** Veteran team owner Robert Yates finally had enough and sold his organization to his son, Doug, after the 2007 season. Unfortunately, Doug Yates has struggled since taking the reins, particularly in finding sponsorship. As 2009 progressed, many began to ask whether the operation would remain together—and if so, for how long. That question was answered during the off-season when Yates Racing merged with Richard Petty Motorsports to form a four-car team. You almost need a scorecard to keep up with the number of drivers who have gone through the Yates camp of late, including David Gilliland, Travis Kvapil, and Paul Menard; then there was a partnership with Hall of Fame Racing that had Bobby Labonte as its driver. And now the merger has changed the roster even more. About the only thing that has remained a constant is that Yates will most likely never quit being a Ford-powered team.

# What Was the Worst Race in NASCAR History?

Elsewhere in this book, I have related my belief that you can never really single out a particular race as the all-time best or worst in NASCAR history. With more than 2,250 Sprint Cup, Winston Cup, Grand National, or Strictly Stock races in the NASCAR history books from 1949 to the present, you could conceivably find at least 2,250 people in the United States who would each pick a different Cup-level race as NASCAR's best or worst.

But there is one "race"—and I use that word loosely—that is very unlikely to be repeated (at least I hope it isn't) and that will go down in NASCAR annals as the worst-ever run. Anyone would be hard-pressed to give a better example than the fiasco I'm about to discuss. I'm not talking about some multicar wreckfest that took out more than half the field at Talladega or Daytona. Nor am I talking about snoozefests at places like Watkins Glen or Infineon Raceway.

Without question, the "worst" race, at least during NASCAR's modern era (since 1972), occurred on July 27, 2008, at Indianapolis Motor Speedway during the fifteenth running of the Allstate 400 at the Brickyard (commonly known as the Brickyard 400). In what was nothing short of one of the biggest calamities in NASCAR history, tire manufacturer Goodyear produced tires for the race with a rubber compound that simply could not stand up to the track's grainy and abrasive racing surface.

It was an absolutely incredible and abominable error for the second biggest race of the year, after the season-opening Daytona 500. Even the ill-fated Formula One race at Indianapolis in 2005, when all but six teams refused to compete because of safety concerns over tires, was not as much of a joke as this Sprint Cup event would ultimately prove to be. Goodyear was publicly caught with its pants down, so to speak, and it wasn't like the tire company didn't know what could potentially happen. Testing at the track earlier in the year had shown a need for a much different rubber compound from what is used for tires at any other track.

But somehow, Goodyear engineers hoped for the best, only to go down miserably. The rubber compound proved to be so bad that NASCAR had to call an unheard-of nine competition caution periods during the 160-lap event (with two other cautions called for crashes) so that the teams could continually change their tires, which kept shredding like the husk on an ear of corn.

There was enough advance notice—during the practice sessions on that Friday and Saturday—that the teams had begun preparing for what might happen. But no one really knew what to expect come race day. Everyone hoped and prayed for the best, but the drivers wound up with a situation that unquestionably was worse than anyone had ever seen before in a NASCAR race.

One highly placed executive for a major Cup team personally warned me early on race-day morning that we would be witness to a debacle unlike any we'd ever seen in NASCAR history. I didn't want to believe him, but given his experience, status, and expertise in the sport, I had no choice but to take him at his word—which ended up being prophetic as well as an understatement. Many on pit road knew it would be bad, but it's likely that no one could have predicted just how bad it would become.

Over and over, we saw cars get up to speed, do some passing and side-by-side racing, and then, just as they began to hit their stride, it was back into the pits for the next set of rubber. It was like clockwork; a car would run eleven or twelve laps at a time, then NASCAR would throw a competition caution to change tires that were mysteriously self-destructing in a manner never seen before in stock car racing, let alone motorsports history.

"Nobody likes to race like this," admitted Greg Stucker, Goodyear's director of race-tire sales, after the checkered flag mercifully fell. "I think the teams are going to be upset, probably rightly so."

Lost in all of the focus on the tread-wear debacle was Jimmie Johnson's second career Brickyard win. But if there's ever a win a race car driver would essentially like to forget about, this would be it. It was far from Johnson's most stellar effort; it was more like a battle of survival than a battle of one man and his machine against forty-two others.

Still, Stucker had the audacity to tell reporters after the race, "It's nobody's fault. It's the package [the combination of the tire and the new Cup car, the so-called Car of Tomorrow], and that's what we need to understand. We came up with the best tire we had for the conditions and we fell short of that. So we're going to turn around and try to do everything we can to make sure we get it right."

Unfortunately, Stucker then went on to say that he could not completely guarantee that such a perfect storm of incompetence and missing the mark wouldn't happen again—be it next year or ten years from now.

As for NASCAR's take, you couldn't help but feel sorry for guys like chairman Brian France, president Mike Helton, or vice president of competition Robin Pemberton. They did the best they could under the most trying circumstances they've probably ever endured. To their credit, they quickly realized just how major a problem they had on their hands, and they immediately moved to minimize the risk to the drivers, the teams, and the fans. They succeeded: only four cars were involved in wrecks, and no drivers suffered any injuries.

"We'll just try to learn from this and come back here and try it again next year," Pemberton said, shrugging his shoulders.

Goodyear tried to make good by offering partial refunds to the teams that had paid $1,700 per set of tires for up to ten sets. It's too bad that the 240,000 or more fans who showed up that Sunday afternoon didn't get a refund, too, because they're the ones who deserved it the most.

# What Are the Worst Racetracks in NASCAR?

Obviously, you can't pontificate on stock car racing's best tracks, as we did in the first section, without giving equal time to the worst tracks. These are the last places you want to see—or be seen at—a NASCAR race. The best tracks have a certain charm or joie de vivre that make them must-see locations; the worst tracks leave little to be desired, ranging from boring to downright monstrosities that don't deserve your hard-earned cash, let alone your precious time.

Choosing the five worst tracks is subjective, but I challenge anyone to prove that these choices are anything but bad in the overall scheme of things:

1.  **Pocono Raceway** (2.5-mile triangular oval, 85,000 capacity). Stay as far away from this place as possible. Now more than thirty-six years old, Pocono looks pretty much the way it did when it opened in 1974. The only things missing are leisure suits and disco balls. In other words, there have been very few improvements or amenities added since owners doctors Joseph and Rose Mattioli, who are now in their eighties, threw the gates open for the first time. *State of the art* and *Pocono Raceway* are definitely not synonyms. Pocono is the closest track to New York City, but it is not the kind of showplace facility that NASCAR needs if it's ever going to build a track in or near the Big Apple, which is one of chairman Brian France's biggest goals.

2.  **Watkins Glen International** (2.45-mile road course, 50,000 capacity). This is a close second to Pocono, but it's arguably the worst road course in existence—or at least in NASCAR. If it wasn't owned by NASCAR's International Speedway Corporation arm, it would have been off the Cup schedule a long time ago. The facilities have been nothing short of horrendous. But there's a ray of sunshine on the horizon: the nearly fifty-five-year-old media center was rebuilt in time for the 2008 season. There have also been other incremental facility improvements in the last few years, with more to come. But this track has a long, long way to go if it's ever to approach the aesthetic beauty and state-of-the-art facilities of the other road course on the circuit, Infineon Raceway.

3.  **Auto Club Speedway of Southern California** (2.0-mile oval, 95,000 capacity). If there was ever a track that does not deserve two races per year, it's this one. Formerly known as California Speedway, it still struggles to draw fans—even in the Southern California market, and particularly to what was its Labor Day

race, which came west in 2004 after a fifty-three-year run at Darlington Raceway. (In 2009 this race was moved to early October as part of the Chase for the Sprint Cup.) So many things work against the speedway in its attempt to be a success: location (roughly fifty miles from downtown Los Angeles); type of track (too long, not enough banking); lack of appeal to drivers; proximity to other tracks (Las Vegas and Phoenix); a general lack of interest in NASCAR by most Southern Californians; and fan indifference. Even outreach programs to attract new fans have been only marginally successful; unfortunately, these same programs haven't stopped a large exodus of former ticket holders. Plans to reconfigure the track someday are rumored to have already been drawn up, but it's doubtful that this track will ever be one of NASCAR's best, even if it is reconfigured. Some critics believe the best solution is to simply blow up the place and start over from scratch.

4. **Kansas Speedway** (1.5-mile oval, 85,000 capacity). One word describes this hovel in America's heartland: *boring*. It's no wonder that lots of fans write or call me to complain about so many 1.5-mile cookie-cutter tracks. The racing action at Kansas can best be described as monotonous and predictable. This track is not worthy of one of the ten races in the Chase for the Sprint Cup (the race should go to a track that deserves a second race, like Las Vegas). One of the main reasons it remains in the Chase, however, is that Sprint's corporate headquarters are just a few miles away.

5. **Martinsville Speedway** (.526-mile, capacity 65,000). The oldest track on the circuit doesn't look as if it's changed much since it opened in 1949. While the southwestern Virginia track has a unique charm to it, it's seriously lacking by most Cup standards. Let's face it, when a track has to brag about the type of hot dogs it sells ("famous Martinsville dogs"), something's seriously wrong. It wasn't too long ago, just before International Speedway Corporation bought the track for $192 million in 2004, that rumors abounded about the track's future—that it might lose one, if not both, of its yearly Cup races. But since the

corporation purchased the track, a favorite of NASCAR vice
president Jim France's (brother of the late Bill France Jr. and
uncle of Brian France), rumors of Martinsville's demise have all
but ended. Why NASCAR would want to keep two races at a
place that draws less than half the crowd that could be drawn
at a place like Las Vegas (or perhaps at a current non-Cup track
like in Kentucky) is beyond me. Actually, I do know the reason:
International Speedway and NASCAR don't own those tracks.
Hence, all money earned at Martinsville stays within the France
family. And as long as that continues to be the case, Martinsville's
two Cup dates aren't going anywhere. Too bad.

DISHONORABLE MENTION: **Homestead-Miami Speedway**, which is
literally built in the middle of a swamp, complete with alligators
and snakes nearby—it's definitely not where each season should
conclude or where a champion should be crowned • **Atlanta
Motor Speedway**, a once-great track that has been dying a slow
death ever since Richard Petty ran his last race there in 1992, and
where Jeff Gordon ran his first Cup event the same day—don't
be surprised if this track loses one of its two race dates to Las
Vegas or Kentucky by 2012, if not sooner.

# What Are the Worst Tracks for Ingress
# and Egress?

I was quite laudatory in the Green Flag section about several tracks
that have gone to great measures to significantly improve the ability of
fans to drive to and from them in relatively short order. Since I believe
in being fair, even if it's in a negative connotation, here are my picks
for the tracks that have the worst ingress and egress—that is, the tracks
that are the most pronounced pains in the butt to get into and out of:

1. **Las Vegas Motor Speedway.** This track is by far the worst of
   the worst, no question about it. I have friends in the Nevada

Highway Patrol, but even so, I must say that these guys simply have no clue when it comes to directing traffic. The Las Vegas Metropolitan Police Department, which directs traffic along Las Vegas Boulevard, is equally bad. I can't count the number of times I see police officers simply lounging around rather than doing what they're paid to do: keep traffic moving. And don't even get me started on the absolutely goofy traffic patterns, particularly along the normally expansive Las Vegas Boulevard. It's enough to drive you nuts. If you think you're going to catch a quick flight after the race, forget it. The *average* time it takes to get out of the parking lot is two to three hours. I've left the track four hours after a race, and it still took me another hour or more just to put the track in my rearview mirror.

You don't believe it's that bad? Let's put it this way: there are several helicopter companies that make tons of cash on race weekends flying folks to the track (and it's not cheap: typically a hundred dollars or more per person). I don't understand the problem; there's terrific access, and the track sits between I-15 and the boulevard. Maybe if the cops did their jobs, traffic would not be the number one thing that spoils a great race day. Two tips: First, if you can, try to come in from north of the speedway off I-15. Second, although the police tell the fans to come early to "avoid traffic," you typically can do pretty well if you come within two hours or less before the race starts, particularly along the boulevard. For years the track officials have tried to get the two major police agencies to work on improving traffic, particularly for egress, but to little avail. This track could learn so much from places like Michigan and Kansas.

2. **Talladega Superspeedway.** It takes three to four hours to get into the track and three to four hours to leave the track, at the very minimum. That's pretty much it in a nutshell. In fact, you typically wind up spending close to twice as much time in your car getting to and from the race than you do in your seat watching the race. Even though I-20 runs just a mile north of the track, Speedway Boulevard is a parking lot in either direction, both before and particularly after a race. It's no wonder so

many people choose to camp around the speedway: it's so much easier to leave the next morning. There are a few shortcuts that get you close to the track, but once you get within a couple of miles, it's still gridlock time. Making matters worse (although I do understand the safety aspect of it) is that the Alabama state troopers walk through traffic on Speedway Boulevard after a race looking for impaired drivers and those who are drinking while driving; they also tie up traffic by forcing those who are not wearing seat belts to pull to the side of the road. I've met several state troopers, and they're pretty good folks. But traffic control does not seem to be their forte.

3. **Bristol Motor Speedway.** I have one word for this track: *argh!* (I can think of other four-letter words, as well.) Let's face it, those of you who have attended races here know that traffic is nothing short of a nightmare. At times I have left more than three hours after a race (after writing my race story from the track) and have *still* run into gridlock. It doesn't help that the Bristol police keep the traffic from several parking lots from departing for at least one hour after the race. That's why, if you're looking for a relatively quick way to get out, park in the most outlying lot that your feet will allow (private lots are particularly good). Route 11 East is the main entryway to the track. The only shortcuts you might be able to find come from north and east of the track, but you really can't get to them if you come in from the west or the south (particularly I-81). And forget shortcuts from the west: there are none. Be prepared to spend several hours in your car trying to leave the area. Let's just hope you don't suddenly have an urge to go the bathroom, because if you do, you're out of luck.

4. **Charlotte Motor Speedway.** "Come early, leave late" is the unofficial motto for fans coming to this track, which was formerly known as Lowe's Motor Speedway. Even though there's great access with I-85 (and the connecting Bruton Smith Boulevard, formerly Speedway Boulevard) and I-485, as well as Route 29, which runs alongside the speedway, you easily will spend an hour or more waiting to get into the massive compound. My personal record is three hours to get to the track—from a hotel that was less than five miles

away! Although egress has improved in recent years, it'll still take you two or more hours to leave the area. Tips: Try to come in from the north (on either Route 29 or Route 49), park in outlying lots (to get out more quickly), or, if you can, take public transportation.

5. **Richmond International Raceway.** The first time I went to this track, I figured I'd take Laburnum Avenue, which runs right alongside. Big mistake! Three hours or more were spent just *getting* to the track, and my hotel was only seven miles away. I recall another time when my buddy from ESPN, Mike Massaro, got stuck in legendary prerace traffic here; it took him four hours to go roughly five miles from his downtown hotel to the track! It is horror stories like this that prompted me to find what is arguably one of the best shortcuts I've ever devised—and I'm not telling anyone. Let's just say that I can make it from the same hotel as my previous three-hour adventure to the track infield in less than twenty minutes. Eat your hearts out—and stay off Laburnum!

DISHONORABLE MENTION: **Watkins Glen International**: the road running past the track only has two lanes, so there are miles-long backups ▪ **Pocono Raceway**: bring lunch or dinner to eat in the car, because you won't be moving very far or very fast, that's for sure ▪ **Martinsville Speedway**: if you come from the north, west, or east, you're okay, but if you come from the south you will age quite a bit while waiting for traffic to move ▪ **Indianapolis Motor Speedway**: there are lots of streets you can take, but you're invariably going to be stopped by traffic at least a mile or more out in any direction. This is simply a place where you have to patiently bide your time.

# What Are the Worst Cities in NASCAR?

In the numerous e-mails I receive from readers each week, two cities stand out as the worst locales for NASCAR, offering the least amount of support, civic pride, and attention. (Had a racetrack been built on

Staten Island, however, New York would have zoomed to the top of this list). Here are the two picks:

1. **Los Angeles, California.** Without question, the Greater Los Angeles metro area is the most apathetic market in NASCAR today. Can someone tell me then why it plays host to not one but *two* Sprint Cup events per year? I give a great deal of credit to Gillian Zucker, the president of the Auto Club Speedway of Southern California (formerly California Speedway), for making extensive outreach efforts to virtually every ethnic community in Southern California to try to get a buzz going and attract new fans, but her efforts have had marginal success at best. Even with Hollywood and Disneyland within a short drive, you can't force people to like a sport that they obviously don't have much interest in. After all, if you can't fill a 92,000-seat racetrack from a greater metropolitan area of more than eight million people, you'd think that NASCAR would take the hint that it's really just not wanted. Even though Southern California is steeped in the automobile culture, it simply isn't NASCAR land.

2. **Miami, Florida.** There's plenty to do at South Beach, Key West, or Fort Lauderdale, but ask most Greater Miami residents what the third weekend of November means to them, and they'll probably say "high tide" or something like that. Let's face it, Homestead-Miami Speedway isn't the garden spot of the NASCAR world. Even worse, it was built in the middle of a swamp. Yes, that's right: an alligator and snake-infested swamp. If you get too far afield from the speedway, you can still see some gators and snakes slithering around. But there's more that leaves a lot of fans with a bad taste in their mouths after visiting this track. The Homestead community deserves a big pat on the back for its rebuilding efforts since Hurricane Andrew leveled it in 1992, yet the fact remains that parts of Homestead, adjacent Florida City, and nearby Cutler City are some of the most dangerous parts of the Greater South Miami area. If you're a visitor and get lost, good luck—you're going to need it. I recall the first time I visited this track in 2001: I was one of the unfortunate

visitors who did indeed get lost. I wound up being chased by three would-be robbers who noticed that I appeared lost in a very dark and desolate area on the fringe of the Everglades. They drove up from behind, intentionally rammed my rental car, and the race was on. Fortunately, in my role as a motorsports writer, I've been afforded the opportunity to attend several race-driving schools, and it was that training that no doubt saved my life and my wallet that evening. It's not every day you travel 85 miles an hour on a 35-mile-per-hour street (and do it with relative safety, despite being pursued by armed thugs). If you stay on U.S. 1 or the Florida Turnpike, you should be okay. But venture a few blocks off that well-traveled path, and you had better hope that your life insurance policy is up to date, just in case.

## Why Would NASCAR Be a Flop in New York City?

To many, New York City is the greatest city in the world. Frank Sinatra claimed that if you could make it in the Big Apple, you could make it anywhere. Except if you're NASCAR, that is.

Don't get me wrong; there are plenty of NASCAR fans in the tristate area of New York, New Jersey, and Connecticut. But in a metropolitan area of more than ten million people, the number of NASCAR and stock car racing fans is practically a drop in the bucket.

That's why NASCAR has always had little more than a chilly reception, at best, every time it has brought its traveling circus to New York. Beginning in 1981, the famed Waldorf-Astoria Hotel played host to the sport's annual season-ending awards-dinner banquet in late November or early December.

Late NASCAR chairman Bill France Jr. believed that moving the banquet to New York City would help put the sanctioning body and the sport in a much greater and broader light, especially since New York City is the largest media market in the world. New York was also home to many of the major corporations that had increasingly become sponsors of various NASCAR teams.

France figured that if he couldn't get major TV and radio networks and major publications like the *New York Times* and the *Wall Street Journal* to come to Daytona Beach, Florida (where the awards banquet was previously held), he'd bring the whole show to the Big Apple. It was a costly proposition, but if it meant getting large-scale media coverage—even if only for a week, while the biggest names of the sport were in town—France thought it was money well-spent.

For the most part, New York City tolerated NASCAR for twenty-five years. Then things started taking a decidedly quick plunge downward.

First there was NASCAR's attempt to build an 80,000-seat, .875-mile track on swampland on Staten Island. Promising a state-of-the-art, high-tech racing facility, the sanctioning body spent $100 million to purchase 440 acres of land, then spent even more later to buy an additional 235 acres, giving it a 675-acre footprint for the racing facility itself, as well as abundant parking.

The project was seemingly doomed right from the start. The majority of island residents didn't want a track, particularly with all the extra traffic it would bring (even though NASCAR assured the locals that it would utilize a network of 950 buses and more than 100 ferries to shuttle people to the race site).

Then environmentalists became involved. The place was a dump in more ways than one; it was the site of a former oil-tank farm, with hazardous materials interspersed with a very fragile ecosystem. NASCAR would have to drain the area and clean up the contaminated area, a project that some experts estimated might cost more than the value of the land itself.

Then there was political corruption, with a supervisor of an International Speedway Corporation (ISC) subsidiary being convicted for extortion. Finally, just slightly more than two years after NASCAR and ISC had proposed building the Staten Island facility, they threw in the towel in December 2006. But that doesn't mean that NASCAR has given up its hopes of racing in the Big Apple area soon.

"While we are disappointed that we could not complete the speedway development on Staten Island," ISC president Lesa France Kennedy told the Associated Press, "our enthusiasm for the metropolitan New York market is in no way dampened. We continue to view the region as a prime location for a major motorsports facility."

The global recession in 2008 and 2009 further delayed NASCAR's hopes to have a race in the New York area. But instead of optimistically hoping for 2011, NASCAR is now thinking that we won't see a race, or even the construction of a new racetrack, until 2013 or 2014, at the earliest. If ever.

Things got progressively worse after NASCAR pulled out of the Staten Island project. In 2007, during NASCAR's second Victory Lap around Times Square and midtown Manhattan, Mayor Michael Bloomberg's office was flooded with hundreds of phone calls by angry commuters who were late to work because a one-square-mile area in the heart of Manhattan was mired in gridlock, both vehicular and pedestrian traffic.

It was incidents like this that made NASCAR kill a short-lived idea of a street race through Manhattan, which would essentially turn what already is an island into an island on an island.

By 2008, NASCAR had all but been given a "not welcome" sign by New York. Major media outlets virtually ignored the awards banquet. Drivers, team owners, and the thousand or so attendees complained quite vocally about hotel rooms that cost five hundred dollars or more per night, not to mention other financial gouging for food, ground transportation, and airfare.

In fact, many regular banquet attendees decided not to attend the 2008 shindig because of the costs involved. One who decided not to attend was perhaps the most visible chronicler of NASCAR life, the late David Poole of the *Charlotte Observer*. With the parent company of his newspaper, McClatchy, having financial struggles, Poole took it upon himself to save his company a couple of thousand bucks by not attending the banquet.

"For what?" Poole said to me a few months before he tragically passed away from a massive heart attack at the age of fifty in late April 2009. "I don't need to see the dog and pony show and spend all that money when my company is fighting for its economic life. We could put that money to better use elsewhere."

It was less than a week before Poole's death that the sanctioning body announced it would not return to the Waldorf or New York City for its 2009 banquet. It had finally given in to an incentive-laden proposal to shift the event to Las Vegas and the fabulous Wynn Hotel—which, ironically, had been championed for several years by Bruton Smith, chairman of ISC's chief rival, Speedway Motorsports.

What's more, Las Vegas officials promised to allow NASCAR to once again have its Victory Lap anywhere it wanted, be it downtown or along the famous Strip. Finally, moving the annual awards banquet to Las Vegas would also increase the chance of eventually getting a second Sprint Cup race date at Las Vegas Motor Speedway.

As for NASCAR's future in New York, think about it. If NASCAR moves its biggest blowout of the year to Vegas, it would seem that the sanctioning body had given up on any hope of racing in or around the Big Apple anytime soon.

But NASCAR and ISC are a determined, if not stubborn, bunch. They have backup contingency plans for alternative racetrack sites in New Jersey's Meadowlands area; near the Westchester County Airport in White Plains, New York, about twenty miles north of midtown Manhattan; and even around tiny Linden Airport in Linden, New Jersey, roughly ten miles south of Newark.

And with the exception of some necessary adjustments (particularly if they have to shoehorn a track into a particular site), NASCAR and ISC appear committed to the same type of track they envisioned on Staten Island: a .875-mile track, similar in size and makeup to Richmond International Raceway, which is a .75-mile track. Also like Staten Island, the track will likely have two races per year—if it's ever built.

Unfortunately for the sanctioning body and its publicly traded speedway arm, the plan has been "greeted" with NIMBY ("Not In My Backyard") feedback from residents in all of those alternative sites. But don't fret, stock car fans in New York, New Jersey, and Connecticut. Even if you never have a track in your own neck of the woods, you will still have plenty of venues nearby at which to see guys like Kyle Busch, Jeff Gordon, Tony Stewart, and Dale Earnhardt Jr. Here are a few:

- **Pocono Raceway.** About 100 miles (a two-hour drive), and practically another world, away from midtown Manhattan, Pocono is arguably one of the worst tracks on the circuit. It's not exactly a sterling example of what NASCAR racing is like, but it's still part of the stock-car circus (for now).

- **Dover International Speedway.** The adopted "home track" of rising Sprint Car star Martin Truex Jr., Dover International is less than 175 miles away from Manhattan. It's very underrated, and it has a casino and a hotel attached to it, which makes for a fun-filled weekend—if you're winning at either the track or the casino, that is.
- **Watkins Glen International.** This sprawling road course is roughly 250 miles from the City, in upstate New York. It's one of my least favorite tracks because of poor facilities, but it is slowly trying to build its way into the twenty-first century.
- **New Hampshire Motor Speedway.** About 275 miles away from the City, in bucolic Loudon, New Hampshire Motor Speedway is one of the most underrated tracks on the circuit. It's also flat, fast, and right in some of the most pristine resort areas in the country. It also has arguably some of the best seafood restaurants you'll find anywhere.
- **Richmond International Raceway.** Richmond is roughly 350 miles away from the City (about a six-hour drive). If you want to see a track that would be the closest to what NASCAR has in mind for New York, this is the place to go. You can also swing through Washington, D.C. (100 miles to the north), for a little sightseeing, while you're at it.

With five tracks hosting nine of the thirty-six races on the Sprint Cup schedule within a six-hour radius of New York City, I have just one question remaining for NASCAR on its adamancy in having a track in the New York City market: *Why?*

## Who Are NASCAR's Biggest Enemies?

There's no question that NASCAR has a lot of fans—millions across the country and around the world. The sanctioning body also has lots of friends, particularly in high places. It's no wonder that we've seen presidents and vice presidents make numerous appearances at tracks over the years, not to mention A-list entertainers (even if they're typically paid for their appearances). Face it, being a NASCAR fan is definitely politically correct for a politician, be it on the local, state, or national level.

But in addition to all its friends and fans, NASCAR has a number of foes: individuals and groups who are not keen on some of the sport's policies or strategies. Before I get into who I consider to be the top five enemies of the sport, let me share with you an incident from 2007 that illustrates how far some opponents of NASCAR will go in their distaste (that's a better word than *hatred*) for the sport.

In October 2007, just prior to the fall race at Lowe's Motor Speedway, Congressman Bennie Thompson (D-MS), then chairman of the House Committee on Homeland Security, instructed his staffers to be inoculated for a variety of diseases—including hepatitis A, hepatitis B, diphtheria, tetanus, and influenza—before they visited Talladega Superspeedway and Lowe's Motor Speedway.

Thompson's fear was that the staffers might get the cooties from Bubba and Bobbie Sue—typical NASCAR fans, whom the congressman's office apparently believed to be disease-infested and acutely contagious. Shucks, you know NASCAR fans and their loose morals and lifestyles, right?

Officially, the immunizations were supposedly part of a broader review of the federal response to massive emergencies at a large, crowded venue like a NASCAR track. If Bubba cut a long-winded and stinky fart while sitting in the stands, how many hazardous-material teams would be required to sanitize the situation? Or if Bobbie Sue forgot to put on clean clothes in the morning, would she have to be fumigated?

As I said in my Yahoo! column the day the news broke, Thompson's staffers likely considered NASCAR fans this way: "Y'all are nothin' more than a walkin', talkin', fire-breathin', beer-drinkin', tobacco-spittin', cussin' and cheerin' sumbitch who is carrying enough pestilence and pathos to bring the good, old U.S. of A. to its knees."

In essence, Thompson's office believed NASCAR fans as a whole to be a bunch of sickos—most likely both literally and figuratively. Why else would staffers be ordered to make sure that they were up-to-date on all their shots? As I also said in my Yahoo! column: "Granted, there are some NASCAR fans that are, shall we say, socially challenged—the type that sometimes forget their weekly shower, eschew deodorant in favor of the 'natural' smell and have ample beer bellies that should have Goodyear stamped across 'em—but that doesn't mean they're disease-carrying threats to our national security."

I was not surprised when I received thousands of e-mails from readers and NASCAR fans—among the most mail I've received on any one subject during my career—who were understandably angry at being stereotyped by the congressman's office and at the idea that they'd in any way be threats to the nation's health.

Unfortunately, Thompson just didn't get it with his "the sky is falling" hysteria. Even when backed into a corner and criticized by members of his own political party, he refused to admit that a mistake had been made. Rather, he just kept digging himself deeper into a hole. In one memorable debate on CNN with Representative Robin Hayes (R-NC) on CNN, Thompson had the gall to tell Hayes that he "ought to be ashamed" for criticizing the efforts to protect Thompson's committee staffers—to which Hayes deadpanned (and responded in kind to Thompson), "We got our shots when we were born."

The issue eventually died, and Thompson's staffers went on with their review of emergency response procedures. But the embarrassing fallout was another black eye on the sport that NASCAR just didn't need.

As I concluded in my column on a lovely October day in Charlotte, I tried to put the whole situation in perspective: "As for me, I'm going to be a bit more careful the next time I refer to you die-hard NASCAR fans as 'rabid.' Apparently, you might just be."

Okay, on to the broader list of those who also aren't members of the NASCAR fan club:

5. **Politicians.** Bennie Thompson proved that not all elected government officials are NASCAR fans. NASCAR likes to tout its connections with significant politicians, including presidents, vice presidents, and individual state governors. It has a decided pro-Republican leaning and utilizes things like honoring and giving marked and deserved public support to our armed forces as a way

of currying favor with fans, voters, and politicians. Nevertheless, there are plenty of politicians who don't want to have NASCAR anywhere near them. Need I remind you of the civic leaders on Staten Island when NASCAR wanted to build a racetrack on swampland a few years ago? Or how about the nearly unanimous opposition from leaders in Washington state that stymied NASCAR's efforts to build a racetrack? Several locations were all deemed unsuitable by these leaders.

4. **NIMBYs.** Close behind anti-NASCAR politicians are people who live near existing or proposed racetracks. They don't want the noise, the traffic, the pollution, and the crowds (which can surpass a hundred thousand people) that are associated with the sport. Let me give you two examples. New Hampshire Motor Speedway has an understanding with the residents of nearby villages (such as Loudon, Canterbury, and Shaker Village) that there will not be a significant expansion of the racing complex. For anything of that nature to happen, the local residents would have to approve the revisions first. When Bruton Smith bought the track in 2008 and promised a significant makeover, the local residents let him know that whatever plans he had in mind would not be easily approved. This leads me to my next example, also involving Bruton Smith, who owns Charlotte Motor Speedway (formerly Lowe's Motor Speedway) as well. When some nearby residents voiced disapproval for a planned drag strip that would abut their neighborhoods, Smith pulled a power play and threatened to close the speedway and relocate to another part of North Carolina—thus devastating the local economy, which relies heavily on the taxes and the income generated from the speedway and the surrounding businesses. Smith eventually got his way, but there are still a lot of unhappy neighbors who essentially were left helpless in their plight.

3. **Environmentalists and racial diversity groups.** I am putting these disparate groups under the same category, even though their ideals and demands may be different. Environmentalists, much like NIMBYs, do not like things like traffic and pollution mucking up the fragile ecosystem that can be found around some current racetracks. Racial diversity groups typically make one or

two select appearances every so often to demonstrate their dis-
pleasure at NASCAR's ongoing lack of minority representation
within the sport, even though the NASCAR-sanctioned Drive for
Diversity program is starting to make inroads in bringing more
minorities and women into the sport.

2. **Sports editors.** NASCAR's downturn in TV ratings and at-track
attendance began around 2006. Not coincidentally, it was right
about that time that newspapers across the country started losing readers and advertising revenue, first at a trickle and then as
a full-fledged hemorrhage. By 2008, thousands of reporters had
been laid off, including a number of sportswriters who special-
ized in motorsports, particularly NASCAR. The travel budgets
for the reporters who remained to cover NASCAR were severely
cut, if not outright eliminated, which allowed for coverage only at
local tracks. The trend even included online reporters like myself;
I was laid off by Yahoo! after four and a half years as its national
NASCAR columnist, primarily because the number of readers
did not justify the cost of maintaining the beat full-time. If that
doesn't show how low on the journalistic totem pole NASCAR has
fallen, nothing does. Is it any wonder that the sport has embraced
"citizen journalists" to fill what has become a very deep chasm?
When media centers go from bursting at the seams, packed with
reporters and photographers from around the world, to half full
in just a matter of a few years, something is obviously wrong.
Whether we'll ever see the sport regain the media attention it
once enjoyed is anybody's guess. But it's pretty clear that even
with citizen journalists, it still has a long, long way to go to even
start coming close.

1. **Bean counters.** Nothing makes a driver, a crew chief, or a team
owner break into a cold sweat more than this: a representative of a
team's primary sponsor calls and says, "Based upon changing needs
and strategies, not to mention the economic climate, we have
decided to reallocate our funding and sponsorship to other initiatives." In other words, the sponsor just bailed out, leaving things in
a financial lurch. Now it's time to hustle and try to find a replacement sponsor or cobble together a group of sponsors to fill the

void, if possible. Given the woes the economy has gone through the last few years, such a void has increasingly become far more difficult to fill. Let's face it, the day of one primary sponsor willing to spend in excess of fifteen or twenty million dollars to fly its colors on a race car have become almost as extinct as the dinosaur.

For example, Jeff Gordon has spent much of his career aligned with DuPont paints, but in recent years companies like Nicorette and Pepsi have had to fill in the void of the races that DuPont would not sponsor. Sponsors are increasingly trying to rationalize to their corporate bosses and their stockholders the need to stay in the game, only to find that the costs are too high to truly justify the publicity and marketing return on the investment. After 2009, several sponsors left NASCAR, including the first two whiskey manufacturers to come into the sport (Jim Beam and Jack Daniel's) and longtime industrial tools manufacturer DeWalt. There was also the highly publicized decision by Lowe's to not renew the naming rights for Lowe's Motor Speedway (which reverted to its original name, Charlotte Motor Speedway, in 2010). As the old saying goes, if you want to play in NASCAR, you have to pay. Ten years ago, being part of the sport was practically mandatory if a company wanted to get great attention for its product, but in recent years, more and more companies have, unfortunately, simply been priced out of the remaining part of the NASCAR community.

That said, maybe NASCAR's worst enemy ultimately is itself. It makes you wonder, doesn't it?

# What Are the Worst NASCAR Movies of All Time?

In the Green Flag section, we discussed the best NASCAR movies of all time, even though many of them left a lot to be desired in terms of believability. Now we give the counterpoint: the worst NASCAR movies of all time. How bad are these? Let's put it this way: if you get one of these DVDs as a gift, and the person who is giving you the gift knows you're a big NASCAR fan, you might want to question how much he or she really likes you.

Okay, hold your nose, bite your lips, and cover your eyes, because here are the worst of the worst:

1. *Herbie Fully Loaded* (2005). Come on, a VW Bug that wants to race in NASCAR? Yeah, right, that's a realistic story line. So what do I really think about this movie? Remember Valley Girls and Val-speak from the 1980s? I never thought I'd write anything that would pay homage to that, but the verbiage that found its way into our language is the perfect backdrop for my thoughts about this incredibly terrible movie: "Like, oh my God! Ewwwwww. Lindsay Lohan? Gag me with a spoon!" Enough said, don't you think?

2. *Stroker Ace* (1983). This movie is so bad that it's good in its own unique way. Frankly, I was ready to put it on the "best" list of NASCAR films, given how many people I know who like it. But I had to be true to my critical assessment of this movie: it is one of the most unbelievable, laughable jokes of a sports movie that I've ever seen. Even *Talladega Nights* has more credibility. The only reason so many people seem to like this movie is that it stars Burt Reynolds and Loni Anderson, who were both near the top of their respective careers at the time. Admittedly, Burt is or was a man's man type, and Loni is or was one of the hottest women of her generation. But, come on—a movie based on Reynolds's character complaining about having to dress up as a chicken to placate his chief sponsor (a fried-chicken king)? I don't know about you, but I never saw Dale Earnhardt Jr. dress up as a Budweiser can. The chicken gag is just that, a gag, but it makes this movie a real clucker (and I don't mean that in a positive fashion). Think *Cannonball Run* meets *Talladega Nights*, and you get the gist of this movie.

3. *Redline 7000* (1965). Many racing fans would put this one too in their "best" category. But the acting (even with the budding star James Caan), the racing action, and the overall movie are just so

bad that I can't see how anyone would put this on the plus side of the ledger. And let's not forget one of the main characters who seemed so out of place: George Takei, aka "Mr. Sulu" of *Star Trek* fame. How bad was this movie? Legend has it that when it premiered in Charlotte, ten minutes into the movie legendary driver Curtis Turner yelled over to good buddy Tiny Lund and said, "This is terrible, Tiny. Let's get the hell out of here!" Enough said, don't you think?

4. *Six Pack* (1982). Think of a stock car racing version of *The Bad News Bears*, and you get this forgettable movie that starred singer Kenny Rogers, who should have stuck to his day job. This movie has another typical "realistic" story line, with six kids serving as the pit crew for the down-on-his-luck Brewster Baker (Rogers). And even though budding starlet Diane Lane, at seventeen years old, is in this film, she can't save it from the depths of cinematic hell. Putting a lock on just how bad this movie is was the appearance of mousy, pesky actor Anthony Michael Hall. But wait, there's more. Although the film's producers were able to get real-life announcer Chris Economaki to make a cameo, he was paired with the far-from-believable Chuck "Love Connection" Woolery. I'll repeat the three words a lot of people probably said after sitting through this flick: "God, that sucked!" And nearly thirty years later, it still does!

5. *Speedway* (1968). This is yet another example of why Elvis Presley should have stuck to singing. In one of Elvis's last movies (thank goodness), he stars with Nancy "These Boots Are Made for Walkin'" Sinatra as a race car driver who is trying to pay off a huge IRS bill for back taxes that was incurred by mismanagement from manager Bill Bixby. (Presley's trying to romance Sinatra, who happens to be the IRS auditor, at the same time.) About the only good thing in this movie is that much of it was shot at Charlotte Motor Speedway (formerly Lowe's Motor Speedway), and it also includes cameo appearances by several drivers, including the *other* King, Richard Petty.

DISHONORABLE MENTION: *Thunder in Carolina* (1960): About the only thing notable or memorable about this movie is that much of it was shot in and around the 1959 Southern 500 at

Darlington Raceway. It starred Rory Calhoun and Alan Hale Jr., who would survive this bomb to go on to fortune and fame as the "Skipper" in *Gilligan's Island.* How's that, Little Buddy?

• *43: The Richard Petty Story* (1973): Just as Elvis should have stuck to singing, Richard Petty should have stuck to driving. Still, you have to give him credit for having the nerve to star in a movie as himself at the peak of his career. What Petty lacks in acting ability is more than made up for by the great racing action. But come on, the late Darren McGavin as Richard's father, Lee Petty? Not even close in looks or personality. This is arguably one of the hardest NASCAR movies to find today, but if you stumble on one, buy it even though it's bad. You'll especially get a kick out of The King's stiffness as an actor.

# Who Were NASCAR's Biggest One-Hit Wonders?

*That Thing You Do* was a movie produced and directed by Tom Hanks about a fictitious rock 'n' roll group that hit the big time with a song of the same title, only to never be heard of again in just a few months. The group was known as the Wonders, but they should have been called the One-Hit Wonders.

That's the concept for this section: guys who beat the best of the best once, maybe twice, but they were never really able to build on that success.

Let me clarify one thing: I'm not necessarily talking about drivers who only won 1 Cup race in their careers. I'm talking more about drivers who outdid their peers in the biggest way, only to essentially fade from sight shortly after the big event, or drivers who won 1 (maybe 2) big races but are known more for all the times they didn't win. To make things more current and allow readers to relate, I'm limiting my picks to drivers only in the modern era of NASCAR.

One other element of the decision-making process was how to be fair to drivers. It's hard to pick success at one venue over success at a different venue. Comparing success at Talladega and Watkins Glen is like comparing apples and oranges. So I chose the track that has come to epitomize the NASCAR experience, not to mention being the sport's most well-known facility: Daytona International Speedway.

I believe it was Darrell Waltrip who once said, "If you can do well at Daytona, you can do well anywhere." Whether it's success in the Daytona 500 or in July's Pepsi (now Coca-Cola) 400, a win at Daytona is still a win—even if it is the only win, or one of the only wins, a driver earns in his career. The five drivers I've chosen for this category won one of NASCAR's biggest races at the big D and then essentially disappeared, or they had a few moments of glory in Daytona that ultimately belied the rest of their racing résumé.

Let's count 'em down, Letterman-style, starting with two honorable mentions:

HONORABLE MENTION: **John and Mario Andretti.** John won just 2 Cup races in his career, with the biggest being the 1997 Pepsi 400 at Daytona (the other win came two years later at Martinsville). As for Mario, he's a bit of a ringer. Although he was one of the greatest race car drivers of the twentieth century, Mario made just fourteen Cup starts in his career and was able to win only 1 race. But that wasn't just any win, it was the biggest prize of it all: the 1967 Daytona 500.

5. **Michael Waltrip.** He's a funny guy with a great personality, and he would give you the shirt off his back. But when it comes to success in Cup racing, Darrell's younger brother was not a chip off the old block. Michael won the 2001 and 2003 Daytona 500s—the former was the race in which Dale Earnhardt (and Waltrip's boss at the time) was killed, and the latter helped to reaffirm that the 2001 win was not a fluke. But as an overall driver, Waltrip, who has shifted to part-time status in 2010, will be graded by many as mediocre, at best, with just 4 wins in a career—all at restrictor plate tracks—that has spanned more than 775 Cup starts. He earned just 2 other wins in his Cup career: a triumph at Daytona in the 2002 Pepsi 400 and another at Talladega in the 2003 EA Sports 500.

4. **Jimmy Spencer.** "Mr. Excitement" made things happen in the sportsmen ranks in and around his Berwick, Pennsylvania, home, but once he got to Cup racing, Spencer actually was more like "Mr. Boring." Spencer, who is actually a better Cup analyst on Speed TV than he was a driver in his Cup tenure, won just 2 races in his fabled career (well, it probably was fabled to him). Both were in 1994 and while driving for legendary team owner Junior Johnson: at Daytona in the Pepsi 400 and a few weeks later at Talladega in the DieHard 500. That race name pretty much sums up Spencer's career: it died hard. In fact, Spencer may have earned the greatest notoriety of his racing career when he wasn't even behind the wheel: the day he punched Kurt Busch in the nose after an incident in 2003 at Michigan International Speedway. Then again, Kurt went on to win the Cup championship the following year, while Spencer was essentially on his way out of NASCAR. Talk about ultimate payback.

3. **Sterling Marlin.** Marlin is somewhat of an anomaly in this category. For although he won 10 Cup races in his career, his defining moments in Cup racing were in 1994 and 1995, when he became one of only three drivers (with Richard Petty and Cale Yarborough) to win back-to-back Daytona 500s. Marlin won a third time at Daytona in the 1996 Pepsi 400 and twice at Talladega, among others, but he'll always be remembered most for being the two-hit wonder at Daytona.

2. **Ward Burton.** A veteran of 375 Cup starts, Burton was an average to above-average driver, except when it came to wins. The Virginia native had 24 top-five and 82 top-ten finishes in his career, but just 5 wins. None was bigger than his triumph in the 2002 Daytona 500 for team owner Bill Davis. To show how fleeting fame can be in NASCAR, however, in October 2003, just about a year and a half after his and Davis's greatest triumph, Burton was forced out of the team, and 2004 was his final full season in the sport.

1. **Derrike Cope.** Like John Andretti, Cope is also a two-time Cup race winner, but the Spanaway, Washington, native is still NASCAR's ultimate one-hit wonder by winning the 1990 Daytona

500 and then essentially dropping off the face of the earth in terms of performance. He also won at Dover International Speedway just a few months after his Daytona triumph, but Cope never finished higher than fifteenth in a single season. He had just 4 other top-five and 26 other top-ten finishes in 408 career starts and became the ruler by which all other one-hit wonders since have been measured.

## What Are NASCAR's Worst Rules?

Oh boy, this is going to create a heck of a stir. Get a group of NASCAR fans together, and I guarantee that when the discussion turns to what's right or wrong with the sport, the subject of rules quickly becomes one of the most talked about. We all know that rules are necessary to maintain a safe and competitive race. Unfortunately, some rules are nearly ludicrous, if not downright asinine. As most of my regular readers will tell you, I've long railed against some of the moronic rules that are in place.

But putting my thoughts on the subject of rules into this book actually proved harder than I thought. You see, in my mind, there are a lot more than just five terrible rules in the sport. Other sections of this book deal with the five best rules and the top five rules that NASCAR should have, but here I could actually come up with ten rather than five worst rules. So I did. Here they are, from tenth to first:

10. **One engine rule.** As part of a measure to contain costs, NASCAR elected to allow teams the use of just one engine per race weekend in 2002, and the practice continues to this day. Previously, some teams used different engines for qualifying, practice, and race day. If something happens to the lone race engine, the team can replace it with a backup, but the team is forced to start the race at the back of the field (unless the engine change occurs before qualifying). Unfortunately, the original

intention of the rule, to cut costs, has been minimal, at best; the teams have appropriated whatever savings they've earned for things like more dynamometer or wind-tunnel testing to further test the endurance of the motor.

9. **Impound rule.** This is another cost-saving measure, although the actual savings are a bit more suspect in this case, in my opinion. Typically, the teams are locked out of the garage from early in the evening prior to race day until the next morning before all the pomp and circumstance begins, and no work is allowed on race cars during that period. What's more, when the teams do return on race day, they are limited in what changes or revisions they can make without running afoul of the impound rule.

8. **The race is ruled "official" one lap after halfway.** I have a love-hate relationship with this rule. On the one hand, if there's inclement weather that will affect the outcome of the race or shorten it, I can understand the need to have this rule in place. After all, would you want to come back the next day to watch the final thirty laps of a race? On the other hand, we've seen races that have been shortened far too soon. A good example of that was the 2008 spring race at New Hampshire, won by Kurt Busch. An hour later, the rain was gone. Ditto for the 2009 Coca-Cola 600, which actually was pushed back to Monday after rain on Sunday, then David Reutimann wound up winning the rescheduled and rain-shortened event the next day. I've been at too many races in which NASCAR pulled the trigger and called the race way too soon. If NASCAR had only waited a little longer, we could most likely have had a complete race. It takes longer to dry a wet racetrack, particularly the longest ones (Daytona, Talladega, and Indianapolis), but I think that most race fans will agree with me that if we can wait out two- or three-hour rain delays at major league baseball games, we can do the same at Cup races.

7. **Keeping pit road closed on a caution.** This rule makes absolutely no sense to me, particularly when a car that is involved in a wreck yet is still semidrivable is not allowed to come onto pit

road without being punished because the pits are "closed" at the time. So what happens? The car is forced to either take the penalty or try to limp around the track for another lap, spewing more debris that makes for a much longer cleanup than if NASCAR had simply opened the pits for the damaged car.

6. **The "lucky dog" rule.** Another rule I hate, which allows the first car one lap down to the leaders to get back on the lead lap at the tail end of the longest restart line during a caution period. The implementation of double-file restarts in 2009 took a big bite out of this rule, minimizing opportunities for other, subsequent cars to get the lucky dog—or "free pass," as Fox TV, ESPN, and ABC like to call it—by starting alongside the leaders on restarts. Now, if NASCAR would just euthanize the lucky dog completely, I'd be real happy.

5. **Debris cautions.** This is perhaps the most overused and abused rule in the rule book. How many times have we seen a yellow caution flag fall for a piece of debris that might be the size of a thumb, prompting the field to be artificially bunched up, ending any domination a particular driver might have had prior to the caution flag dropping? What's more, how many debris cautions have we seen over the years that were essentially phantom calls, in which no one but maybe God saw any type of debris that was a potential threat or an interference to the racing at that particular moment? Things got so bad from around 2004 to 2007 that some jaded media members or fans began referring to some debris cautions as "Junior cautions," essentially artificial stoppages due to some phantom piece of debris that, more often than not, helped Dale Earnhardt Jr. to either get back into the race or advance his position and give him a chance to win the race. Fixed? Scripted? You tell me.

4. **Five points for leading a lap.** Let's see, there are no points for qualifying first, but if you're a back-marker car that happens to stay out on a given caution period, you pick up five points for leading a lap in a race in which you are otherwise a nonfactor. Can someone explain the sense of that to me, please?

3. "Actions detrimental to stock car racing." This is NASCAR's catch-all rule that can be used for any infraction, minor or major, even if there is not actually a written version of that rule. If NASCAR thinks you've done something bad, your actions are immediately ruled detrimental to the sport, whether or not they truly are.

2. **No speedometer on cars.** Can someone explain to me why NASCAR goes through the same foolhardy exercise before every race during the prerace drivers' meetings, telling drivers to make sure that the tachometer is showing a certain number of engine revolutions per minute between two points? Why can't NASCAR just do the simple thing, come into the twenty-first century, and allow digital speedometers? If there's so much concern that teams or crew chiefs will try to alter the speed, there are plenty of "sealed" and calibrated speedometers that cannot be tampered with that could be used. Furthermore, NASCAR could use the same concept with speedometers that it does with restrictor plates: it passes them out before practice, qualifying, and the race and then collects them after the race is completed. Right now, drivers have little ability to counter NASCAR's findings if a driver is judged to be "speeding" onto or off pit road, even if he's carefully watching the tachometer to be within the guidelines that NASCAR itself set. If police cars can have calibrated speedometers whose results stand up in court as evidence against speeders, can't NASCAR bring itself into the modern age, as well?

1. **Top thirty-five guaranteed spots.** This is the stupidest rule of all in NASCAR. To curry favor with the sport's biggest sponsors, NASCAR implemented the top-thirty-five rule, which essentially puts cars that are within the top thirty-five in owner's points to have automatic guarantees to make the field for a particular race. NASCAR believes that doing so rewards the sponsors for all the millions of dollars they spend in support of a team, a driver, and the sport. But can't an argument be made that because so much money is being spent, the company is essentially bribing its way into a race just so that its colors and its logo can be seen by the fans in the stands and millions more in front of their TV sets? Why can't we go back to the days when the fastest forty-three cars made the field and the slowest ones went home? It was so much simpler then.

# What's Wrong with the Chase for the Sprint Cup?

I talked in the Green Flag section about what's right with the Chase for the Sprint Cup. I remain a proponent of the Chase format to a certain extent, but my passion and excitement level has waned in the last few years as the once exciting Chase (the inaugural version in 2004) has evolved into a relative boring affair, in many cases.

Jimmie Johnson's supremacy and domination of the Chase in the last few years, while admirable, has also caused a backlash effect, with the fans growing weary of Johnson's ability to constantly outdo his peers in the ten races that count the most in the season. Is it any wonder that the TV ratings in the Chase have gone down in just about the same amount of time that Johnson has shined each year? Could this be a coincidence? I think not.

So I'm playing devil's advocate. Here are the top five things that I—and many others, judging from the e-mails and phone calls I've received—see as being wrong with the Chase:

1. Competitors need a revised points system that more accurately reflects performance during the ten-race Chase for the twelve qualifiers. In other words, if a driver has a bad race and finishes, say, 35th, he shouldn't be awarded the equivalent of 35th place in points. Instead, if he's the lowest Chase finisher in that particular race, he should receive no lower than 12th in points earned. If we set the twelve Chase qualifiers apart from the rest of the other thirty-one non-Chase drivers when the point standings are reset prior to the first Chase race, then those twelve drivers should have their own separate point system, as well.

2. Track selection does not adequately reflect NASCAR's top markets. How can one of the most popular venues in the sport, Bristol Motor Speedway, not be included in the Chase? What about Las Vegas, which consistently sells out its early spring race every year? And what about Chicagoland Speedway, home of the third largest media market in the country? Why doesn't it have a slot in the Chase? Some fans even argue that if the Chase is supposed

to mirror the entire schedule, perhaps even a road course should be part of the final ten races. Instead, and with all due respect to those venues, we have places like tiny Martinsville and boring Homestead in the Chase instead. Something is definitely out of whack here. A sport's marquee event should include its largest and most popular venues. With NASCAR, that is far from the case.

3. Even after six years, fans still don't like the format. There have also been several format changes during those years that have only served to confuse or alienate fans even more, such as expanding the field from the original ten drivers to twelve and using the wins earned during the first twenty-six races to generate a seeding system of sorts going into the Chase. In addition, the fans of drivers who fail to make the Chase are more apt to stop watching or attending races if their driver has little to race for and will finish no better than as an also-ran.

4. Many people think it's a contrived system designed only to promote TV ratings. If that's the case, it isn't doing a very good job, considering how overall TV ratings have slipped by close to 20 percent since 2006 (although, to be fair, overall Chase ratings haven't fallen as much as "regular season" ratings have). Others think the system is contrived to build false excitement and false expectations.

5. The almost robotic reign of Jimmie Johnson in four straight championships from 2006 to 2009 turned a lot of people off, particularly the fans of drivers who either didn't make the Chase or who struggled once the ten-race play-off was underway. Johnson and crew chief Chad Knaus are to be commended for working the system to their benefit, but it also has triggered a backlash of fan allegations of cheating, boring racing, and the inability of other drivers to compete with the Johnson-Knaus juggernaut in the Chase.

# YELLOW FLAG

## Things to Make You Think

# Why Do I Hate Dale Earnhardt Jr. So Much?
## (I Really Don't)

Let's make this very clear from the start: regardless of how this question is posed, I unequivocally do not hate Dale Earnhardt Jr., not as a driver nor as a human being. In fact, I give him credit for being NASCAR's most popular driver for the better part of the last decade.

But for some reason, many diehards within Earnhardt's huge fan base have taken to calling me a Junior-hater and worse because of some of the critical things I've written or said about him over the years. It's become nothing short of a running joke, and I seem to be the punch line or the butt of the joke.

Some of the questions from my readers and listeners border on the fringe of lunacy: Do I have a long-simmering beef with him that has clouded my judgment? Did he steal my girlfriend? Did he stiff me for a dinner or bar bill? Do I have such a fragile ego that I get an almost orgasmic rush if I blast Earnhardt? Don't I understand how much he must still hurt at the tragic loss of his father, Dale Earnhardt? The answers to these questions are: no, no, no, no, and yes. Let me explain.

Like a savvy politician or a TV preacher, the younger Earnhardt has unquestionably—and in the fine fashion of a world-famous virtuoso— played the media, the advertising world, and his fans like a fiddle. He's larger than life, and having the Earnhardt name and the tragic loss of his father hasn't hurt in developing his legacy.

Yet his fans still can't understand. They just don't get it. They are completely oblivious to his talent level, his career statistics, or anything that shows him as anything less than the greatest driver the sport has ever seen. I've received numerous letters saying this. Many of them act as if Junior is entitled to superstardom and championships just because of his surname and his father.

Because of marketing prowess and the advice of his handlers, Earnhardt has been painted as an all-American boy, the boy-next-door type that any parents would love to have take out their daughter and even marry her.

There are also folks who say that I'm jealous of Junior's fame and fortune. That couldn't be further from the truth. (I admire the millions of dollars and the fame he's received, but that's it. I've never asked him for a handout or a loan and never would.)

The bottom line is this: Junior never has been and never will be the greatest driver in NASCAR history. If I've said it once, I've said it a thousand times: Junior is a *good* driver, but that's as far as I go. He is *not* a great driver. He's made a career that has been marked by way too many driver errors, too many lapses in judgment, too much arguing with his crew chiefs, and a tendency to let off-track interests and pursuits distract him from his day job. He has built his career simply by believing many of the fawning newspaper and magazine stories that have been written about him, many by writers who were simply trying to curry favor with NASCAR's most famous redhead.

This isn't just me talking. Take an objective look at the course of his career, and you will find that I'm 100 percent correct on all these counts. If Earnhardt truly were as great as his fans believe, we would not have come into 2010 with him still desperately in search of his first Cup championship. We also would not have to look into the NASCAR record book to see that in his first ten Cup seasons (through 2009), he had just three top-five seasons (in which he never finished higher than third, and two other times he was fifth), one top-ten season, and six other seasons in which he finished outside the top ten (including four times outside the top fifteen).

And let's not forget 2009, his second year with Hendrick Motorsports. After much outcry from his fans and the media, Junior finally parted ways with longtime crew chief and cousin Tony Eury Jr., who was replaced by Lance McGrew. Team owner Rick Hendrick thought that

Junior needed some new blood—and not a relative's blood, at that—to direct his career. Unfortunately, McGrew proved to be worse than Eury in the short run. Instead of McGrew leading Earnhardt to victories and a Chase appearance, Earnhardt finished with the worst season (25th) ever in his Cup career.

I can spout statistics and facts until I'm blue in the face, but Earnhardt and his handlers have done such a great job of brainwashing Junior's posse with all his supposed great ability and talent that anything I say simply comes out sounding like sour grapes. It's very frustrating when you try to tell someone that their favorite driver is a cross between a good driver and a poser. I'm just looking at things from an objective standpoint, not through rose-colored glasses.

In terms of statistics, Earnhardt would fall in the same category as Kurt Busch or Matt Kenseth (both have similar overall career stats as Junior). Yet, those two have already won one Cup championship apiece—whereas Earnhardt is still seeking his first title, a pursuit in which he may never wind up ultimately finding Camelot.

Despite all this, who is the most popular driver in NASCAR? Earnhardt, for reasons that will always remain mysterious to me.

As much as I hate to say it, I predict he'll continue to seek that elusive first Cup crown for many years to come. And though I admit I would like to give his fans something to be proud of if he were to finally win a championship, I also want to be there ten years or so from now, after he retires, to simply say to all those hoodwinked fans who think their driver deserves to be in the same category as his late father, Richard Petty, Darrell Waltrip, David Pearson, and so many others: "See, I told you so. He was good, but never great."

Will all those fans who called me crazy or a Junior-hater finally believe that I was only preaching the truth and backing it up with facts, not emotion? Wait, we're thinking about the hear-no-evil, see-no-evil, speak-no-evil Junior Nation here. Nope, it'll never happen; they'll never see what I've been saying all along. And you wonder why I'm so frustrated and hate Junior—even though I really don't.

# What Were the Biggest Tragedies to Befall NASCAR?

Every time a driver climbs into a race car, he is faced with the possibility that it could be the last time he ever does so. By climbing behind the wheel, a driver acknowledges and accepts what is the unofficial race car driver's credo: "If I die, I want to die doing what I love, and that's in my race car." It's that passion that makes race car drivers special: the passion for speed, for dangerous thrills, for competition, and for life—even if it possibly means death.

NASCAR has lost nearly two dozen Sprint Cup, Nationwide, and Camping World Truck series drivers over the years in a variety of ways, both on and off the track. Many have died in racing- or practice-related wrecks, but several others weren't even in their race cars when they perished. Some were in planes, and at least one was in a helicopter when his time on earth was up.

I know this is a debates book, but trying to quantify the most tragic deaths, ranking them by the severity of how they died, is foolhardy and only serves to unnecessarily malign those who have died unexpectedly. No one deserves to die in any kind of accident, no matter what kind.

Nevertheless, certain deaths stand out because of the impact they had on the sport. So, even though I don't want to offend anyone with my list of the most notable drivers and other individuals and how they perished, I must call attention to how much of a blow their sudden and tragic departure was—not only to their own families and their teams but to millions of race fans around the world.

Here they are:

1. **Dale Earnhardt, race-related crash, February 18, 2001.** Less than two hours after Earnhardt crashed on the final lap of the Daytona 500, NASCAR president Mike Helton, with tears

welling in his eyes, uttered arguably four of the most shocking words that the sport and its fans have ever heard: "We've lost Dale Earnhardt." The resulting mourning reverberated around the world, akin to when rock 'n' roll great Elvis Presley died in 1977. The driver of the all-black No. 3 Chevrolet Monte Carlo owned by Richard Childress Racing, Earnhardt was an iconic figure who almost single-handedly transformed NASCAR from a primarily Southeast-based sport into a strong national series that eventually led to it becoming the second most popular spectator sport in the country, behind only pro football. Known as The Intimidator for his all-or-nothing style of racing, including pushing drivers out of the way if he had to, Earnhardt was a true blue-collar hero, emerging from the cotton mills of Kannapolis, North Carolina, to become one of the greatest drivers the sport has ever known. A seven-time Cup champion, who is tied with the legendary Richard "The King" Petty for most championships won, Earnhardt died less than three months short of his fiftieth birthday.

But Earnhardt's death was not in vain: it resulted in a revolutionary and sweeping change within the sport to greatly increase safety and protection for drivers, crew members, and fans. Some of those improvements were head-and-neck restraint devices (Earnhardt died from a basilar skull fracture), steel and foam energy reduction barriers (which greatly improved impact absorption when a car hit a racetrack wall), more strenuous safety inspections of race cars (particularly driver seats and seat belts), and the controversial Car of Tomorrow, which brought NASCAR into a pioneering and leadership position within motorsports with its state-of-the-art safety design and internal elements. During an interview on Fox TV (NASCAR's first broadcast as part of a new multibillion-dollar, multinetwork TV package) just hours before his fatal wreck, Earnhardt promised viewers, "You're going to see something today that you've never seen before." Truer, more prophetic words were never spoken.

2. **Hendrick Motorsports (HMS) airplane crash, October 24, 2004.** Less than four years after the largest tragedy the sport has

ever seen, its fans were once again left reeling when a small plane carrying ten passengers and crew members, most affiliated with Hendrick Motorsports, crashed into the side of Bull Mountain, just outside Martinsville, Virginia. Those on board were headed to the race that day at Martinsville Speedway. The cause was eventually determined to be pilot error, compounded by extremely poor weather conditions. Those killed were John Hendrick (HMS president and brother of team owner Rick Hendrick); his twin daughters, Kimberly and Jennifer; former Busch Series driver and team owner Ricky Hendrick (the only son of Rick and Linda Hendrick); chief engine builder Randy Dorton; HMS general manager Jeff Turner; Scott Lathram (helicopter pilot for Tony Stewart), who was merely hitching a ride to Martinsville so he could say good-bye to Stewart before shipping off the next day to serve with the National Guard in Iraq; Joe Jackson (an executive of Jeff Gordon's primary sponsor, DuPont); and pilots Elizabeth Morrison and Richard Tracy. Team owner Rick Hendrick was scheduled to be on that flight but stayed home due to illness.

3. **Davey Allison, helicopter crash, July 13, 1993.** Legendary NASCAR driver Bobby Allison and his wife, Judy, lost their son, Davey, exactly eleven months to the day after the death of their other son, Clifford (August 13, 1992), in a crash during practice at Michigan International Speedway. A budding superstar on what was then the Winston Cup circuit, Davey Allison was considered by most of his peers as a future champion in the making. The question wasn't *if* he'd be a champion, but how soon and how many times throughout the years. Tragically, his life was cut short, so he never earned a Cup championship. He died from his injuries after his brand-new helicopter, which he was flying on a leisure trip to see Neil and David Bonnett practice, crashed while he was attempting to land in the infield of Talladega Superspeedway. Davey did not regain consciousness and died the next morning. So-called Alabama Gang cofounder Red Farmer was also in the chopper and suffered serious injuries, but he eventually recovered and raced again, long into his seventies.

4. **Alan Kulwicki, airplane crash, April 1, 1993.** Kulwicki was the last combination owner-driver to win a Cup championship, capturing the 1992 Winston Cup title in thrilling fashion and finishing just high enough in the final race of 1992 to beat Bill Elliott by 10 points. Unfortunately, Kulwicki would not be able to enjoy the spoils of that championship for very long. Less than five months after being crowned the sport's top driver, he died along with three others in the crash of a small airplane only miles away from Bristol Motor Speedway. The cause of the crash was determined to be ice on the plane's wings and pilot error. It was most certainly a far-too-early demise for a driver who had left his native Milwaukee just seven years earlier to earn his fame and fortune racing against NASCAR's best. At the age of thirty-eight, he became the best of the best of the 1992 season.

5. TIE: **Fireball Roberts, race-related crash, July 2, 1964, and Joe Weatherly, race-related crash, January 19, 1964.** Two of the sport's best drivers and most colorful characters were lost less than six months apart. Edward Glenn "Fireball" Roberts suffered devastating injuries in a horrific end-over-end crash and fire that left him with second- and third-degree burns over 80 percent of his body during the World 600 at Charlotte Motor Speedway on May 24, 1964. Roberts was never able to fully recover; he eventually developed pneumonia and succumbed to his injuries six weeks later. When Roberts was hurt, NASCAR was just starting to recover from Weatherly's tragic crash at Riverside International Raceway. The reigning 1963 Grand National champ, Weatherly slammed his car broadside into a retaining wall. With window nets still seven years away from being made mandatory, the force of the crash carried Weatherly's head directly into the same retaining wall with such force that he was killed upon impact.

Postscript: We'd be remiss if we didn't include Adam Petty. In the overall scheme of things, he was just one of several drivers who died far too young (we could also include Neil Bonnett, Kenny Irwin, Tiny Lund, John Nemechek, J. D. McDuffie, and Tony Roper, among others, in this category). However, because he was Richard Petty's grandson, his death meant that the Petty racing legacy had essentially ended. Adam was just two months shy of his twentieth birthday when he was killed in May 2000 as he was practicing for a Busch Series event at New Hampshire International Speedway. He had a promising future ahead of him, and by many accounts he had the talent to be a great success. It's tragic; we'll never know just how much success he would have enjoyed.

# How Will Danica Patrick Fare Long-Term in NASCAR?

People who have accused me of being anti–Dale Earnhardt Jr. have also charged that I'm anti–Danica Patrick. I'm sorry if the fans of both drivers think that, but I call it like it is.

Back in 2006, I said that Danica was nothing more than "flesh and flash," a comment that was picked up worldwide—and I still stand by my words. Even with her first career win in Japan in 2008—in a fuel-mileage decision, no less—she is still one of the biggest underachievers in the Indy Racing League, for the amount of talent she is supposed to have.

She has "succeeded" in the Indy Racing League—and I use that word loosely—because the cars are state-of-the-art, technologically advanced vehicles that are not that hard to drive, compared to the cars in other motorsports.

First, they have the luxury of a number of electronic aides within the cockpit that drivers in racing series like NASCAR, drag racing's National Hot Rod Association (NHRA), World of Outlaws, and other U.S. series simply don't have. Second, an Indy car is roughly twenty-two hundred pounds, compared to a NASCAR Sprint Cup car, which weighs around thirty-six hundred pounds.

Third, it takes a large amount of muscle to wheel a Cup car around a racetrack, but the power assists on an open-wheel Indy car make traversing ovals, road courses, and street courses significantly easier than their stock-car counterparts. Fourth, Danica really hasn't proven that she's ready and able to jump from the Indy Racing League to NASCAR's premier circuit.

All this changed in 2010, when Patrick began her foray into stock car racing by running a healthy combination of Automobile Racing Club of America (ARCA) and Nationwide Series events during some of her weekends off from Indy, as a possible prelude to eventually moving full-time from Indy cars to Sprint Cup. In other words, she's getting her feet wet and seeing what this stock car business is all about—and whether she can handle it.

Prior to announcing that she was coming to NASCAR on a part-time basis, Patrick had no experience, period, in a stock car, not in Nationwide or even ARCA. Danica is physically beautiful, but beauty doesn't win races. I've seen some of the ugliest male drivers in the world smiling broadly in a Cup victory lane.

Moving to NASCAR will be a public relations and media bonanza for both Danica and the sanctioning body. She'll get tons of public-ity and face time on TV, and she'll become as much (if not more) of a media darling than Dale Earnhardt Jr. Unfortunately, like Junior, she's a good driver but not a great driver. Neither of them will ever be able to claim greatness as their careers continue in the next few years.

If Danica truly wants to move to NASCAR full-time, she has to pay her dues. She has to log at least five to ten thousand miles in a Nationwide Series or an ARCA race car. But logging miles is easy; it's being competitive that's much more difficult.

One of Patrick's Indy counterparts, Canadian Paul Tracy, who won the Championship Auto Racing Teams championship in 2003, hoped to one day become a full-time NASCAR driver, but he strug-gled greatly in a handful of Nationwide and Camping World Truck series races. In fact, to date, Tracy's best finish in a Nationwide Series race was twenty-fourth, and his best (and only) Truck Series finish to date was twentieth.

If Danica wants to become the Anna Kournikova of NASCAR, let her have at it. But if she really wants to try and improve her overall lot as a race car driver, she's not going to do it in stock car racing. From a marketing and sponsorship standpoint, sure, she'll be great. She'll probably quickly come to rival Dale Earnhardt Jr. as the most popular driver and endorsee. But as we've seen Earnhardt's career ride a rocky roller coaster—and with nary a Cup championship in sight—Patrick will become known as one of NASCAR's beautiful people but not as one of its great drivers, plain and simple.

# Why Is It So Hard for Open-Wheel Drivers to Make It in NASCAR?

Tony Stewart can pilot just about anything on four wheels: a stock car, an Indy car, a late model, a modified, a tractor, and even a forklift. "I can drive any forkin' thing," he once said with a big laugh. Yet for almost anyone else who has tried it, the transition from open-wheel Indy cars to closed-body stock cars has not been easy.

Robby Gordon went from being a better open-wheel driver—particularly with Indy cars and off-road vehicles—to a career in NASCAR, where he's been a mediocre driver at best (just 3 wins and a little more than 12 top-five finishes in nearly 350 career Cup starts). By comparison, Gordon has 2 wins, 18 top-five finishes, and 46 top-ten finishes in 107 career Indy car starts.

The stats speak for themselves. It's not that Gordon isn't talented as a NASCAR driver. Rather, his racing style and ability just seem suited better for an open-wheel ride than a stock car.

John Andretti, who much like Stewart has proven he can drive pretty much anything (he even spent a season driving Top Fuel dragsters in NHRA drag racing competition in the 1990s), has also had success in the open-wheel world, but he has never been able to do the same in stock-car racing.

Since the influx of Stewart, Andretti, and Gordon into the stock car world in the 1990s, only two other former open-wheel drivers of note have had any semblance of success in stock car racing.

First, of course, is Juan Pablo Montoya, who came to the Sprint Cup Series full-time in 2007. The Colombian native took to stock car racing almost as quickly as a duck takes to water. Unfortunately, he didn't have the right team or the right equipment around him in his first two seasons, but perseverance—and the merger of Chip Ganassi Racing with Felix Sabates, which had a long history with Montoya in Indy cars, and Dale Earnhardt Inc. after the 2008 season put Montoya on the right path in 2009. He qualified for the Chase for the Sprint Cup for the first time in his career and proved to be a strong contender in the Chase's first several races, finishing a career-best 8th in the final standings.

Montoya actually made it look easy at times. With just one previous Cup start under his belt, he undertook the full thirty-six-race season in 2007, finishing a surprising 5th in Atlanta (his fifth career Cup start), and followed that up three races later with an 8th-place showing at Texas. Then, to cap things off, roughly two months later he went on to win on a track that was more to his liking and experience level: the road course at Infineon Raceway.

Still, Montoya finished 20th in his rookie campaign, then dropped to 25th in his sophomore season in Sprint Cup in 2008. In 2009 things finally began to come together for him; he became a consistent finisher, with more than a dozen top-ten showings to his credit during the season.

After some clouds in his first two years, the future is looking significantly brighter for Montoya, who could, conceivably, become the second driver to win both an open-wheel and a Cup championship. (The first was two-time Cup and former Indy Racing League champ Tony Stewart.) Don't forget that Montoya was the 1999 CART champ, not to mention the 2000 Indianapolis 500 winner, a trophy that Stewart still covets.

One other former open-wheel Indy car driver who is just starting to come into his own after an admittedly trying apprenticeship in stock car racing is former Indy Racing League and Indianapolis 500 champion Sam Hornish Jr.

It took Hornish quite a bit more than one full season in Sprint Cup competition, aided by more than a dozen starts in the Nationwide

Series, before he was finally able to start making a successful transition to stock car racing—particularly in 2009, when he earned the first top-five and top-ten finishes of his Cup career.

But Hornish and Montoya have proven to be exceptions to the rule. Others cut from the same open-wheel-racing mold have had far greater difficulty. Let's look back to the start of the 2008 Cup season. The NASCAR world was abuzz that four open-wheel stars from the Indy, CART, and Formula One worlds were joining Montoya in the Cup ranks.

NASCAR chairman Brian France bragged about how his series was a natural magnet to draw some of the best racers in the world to challenge and test themselves against the best drivers in America's best racing series. Unfortunately, three of the four were gone by season's end:

- **Jacques Villeneuve.** This Canadian native and former CART and Formula One champ made just two career Cup starts and one Nationwide Series start before bailing, reportedly due to a snag in contract negotiations and sponsorship issues.
- **Dario Franchitti.** His team failed to acquire sponsorship for a full season, even though he was the defending Indy Racing League and Indianapolis 500 champion, and it shut down before the halfway point of the season. However, he bounced back in 2009 to once again win the Indy Racing League championship.
- **Patrick Carpentier.** A versatile open-wheel and sports-car driver, this Canadian native was pushed out of the way late in the season at Gillett Motorsports (previously Gillett Evernham Motorsports) in favor of A. J. Allmendinger.

Three foreign drivers, looked upon as the linchpins of the increasing foreign popularity of NASCAR, didn't even finish their first season in the sport. When asked if he thought he'd ever come back to NASCAR some day, the Scottish-born Franchitti (who is the husband of actress Ashley Judd) was quite adamant when he replied, "Not for a very, very long time. I wouldn't hold my breath or lose any sleep hoping I'll be back anytime soon."

The only driver of the four to have any success (and as I've already said, it was a long and difficult road for him) was Hornish. And, frankly, I'm not totally convinced that Hornish won't return to the open-wheel Indy car world some day. Even though he achieved pretty much everything there is to achieve in the Indy Racing League, including winning three championships and the Indianapolis 500, if he ever gets to the point where he's mired in mediocrity on the Cup level, don't be surprised if Hornish bolts back to the IRL, the series in which he's achieved the most success of his overall racing career.

# Is the Winner of the Chase for the Sprint Cup *Really* the Best Driver That Year?

For much of its first sixty years, NASCAR boasted that the best driver invariably wound up winning the championship. Sometimes, the number one finisher would win the most races that season, or, like Matt Kenseth in 2003, win the title by being the most consistent finisher throughout the thirty-plus race season.

But when Jimmie Johnson and Chad Knaus started winning championships, they employed a new strategy that caught most of their peers completely off guard. Essentially, Johnson and Knaus made sure that they were competitive enough to qualify for the Chase, then they let all their guns blaze in the ten-race Chase, elevating their game to a far higher level.

Critics blasted the way Johnson and Knaus achieved their championship success as nothing more than formulaic winning, essentially keeping their best in reserve until it mattered the most: during the Chase. That includes bringing their best equipment, playing to their strengths at tracks they have a good history at, and settling for a high finish if a win is out of the question. In other words, they followed pretty much the same path that Kenseth traveled in 2003: sheer consistency to win the championship.

On the one hand, you have to give Johnson and Knaus credit, because they found a loophole of sorts in the Chase format and were able to capitalize on it to their advantage. On the other hand, Johnson and Knaus made watching the Chase boring for many fans—not to mention what they did to the thirty-plus other drivers who failed to make the Chase.

But perhaps the biggest victims of Johnson and Knaus's "loophole" were several of the other drivers who qualified for the Chase each of those years only to see their championship hopes end almost before they got started. If a driver had a bad race in the first three events of the Chase, it became increasingly difficult, if not downright impossible, that he could rally back in the remaining Chase events.

Johnson proved to be the exception to that rule in 2006, and it was then that his and Knaus's championship-winning strategy was born. Johnson was 156 points behind after the fourth race of the Chase (Talladega), and he had all but conceded the championship to another driver. Johnson even said after that race that he and Knaus would spend the remaining six races of the Chase getting a head start on the following season. Unfortunately for every other driver in the Chase, but most fortuitous for Johnson and Knaus, they began one of the biggest comebacks in the sport's history, winning the championship that season and the next three seasons as well.

This brings us back full circle to this question: Was Johnson necessarily the best driver all four of those years? Not at all. He simply was able to win and capitalize on things at the right time. Look at 2007, for example, when Jeff Gordon dominated much of the first twenty-six races only to fall short and finish runner-up to Johnson, his Hendrick Motorsports teammate, because of one extra bad race in the Chase. Johnson, meanwhile, ultimately won 10 races that season, including the last 2 going into the Chase and then 4 in a row in the final five events of the Chase.

In 2008, Johnson once again won 4 Chase races (though not in a row) en route to his third straight Cup title, but many observers thought that Carl Edwards (who won 9 races that season) was truly the best driver across the entire thirty-six-race season. Others cited

Kyle Busch, who won 8 races and dominated, from the start of the season in February until August, as the best overall driver of the year. Unfortunately, they don't give championships to guys who did outstanding in the so-called twenty-six-race regular season, only to have nothing short of a miserable Chase, eventually finishing the season 10th as the younger Busch brother did.

In 2009, Johnson again won 7 races in total, including 4 in the Chase, to ultimately achieve something no other Cup driver ever has: winning a fourth consecutive championship.

In the Red Flag section, I showed some of the flaws in the Chase format and why interest and excitement have dropped considerably in the years after the first Chase season in 2004.

Even Johnson admitted that he wasn't necessarily the best driver in each of his four championship-winning campaigns. "All we have to do is perform well enough to finish in the top twelve after [the September race in] Richmond [which decides the Chase field] and qualify for the Chase, and then we go from there," Johnson said. "It's not about what you do in all thirty-six races, it's being the best of the best in the final ten."

I'll concede that even though Johnson wasn't necessarily the best driver each time he won his championship, at least he can proudly say he was the best driver in the final ten races each year. And in the Chase's format, that's all that counts for being the ultimate champion.

## Has the Chase for the Sprint Cup Been Worth It?

When NASCAR chairman Brian France and the new Cup Series title rights holder Nextel (now Sprint) first announced the concept of the Chase for the Nextel Cup in 2004, there were a lot of detractors. A play-off format of sorts in motorsports? It was an unheard-of concept that quickly drew a wave of criticism and predictions that it would destroy the sport of stock-car racing. Even former chairman Bill France Jr. expressed some initial misgivings, only to have those fears downplayed by his young son and successor, Brian.

But after watching Matt Kenseth win the 2003 Winston Cup championship with just 1 victory all season, resulting in great consistency for Kenseth but boring racing for the fans, France decided that something had to be done to give more weight to race wins.

Enter the Chase format. As the 2004 season wore on, the tone seemed to change from misgivings about the Chase to resigned acceptance. Folks actually were starting to be intrigued at how things would play out and whether the new format would become France's folly or nothing short of a stroke of genius. And when the Chase began, there was a sudden influx of excitement and heightened interest in the newfangled concept. People actually were getting into the new format, just as the younger France had predicted.

In the season finale at Homestead-Miami Speedway, a better script could not have been written. Kurt Busch came out of virtually nowhere, survived near-disaster when a wheel came off his car and the car missed hitting the pit road wall by mere inches, and then won the championship on the final turn of the final lap, edging Jimmie Johnson out by the smallest championship-winning points margin in Cup history: a mere 8 points (breaking the old record of a 10-point championship-determining margin when Alan Kulwicki overtook Bill Elliott in the final race of 1992).

Brian France was looked upon as a genius. Other sports leagues quickly wanted to emulate the Chase format, including the NHRA and even the staid and traditional Professional Golfer's Association (PGA). Unfortunately, Brian's stroke of genius wound up being a one-hit wonder.

By 2005, when Tony Stewart won the championship, two of the sport's biggest stars (four-time Cup champ Jeff Gordon and Dale Earnhardt Jr.) failed to qualify for the Chase. As a result, fan interest dropped from 2004.

In 2006, Jimmie Johnson began the first of a four-year reign as champion. Unfortunately, Stewart did what Gordon and Earnhardt did the year before—failed to qualify for the Chase, missing it by a mere 16 points—and thus failed to give the defending champ a chance at truly defending his title. Ironically, Stewart would go on to win 3 of the Chase races and steal a great deal of thunder from the ten Chase competitors.

In 2007, with TV ratings dropping further from the previous year, NASCAR expanded the Chase field from ten drivers to twelve. It also increased the significance of winning races during the first twenty-six races of the season—the so-called Race to the Chase, awarding drivers 10 extra points for a race win. However, those 10 extra points were only used to help seed drivers in the Chase, thus negating some of the effectiveness and reward for winning during the pre-Chase period. And, once again, Johnson and crew chief Chad Knaus used a formulaic strategy to win their second straight title, showing everyone in the stock car world that it's not whether you win or lose during the whole thirty-six-race season, it's only how well you perform in the final ten events.

In 2008, the Chase had become a boring concept to many, as evidenced by the number of fans who had lost interest in the sport. All one needed to do was look at empty seats in the stands for several Chase events, not to mention slumping TV ratings despite outstanding broadcasts from ABC, to see that the Chase had worn out its welcome. That downward trend continued in 2009, but NASCAR still refused to change—or outright scrap—the Chase format.

The Chase was a great concept in theory and at the start, but sustaining it was the key. And as much as France, NASCAR president Mike Helton, and the rest of the sanctioning body's officials tried, they couldn't get lightning to strike twice, producing another year like 2004.

I predict that with realignment rumored for 2011 or 2012, the Chase will remain in name only as a revamped format is introduced to try to regain some of the lost fans and viewers. Unfortunately, those efforts will prove fruitless, and I expect that the Chase format will disappear after 2013 or 2014, particularly if Sprint does not return as title rights holder of the Cup Series, or if the current TV partners—whose contracts with NASCAR expire after the 2014 season—demand an end to the Chase.

If Sprint does not return after the 2014 season as title right sponsor, a new title rights holder will most likely want to implement its own new format, and given how the Chase has faltered, a new format might just be the best thing for the sport—just as the Chase was supposed to be.

## What At-Track Innovation Has Made Life Significantly Easier for the Competitors?

Say what you want about the convenience of private airplanes, which whisk drivers across the country on their schedule, not anyone else's, and without having to wait in long security checkpoint lines at the airport. Nothing has made a driver's life more comfortable, more convenient, and easier than having a motor coach in which to eat, sleep, relax, and hang out—just like home—at every racetrack from Loudon, New Hampshire, to Fontana, California.

Call them what you want—motor coaches, motor homes, coaches, buses, rolling mansions on wheels, or simply trailers—what was once considered a luxury has become an absolute necessity in NASCAR racing. "If you don't have one now, you're an oddball," said the man who introduced the motor coach to the sport (and vice versa), Felix Sabates, minority owner of Chip Ganassi Racing.

It all began with a very natural and human calling for Sabates: he was looking for a bathroom. More on that in a moment.

As NASCAR grew in the 1970s and into the mid-1980s, and race weekends expanded from one to two days and eventually three to four—or more, when you add the nearly two weeks of Speedweeks at Daytona International Speedway into the mix—the commute from hotels to racetracks and vice versa had become an often burdensome routine. The drivers weren't always able to find the closest and most convenient hotels, which meant that they often wound up driving some distance after essentially driving all day on a racetrack, and that was the last thing they wanted to do.

That's where the motor coach came in and how it came to be. Coaches become the home away from home for drivers and their families for two or three days and nights every race weekend. The fans quickly took notice of these coaches and decided to get in on the act themselves. This led to the typical contingent of hundreds of trailers, buses, and coaches that now line the fan parking lots and campgrounds in and around NASCAR racetracks on race weekends.

Because the drivers spend so much time in their homes away from home, they like to personalize their rolling condos (as Rusty Wallace used to call his) with things to make them feel really and truly at home.

Some drivers like to joke that they live in trailer parks for half the year, given that there's usually about fifty to sixty coaches in secured and guarded lots designated only for drivers, crew chiefs, and team owners' buses. But there's no laughing at the art form into which many drivers have turned their motor coaches. A full kitchen, a bedroom, a big-screen TV in a sitting area, a sound system, and even doorbells are de rigueur. From there, things go off in countless tangents, with the options running the gamut from satellite dishes to awnings to giant TVs that pop out from under the bus, allowing for late-night viewing outdoors and under the stars. Some drivers have even installed portable hot tubs that roll out from the rear undercarriage to help soothe aching muscles after a long day behind the wheel of a race car.

Married drivers, especially those with children, customize their coaches to be family-friendly, particularly in terms of accoutrements such as washers and dryers, dishwashers, large stoves and ovens (for, what else, home-cooked meals), and even areas for cribs or for school-age children to do their homework in.

Single drivers, on the other hand, tend to emphasize the bedrooms and have tons of stereo and TV gear—pretty much the kinds of things you'd expect an unmarried guy to have in a bachelor pad. (It's not surprising that some single drivers' coaches are referred to as "sin bins.")

Not only are the motor coaches individualized, they're also very utilitarian, giving a driver virtually every creature comfort he could want after a hard or productive day at the track. And best of all, instead of spending countless hours stuck in traffic while traveling back and forth to an often lonely hotel room, as many of their predecessors once did, the average pre- and postrace commute for today's drivers can be measured in steps and minutes rather than miles and hours.

There is one other perk that most folks simply don't enjoy at their jobs. "The best thing [about a motor coach]," said Cup driver Tony

Stewart, "is if I have a bad day or get into it with another driver on the track that might be parked next to me in the driver's lot, I can just get behind the wheel and move to another parking space. Tell me how many people, if they have a run-in with their neighbors, can say that about, or do that with, their own houses?"

As the drivers have earned greater amounts of money over the years, so too have the accoutrements and the cost of coaches gone up, to the point where you can spend roughly $300,000 for a starter coach or more than $2 million for a handmade customized coach (built upon the Ralph Lauren Collection platform offered by Oregon-based manufacturer Marathon Coaches). Jeff Gordon has one of these. When it was built in 2007, it included a custom-made playpen and crib for his then newborn daughter, Ella. The highly customized coach has special built-in pop-up sections that double the amount of space. When the race is over, Gordon's coach driver brings the sections back down, and it's off on the road again, to the next race.

Many fans may not realize it, but motor coaches have been a fixture in the sport for little more than twenty years. How coaches came to be a racetrack fixture is a great story in and of itself.

Sabates joined the NASCAR community in 1984. The Cuban native immigrated to this country virtually penniless, but through more than two decades of hard work, he eventually became a multimillionaire who was attracted to NASCAR's penchant for speed, excitement, and attention. As he tells it, the whole idea to bring a motor coach to the racetrack boiled down to one thing. "I was looking for a bathroom," Sabates said with a hearty laugh.

"I got involved with NASCAR in 1984," he explained, "and a lot of racetracks, especially the smaller ones like North Wilkesboro at the time, didn't even have bathrooms; they had port-a-johns. And every time I had a sponsor or a guest, they had to use the port-a-johns.

"So I decided one day that I would go look at a motor coach. I started looking at inexpensive Winnebagos and that kind of stuff. I went from one to the next one and the next one, but didn't find anything I liked. A friend of mine told me to go to Miami, Oklahoma, where there's a company called Newell that makes motor coaches. So I jumped in my plane and went out there, saw what they were building, and I fell in love with them. So I bought myself a new Newell. It cost me four hundred thousand dollars. Today, a good coach can run you two million dollars.

"Really, the concept was I was looking for a bathroom. Really. The motor coach was a throw-in. The first [coach] I had even had two bathrooms [most have just one]. And then I put a bathroom in both of my trailers in the garage area, which we had to hide from NASCAR because that was a big no-no in those days."

Sabates brought his brand-new find to Daytona International Speedway in time for the 1987 Daytona 500. No one quite knew what to make of it, other than Sabates. Ever the savvy businessman, he parked his new Newell coach outside the garage area and waited for the reaction. It didn't take long.

"I put a sign outside the door saying, 'Thank you for not smoking.' I used to smoke but I didn't want people to smoke inside this motor coach," Sabates said. "The first day, I was inside [the coach] watching television when all of a sudden the doorbell rang. I looked outside and it was Bill France Jr. He said to me, 'Mr. Sabates, can we have a talk?' I said, 'Yes, sir.' So he comes in and he said, 'Do you have an ashtray?' And I said, 'No.' So then he said, 'Do you have a Coke can or something?' I said, 'Yes, sir.' He said, 'Pour the Coke into the sink and give me the [empty] can so I can light up a cigarette.'

"Then he said, 'Are you stupid or something? Do you know who sponsors this series [then known as the Winston Cup Series]? It's R. J. Reynolds, and they sell cigarettes.' Do not put a sign 'Do not smoke' outside your coach. Then he said, 'Why did you buy this thing?' So, I told him, for a bathroom, and I have a bed in here. He said, 'Is this for you or for the driver?' I told him, 'Well, Mr. France, this is for me, and the driver and his wife [are] welcome to use it.' He said, 'If the driver starts hiding in this motor home, I'm going to call him for a meeting in the office every fifteen minutes. We don't want drivers hiding out in the infield. They have to be in the garage so the fans can see them.'

"He was very nice about it and complimented me about it. Then he said, 'You know, one of these days we're probably going to have ten or twelve of these things, so we may have to have to make a small parking lot next to the garage.' The next race, Darrell Waltrip and

Geoff Bodine both show up with one, so it's now the three of us with a motor coach.

"Lo and behold, we get to Daytona the next year, and there must be twenty of those things. I get a call to come to Mr. France's office across the street. So I go over there, walk in his office and he's laughing. He says, 'Sabates, look at this shit in the garage. I thought maybe eight, ten, or twelve, but now there's more than twenty there.' I told him, 'Mr. France, I hate to tell you, but Newell has six more on order.' He said, 'Oh, don't tell me that.' Then I said, 'Mr. France, some day, every driver is going to have one, every owner's going to have one, and probably every crew chief is going to have one.'"

Needless to say, the drivers quickly fell in love with the concept of motor coaches. It gave them all the comforts of home, they didn't have to worry about fighting traffic to and from the racetrack, they were able to get eight hours of relatively uninterrupted sleep, and eventually the coaches injected a social element into the sport that had been lacking previously: the families gathered together for dinners, shared a few beers and conversation after a day of racing, watched TV, or just simply hung out.

"I never envisioned how big it would grow," Sabates said. "It just took off. And then it became [an issue of] who had the nicest one. Originally, people were fine with what they had, and then all of a sudden each guy starts spending a little more money, and then the next guy spends a little more money. It was like keeping up with the Joneses."

Sabates was witness to one of the funniest bits of NASCAR lore related to France and motor coaches. On the day that Daytona opened for Speedweeks in 1988, one year after Felix came calling with his motor coach, the infield quickly filled with motor homes, prompting France to look out among the sea of glistening sheet metal and sigh.

"Somebody built a goddamn trailer park in my infield," France said, shrugging his shoulders in resignation. But ever the visionary, France ultimately decided if you can't beat 'em, join 'em. Once he realized the coaches were here to stay, he told Sabates, 'Now that we've got a trailer park in the infield, we've got to make it nice. We've got to put [concrete parking] pads, electricity and all that stuff.' So it was his idea to do that. And now Daytona has the nicest facilit[ies]. They have individual [concrete parking] pads, cable TV, and electricity. They're pretty nice."

France eventually was bitten by the motor coach bug; he finally broke down and bought one for himself and his wife, Betty Jane. Let's just say it seemed like a good idea at the time to the Frances—but it didn't last, according to Sabates.

"We were out [for a race] in California, parked next to each other, and we had a ball," Sabates said. (Well, at least for a little while.) "[France's] driver comes over to our bus and asks if he can hook up his electrical cord to our bus. I said, 'For what? You've got a generator, too.' He said, 'Well, yeah, but Mrs. France has got so many hair curlers, curling irons, and hair dryers that they didn't have enough [power], so we wound up running a cord from our bus to the Frances' so there'd be enough power there. And then they wound up spending just one night in the bus. I think that one-night experience for Bill and Betty Jane was it. I don't think they ever slept there after that."

And then there was this time: "One of the drivers had a satellite dish, and they didn't realize that his remote control had the same frequency as the bus parked next to him. There was a driver in the other coach watching some X-rated movie. [He] flipped the channel over, and next door the other driver was standing there with a girl, and his mother turned the TV on, and boom, there it was.

"I have a lot more stories, but nothing you can print," Sabates concluded.

Sabates was a pioneer in the sport because of his ethnicity and for bringing motor coaches into the sport, but also because he was the first team owner to buy a plane specifically to fly his crew members to and from races. In partnership with fellow team owner Rick Hendrick, he purchased the first helicopter for shorter, commuting-type flights to and from racetracks. But it's introducing the motor coach to the NASCAR community that greatly revolutionized the sport and became a big part of Sabates's legacy in the sport.

Sabates is working on the next-generation motor coach, which he envisions at the track in the next couple of years. "Two stories is [what's] next," Sabates said. "I've got something you're going to see, a motor home that will have some way of popping the back off it and then possibly having a third floor, too. I don't think we're too far away from it. There are a couple people already working on it."

Just what we need, an even bigger trailer park.

## Which Event Created More New Fans for NASCAR?

To answer this question, we have to quantify each of the three contenders: the live televising of races, the split of the Indy Racing League and CART, and the death of Dale Earnhardt.

With the live telecast of the 1979 Daytona 500, NASCAR began its transition into a national sport, having previously been primarily a Southeastern-based series. Nevertheless, it took another fifteen years or so before NASCAR really started to show huge gains and strides in TV viewership. The numbers continued to grow almost every year after the 1979 race, but it wasn't until Dale Earnhardt was in his prime and began a long rivalry with Jeff Gordon (around 1994) that the TV numbers took off. And it wasn't until 2001 that NASCAR finally capitalized on its TV popularity with a multibillion-dollar TV contract with Fox, Turner, and NBC.

The death of Dale Earnhardt cast a terrible pall over the sport, but it also wound up being one of the best things to ever happen to the sport, so to speak. I would never speak about Earnhardt's death as a positive phenomenon, but his dying brought millions more fans into the sport, both at the track and on TV. Upon The Intimidator's death, many (if not most) of his fans transferred their loyalties to his son, Dale Jr., creating the so-called Junior Nation. Also, the elder Earnhardt's death was not in vain, for it brought long-overdue massive improvements in driver safety.

Unfortunately, although NASCAR rode high for the following three or four years after Earnhardt's death, things started to slip around 2005 or 2006. The reasons were many, but they mostly involved the Chase for the Nextel Cup (now Sprint Cup) play-off format, which didn't go over very well with many old-time fans, especially those whose favorite driver might have ultimately done better in a particular season if the Chase had never been implemented. Other fans began to fall away from NASCAR, much like followers often fall away from organized religion, due to a general malaise or dismay at how things are being run. There was also the inclusion of Toyota into the Cup Series in 2006, prompting even more fans to depart the NASCAR world.

The Toyota imbroglio, in particular, seemed to be a significant part of the downward turning point for NASCAR. Older NASCAR fans, particularly those who served in World War II (or whose relatives did), sometimes bestowed an anti-Japanese sentiment and rhetoric upon their offspring.

Ironically, Toyota had already been in the sport for the previous five years in the then Craftsman Truck Series, and although there was a bit of anti-Japanese sentiment before Toyota came to the truck world, it was much more subdued—or maybe *accepted* is a better word. This led to an even greater irony when Toyota moved up to Sprint Cup racing. The outcry was significantly louder than before; countless numbers of fans left the sport in protest. In the scheme of things, however, the fan departure was not nearly as large or as loud as the opponents of Toyota would have you believe.

Part of the anti-Toyota sentiment, as I have said, can be traced to World War II. But another element was a sense of nationalism not related to any particular war. Many race fans wanted to know what was wrong with keeping a series that was all-American in its roots—American-born and American-developed, composed of almost all American-born drivers, crew chiefs, team members and owners and race cars—the way, in their minds, it was intended.

This is one area in which I greatly disagreed with many of my readers. Toyota's coming into NASCAR was certainly going to cost the sport some fans, but Toyota's inclusion in the sport also meant lots of jobs for the same Americans whom their brethren in the stands and in front of the TV seemed to forget about.

You could see trouble on the horizon for the big three auto companies—at least, NASCAR chairman Brian France could see it. To his credit, he realized that the U.S. auto manufacturing industry was spinning downward, going from struggle to near calamity, certainly far earlier than others envisioned or predicted. To ensure the viability and long-term survival of his sport, France heavily courted Toyota to come join his party, just as any good businessman would have done.

Toyota thus came into the sport with lots of money to spend and, in the end, less protest than most fans probably expected. And for all the fans the sport lost when Toyota came into the game, new ones (particularly those who own Toyotas) were gained, and thousands of jobs were created, both directly and indirectly. The company was run by, as they say in the South, "fur-in-ers," but how can something that creates jobs and opportunities ultimately be bad, in the long run?

This brings us to the second contender, and the one that I proclaim the winner in this debate. NASCAR needed something to burst forth and become a major league sport in the worst way, and almost by divine providence, it got it when CART and the upstart Indy Racing League went their separate ways in 1996. It all began with IRL forbidding CART to compete in the Indianapolis 500 unless it joined the fledgling IRL. This was practically a form of blackmail, which all CART owners refused to buckle to, much to the chagrin of the race fans who wanted to see their favorite drivers in the fabled 500.

NASCAR couldn't have been in a better place at a better time, because many racing fans who became disenchanted by the politics of the CART-IRL split elected to take their loyalties and hard-earned money to a different racing series—namely, the Winston Cup Series. From 1996 to about 2004, NASCAR was like a runaway freight train, collecting everything in its path as it blazed its way to new heights of popularity, attendance, TV ratings, and, most important, profitability and revenue generation.

Teams were swimming in tens of millions of sponsorship dollars; it seemed that almost everyone in the corporate world wanted to affiliate with NASCAR. The sanctioning body became rich beyond its wildest dreams, not to mention the dreams of founder Bill France Sr., and those of his successor, Bill Jr. NASCAR had gone from a small mom-and-pop operation to a high-flying, multibillion-dollar enterprise that showed no signs of stopping when it came to more teams, more drivers, and more money.

Unfortunately, when Brian France took over from his father, Bill Jr., as NASCAR chairman late in 2003, a slow and gradual decline started that got worse with virtually each misstep the third-generation NASCAR chief took. Had NASCAR not started the Chase format, had it not allowed the inclusion of Toyota, had it not raised ticket prices and concession-stand prices to near-astronomical levels, it would probably not have lost the millions of fans (or at least so many) that it has lost since the youngest France assumed his reign.

I can't count the number of e-mails from fans who back me up on this contention. And, I'm afraid to say, any chance of getting those old fans to return to the sport is probably unrealistic until Brian France steps down as NASCAR's leader, which also seems pretty unrealistic at this time.

France reminds me of Nero, fiddling while NASCAR burns around him. No one in his inner circle seems able to convince him (they're afraid to even try, lest they be ostracized or fired) that he has made far too many moves that have ultimately proven to be wrong.

NASCAR got greedy as a sanctioning body, as a conglomeration of teams, and as a series that made many people rich. It wasn't enough to stay at that level of richness; instead, everyone wanted and had to have more and more, until there was no more to give. Once that happened, the downward spiral began, and it continues to this day. Will we ever see the spiral turn around? Check back with me in about ten years. If we're lucky, Brian France will be gone by then.

Unfortunately, the damage will already be long done by then. In roughly five years, Brian has managed to undo many of the gains his father and his grandfather achieved in more than half a century. It's very, very sad.

# How Would NASCAR Be Affected by an Openly Gay Driver?

"Jeff Gordon's gay! Jeff Gordon's gay! At least that's what them ornery Earnhardt fans always say." When comedian Tim Wilson penned these lyrics in the late 1990s (to a parody song entitled "Jeff Gordon's Gay!") he touched a nerve with all the non-Gordon fans, particularly since Gordon had run roughshod over his competition, winning Cup championships in 1995, 1997, and 1998 (and another to come in 2001).

Gordon's supremacy, coupled with things such as the rainbow-hued colors on his No. 24 Chevrolet (which are actually nothing more than a rolling advertisement for DuPont paints) and his pit crew picking up the nickname "Rainbow Warriors," created frustration and angst among the fans of Gordon's biggest rival, the late Dale Earnhardt.

What better way for non-Gordon fans to retaliate than to spread rumors about Gordon's sexuality as his marriage to first wife, Brooke, was crumbling. (The couple divorced in 2003.) That came roughly a year before Gordon began dating the woman who would become his second wife in November 2006, Belgian-born model and actress Ingrid Vandebosch.

Because songs like Wilson's are considered humorous and comical by some, it makes you wonder how the NASCAR community—in the garage, in the stands, and at home in front of their TVs—might seriously react to an openly gay driver. Would it cause mass homophobic hysteria in the garage? Would competitors be afraid to hang out with an openly gay man for fear that it might have negative repercussions on their own careers? Would some drivers (or even NASCAR medical personnel) even go to the furthest—and lowest, in my opinion—extreme by saying that they'd fear being around a gay man who was bleeding in an on-track crash because he might be HIV-positive?

I'd like to think that in this day and age, we'd be far past these ridiculous stereotypes. Unfortunately, we're not. Just like any other profession, NASCAR is likely to already have gays within its ranks. Unfortunately, though, they remain in the closet for fear that outing themselves would potentially do great damage to their careers. NASCAR likes to bill itself as an all-American family sport—with emphasis on the family aspect.

One current Sprint Cup driver is rumored to be gay, but I won't mention his name, because there is no evidence to support the rumors—or he prefers to remain in the closet, which is certainly his prerogative.

Does being gay preclude being a successful race car driver? Is NASCAR, which claims to be progressive and openly welcomes people of all colors and creeds, still made up of individuals with the redneck ideology that gays, women, blacks, and other minorities have no place behind the wheel of a race car? Does being gay mean he has no business being in a "real man's" sport? Does being gay give a bad name to his fellow straight competitors? Not at all.

We could joke that the only openly gay driver in NASCAR to date is the fictional character Jean Girard (played by Sacha Baron Cohen) in *Talladega Nights*. But let's be serious. Given the advances that gays have made in other professions, why shouldn't there be gay drivers in NASCAR? I can just hear some readers saying, "Is he crazy?" But is it really as outlandish as it sounds?

How about all the male drivers in the sport who have gone through women the way cars go through a McDonald's drive-through? What about all the married male drivers who have been caught having extra-marital affairs and then end up divorced? Some drivers have done this more than once.

Is the sport so homophobic that it would not welcome a talented driver as a legitimate contender, but would instead focus on his sexuality? I can still recall the terrible treatment that female drivers like Janet Guthrie and Shawna Robinson endured in the sport over the years. I would hope that in this modern era, people would judge others solely by their talent.

There actually is at least one openly gay race car driver currently competing in the United States—not on the NASCAR circuit, but with designs to actually get there one day soon. That's Evan Darling, a forty-year-old sports-car driver from Oakland Park, Florida. Darling sold his successful business in 2008 to finance a lifelong dream of being a full-time racer. His progress has been slow, due to the economy, but he's had some success in a variety of circuits, particularly the Sports Car Club of America circuit.

Despite his age, which is advanced by NASCAR standards, Darling still has high hopes of making it in the stock car world in the next few years. Even though he is open about his sexuality, he doesn't flaunt it. I encourage you to check out his Racing for Diversity and Acceptance blog at http://evandarling.blogspot.com.

Being known as one of NASCAR's biggest critics, I admit that I'm curious how the sport will react once a gay driver either comes out of the closet or an openly gay man like Darling comes into the sport.

I mean, is NASCAR chairman Brian France going to prohibit gays, claiming they violate NASCAR's most overused (and abused) rule: "Actions detrimental to stock car racing."

Let's look at things from a radically different perspective. In 1994, J. T. Hayes, a successful Sprints, Midgets, and Karts racer (with more than 500 wins), underwent sexual reassignment surgery to become a woman. Hayes had been born a hermaphrodite, a person with the reproductive organs of both sexes. After the surgery, roughly four years after Hayes's one and only start on the Cup circuit (March 1990 at Rockingham), he changed his identity and legally became a woman known as Terri O'Connell. O'Connell's life story is chronicled in the autobiography *Dangerous Curves: The Terri O'Connell Story*, which was released in mid-2009.

What makes O'Connell's story all the more compelling is that she wrote the book in an effort to restart her long-dormant racing career. While I was writing this book, I learned that the Mississippi native had plans to compete in several ARCA Series events in 2010 as a potential prelude to returning to racing full-time—as a forty-five-year-old woman. If she is successful in restarting her racing career, O'Connell wants to eventually create an all-female pit crew. This might be a bit harder to bring together, but I say, "You go, girl!"

Although it might make some NASCAR officials a bit uneasy in private, having an openly gay or transsexual driver in the sport would speak volumes to the legitimacy of NASCAR's claims to diversity. It would also show that the diversity program is not just about racial or ethnic minorities and women. A diversity program is about giving access to people of all types, isn't it? If people can drive, who cares about their genitalia or their sexual preferences? It's nobody's business but theirs—and certainly not NASCAR's.

## Why Do Fans Love and Hate the Busch Brothers?

"If you think I'm good, wait till you see my younger brother." When Kurt Busch uttered those words in 2002, the world had little idea of who Kyle Busch was. We simply had to take an older brother's bragging as fact. Kurt wasn't lying or embellishing, however. Kyle Busch has become arguably one of the best young superstars in the making in NASCAR.

Although his time at Hendrick Motorsports from 2004 to 2007 was marked with controversy—allegations of immaturity and a showroom full of wrecked cars caused by Busch's youthful exuberance and lack of patience—being fired by team owner Rick Hendrick in favor of Dale Earnhardt Jr. could wind up being the best thing that ever happened to the younger Busch.

Since moving to Joe Gibbs Racing, Kyle has elevated both his game and his stature in the racing community to a whole new level. Barring any unfortunate circumstance down the road, I predict that Kyle Busch is going to win a Cup championship like his older brother and possibly become the more successful of the two siblings.

Kurt has tapered off dramatically since winning his Cup championship in 2004, the inaugural season of the Chase for the (then) Nextel Cup. Kyle, meanwhile, has been coming on like a champion in the making.

Very few drivers show the potential they have when they come into the Cup Series. Jeff Gordon was one, Tony Stewart another. But Kyle Busch has shown a talent, flair, and bravado that draws striking comparisons to the late Dale Earnhardt.

Like Earnhardt, the younger Busch is brash, cocky, and extremely self-confident. Although he has caused a number of wrecks due to his overaggressiveness, that is simply the style he races with—again, much like the late Earnhardt. If you were in The Intimidator's way and you wouldn't move, he'd move you himself. It's the same with Kyle Busch.

Of all the brothers we've seen in NASCAR over the years—Bobby and Donny Allison; Darrell and Michael Waltrip; Terry and Bobby Labonte; Ward and Jeff Burton; Rusty, Kenny, and Mike Wallace; and Geoff, Brett, and Todd Bodine—one sibling always seems to stand out from the others.

Only the Labontes had similar success in the overall scheme of things, with Terry winning two Winston Cup titles and younger brother Bobby capturing one. Of the brothers who have had great success in stock car racing, it's typically been the older one who has far outshined the younger one(s).

The Busch brothers, however, are likely to be just the opposite. Kyle, the younger sibling, is a multiseason champion in the making, with the potential of becoming the sport's biggest superstar since the late Earnhardt.

Say what you want about Earnhardt's son, Dale Jr., being the most popular driver in NASCAR for the last seven years. Kyle Busch's footsteps are growing in the distance. Earnhardt may be the fan favorite, but "Shrub" (Kurt's nickname for Kyle) is on track to ultimately pass and far exceed Junior in career wins, eventual championships, and possibly even in popularity.

But for all the success the Busch brothers have enjoyed on the NASCAR circuit, they are still victims, of sorts: a lot of fans just don't like them—and haven't liked them since they came into the sport.

It's kind of easy to understand. Kurt came into NASCAR with a chip on his shoulder and, as former Cup racer Jimmy Spencer once said, "pissed a lot of people off with his arrogant ways." To prove his disdain for Kurt, Spencer ultimately punched the elder Busch brother in the nose after a race, following yet another run-in between the two.

Kurt was a gracious champion when he won the first Nextel Cup title in 2004, but he was not so gracious the following year, when he got into a widely publicized incident with a sheriff's deputy outside Phoenix. What NASCAR fan can forget Kurt's famous words to the deputy: "Don't you know who I am?" This ultimately led to his premature release from his contract with Roush Racing (now Roush Fenway Racing).

Since joining Penske Racing and replacing the retired Rusty Wallace, Kurt has been a virtual gentleman's gentleman, due in part to the responsibility he has to his primary sponsor, Miller Beer, to maintain a good and positive image. Penske's own code of conduct, which is mandatory for his drivers and employees, also helps.

Where Kurt left off with his arrogant side, however, Kyle seems to have picked up. He's also been called arrogant and cocky—and those are the nicer things that have been said about him (and pretty much the only things we can print about him in this book).

Much was said about Kyle's attitude during his breakout season in 2008, his first with Joe Gibbs Racing after being unceremoniously dumped by Hendrick Motorsports after the 2007 season to make room for Dale Earnhardt Jr. "KyBusch" (a nickname I coined that has been picked up by many of my media peers) went on a tremendous victory tear, not only in Sprint Cup but also in the Nationwide Series and the Craftsman Truck (now Camping World Truck) Series; he won 21 races in the three series in 2008.

Kyle quickly became the man whom people loved to hate. He didn't do himself any favors when he and Earnhardt Jr. "traded fenders" at Richmond in the spring of 2008. This brought out a loud and vociferous reaction from the Junior Nation, and both drivers ending up not winning because their cars went slip-sliding away while winner Clint Bowyer smiled and waved as he drove past.

All that being said, however, the younger Busch has been put in his place a couple of times already, which has somewhat helped his maturity. The first took place when after a tremendous run-up to the Chase in 2008, he literally fell apart in the ten-race Chase, ultimately finishing a disappointing tenth out of twelve drivers.

The other came in 2009. Busch appeared be a lock to repeat as a Chase contestant, but a rough stretch of races leading up to the final Chase qualifier at Richmond in September ultimately cost him a berth in the play-offs, leaving him on the outside looking in, much like Tony Stewart in 2006, when he failed to make the Chase by 16 points after winning the championship in 2005.

Expect an even more refined and demure attitude from the younger Busch brother in 2010. Maybe he'll see what a lot of fans have seen for the last several years: arrogance and cockiness, while good for confidence, can also work against you, not just in the court of public opinion but also among your peers on the racetrack. If Busch learns his lessons well enough and matures further, it may actually bring him the thing he covets the most: a Sprint Cup championship. He has the talent to win the title; the question is if he has the maturity to do so, as well.

In the whole scheme of things, just how good is the younger Busch? At age twenty-five, the Las Vegas native has the potential to become the greatest champion in NASCAR history. That's obviously a very bold statement, but no one currently in the sport—other than maybe Jimmie Johnson, who is already a multiple champion—can match Busch's long-term potential. Given another good fifteen to twenty years of racing, Busch could someday break Richard Petty and Dale Earnhardt's shared record for most Cup championships (seven).

"He's going to show you things you're not going to believe," Kurt Busch said on the day he revealed his younger brother to the world. Right now, he already has. I can't wait to see what the future brings.

## Which Drivers Should Retire?

It's never easy to tell someone that he can't cut it, that he's too old to do the job he's been doing for so many years. The natural response, particularly for a race car driver, is anger: How dare someone question my ability, drive, or competitiveness? I'm as good as I've ever been, he insists.

The problem is that he's *not* as good a driver as he's ever been. Even if he still has ability, drive, and competitiveness, his talent level is nowhere near what it was in the prime of his racing career.

Most drivers who overextend their stay in NASCAR aren't like fifty-one-year-old Mark Martin. His talent and dedication to good health could keep him functioning as a competitive and winning driver for another ten years, at the rate he's going. But Martin is definitely the exception rather than the rule.

Fortunately, some drivers in recent years have walked away on their own terms, realizing that it was the right time for them to step aside rather than hang around far too long. Darrell Waltrip readily admits that he did the latter as a driver. Among those who got out while the getting was good was Rusty Wallace, who stepped out of a race car for the final time at the end of 2005 and has never looked back. Ditto for Dale Jarrett, who raced one last event, the 2008 Sprint All-Star Race, and called it a career, just as his father, Ned, ended his racing tenure: cold turkey.

The last thing I want to do is push someone out of his or her job. But let's face it, some drivers are not only past their prime, they're occupying seats that could be taken by up-and-coming stars of the future. Look at how the flood of young guns earlier in the decade has dropped to a trickle the last couple of years, with essentially just David Ragan, Regan Smith, and Brad Keselowski joining the party. How many seats filled by aging veterans, who have made a nice living for themselves all these years, could go to young up-and-comers, injecting some revitalization and new blood into the sport, much as the arrival of Kyle Busch has?

I have compiled a list of drivers to appease the fans who continually wonder, "When's he going to retire?" When those drivers read this, I hope they understand that I wish them the best—but just as I'm sure I'll do in my own career in a few years, they should move on to the next chapter of their lives.

- **Bill Elliott.** Let's face it, "Awesome Bill from Dawsonville" just isn't so awesome anymore. Elliott said he was scaling back into semiretirement in 2004, but he still competed in six races. Instead of cutting even more events from his schedule each season since then, he has seen a steady increase in his workload. He started nine races in 2005, ten in 2006, and twenty each in 2007 and 2008; he probably would have come close to that number again in 2009 had he not suffered three broken ribs in a dirt-bike accident in the late summer, competing in just twelve races all season. Some retirement. At the age of fifty-four (he turns fifty-five in late 2010), Elliott has done pretty much everything a driver could ever do, including winning a Winston Cup championship (1988). Why he needs to hang on is anyone's guess. Didn't he learn anything from the way Darrell Waltrip's legacy took a big hit for sticking around *way* too long? Considering that Elliott's average finish in sixty-plus races since 2004 is twenty-seventh (and not even one top-ten finish among them), Elliott should face the facts: You're not Awesome Bill anymore. You're now Over-the-Hill Bill.
- **Michael Waltrip and Kenny Wallace.** These crown jesters of NASCAR are hysterical comedians and great broadcasters. Unfortunately, both have seen far better days as race car drivers. Waltrip has at least realized his limitations somewhat: he's scaled back to a part-time schedule in 2010. Wallace, on the other hand, will race whenever and wherever someone wants him to. If you're an owner with a seat open and you've got the money, Kenny's got

the time. And even though Wallace still maintains a full-time ride in the Nationwide Series, his performance in that circuit hasn't been much to write home about: his average race-day finish the last couple of years has been twenty-second. Frankly, these guys are much better in front of a TV camera, and that's nothing to be ashamed of. In fact, they could probably put together one hell of a comedy routine, an Abbott and Costello of stock car racing. Do we need to pass the hat and start up a collection at Cup events to raise money to convince them to hang up their helmets for the final time? It's time, guys, to give it up. Please!

- **Terry Labonte.** The two-time Cup champ made it clear that he was done with racing in 2006, after two seasons of competing on a part-time schedule. But Labonte, now fifty-three, couldn't stay away for too long. He drove three races in 2007 for Michael Waltrip Racing, ten in 2008, and scaled back to just six in 2009. I might point out that since Texas Terry's last full-time season in 2004, he's competed in more than fifty races, with an average finish of 30th. If this doesn't tell you that he's doing it just to pick up some easy cash, I don't know what would.

- **Sterling Marlin.** Marlin's average finish the last two years in fewer than twenty races (he also failed to qualify for several others) is 36th. Your farm in Tennessee is calling you, Sterling. Please pick up the phone. The cows need to be milked. (As of this writing, Marlin said he was now "pretty much retired" as a driver.)

All the above being said, I have to voice my opinion about two guys who recently did retire, but not necessarily by choice. They probably were due to retire anyway, but the way they wound up leaving the sport struck a raw nerve that greatly saddened me.

The first is Ken Schrader. Racing is the fifty-five-year-old Schrader's lifeblood, but when all other options disappeared, he wasn't given a gold watch or a retirement party or anything. He just seemed to simply fade away, a fate that he should not have had to experience. For all the good-will and good times that Schrader has brought to the sport in twenty-five years on the Cup circuit on either a full- or a part-time basis, he deserved a better send-off than what he got, which was absolutely nothing. Still, you don't have to feel sorry for Schrader. He'll do okay. He earned more than $35 million in his Cup career, he is still barnstorming in late-model and modified races across the country, and he owns a couple of small short tracks in the Midwest that promote grassroots racing.

The other driver is Kyle Petty. What happened to him is nothing short of a crime, in my opinion. Squeezed out of Petty Enterprises when his father merged the company with Gillett Motorsports to form Richard Petty Motorsports, Kyle was unceremoniously excluded from the driving roster for 2009 because of the four drivers Richard Petty inherited from the Gillett camp: Kasey Kahne, Elliott Sadler, A. J. Allmendinger, and Reed Sorenson. Through no fault of his own, there just was no room left at the inn for Kyle. At the very least, you would think that NASCAR would have put together some sort of fare-well tour for Kyle in 2009, even if he wasn't racing, for all his tireless support and his involvement as a goodwill ambassador throughout the years. The most significant accomplishment that will prove to be his legacy as a human being is founding and building Victory Junction Gang camp in honor of his late son, Adam, who was killed in a crash while practicing at New Hampshire in 2000. While Kyle is still around at select races as a spectator and is still part of the six-race Turner Sports telecasting package of NASCAR races between the Fox Sports and ABC-ESPN packages (and makes regular appearances on SpeedTV), he definitely deserved a better exit than what he was given. Even though he won only 8 races in his career, compared to his father's record 200 wins, Kyle Petty will go down in NASCAR annals as one of its biggest winners—not so much as a driver but as a humanitarian who cared and put his money where his mouth was.

# Where Do You Find the Two Most Disparate Race Crowds in NASCAR?

Race fans are race fans, no matter where you go, right? Wrong. Maybe they all like to watch races and their favorite drivers, but there are some rather distinct differences among race fans, like economic class and geographic location.

I've visited every Sprint Cup racetrack in the country, and there are several that are virtually identical, both in the makeup of the track and its fans. But without question, you couldn't find a bigger disparity between tracks and fans than Talladega Superspeedway in Alabama and Infineon Raceway in Sonoma, California. Talladega is like living in the movie *Deliverance*, where God, guns, breasts, and beer rule—and not necessarily in that order. Sonoma, on the other hand, is like watching a run-of-the-mill chick flick, where folks are well-mannered and almost dainty, and where wine, stock options, and Mercedes Benzes or BMWs rule—again, not necessarily in that order.

For those of you who have never been to either track (and for those of you who have and are likely to agree with me), I've decided to do a top-ten list of what makes each track stand out from the other. So, without further ado, here are the top-ten differences between NASCAR fans at Talladega and Sonoma:

10. **Talladega:** Best word to describe it is *wild*, where anything goes and usually does. There are plenty of torn jeans and stained T-shirts. Favorite question: "Do y'all wanna party? (Clothes are optional.)

    **Sonoma:** Best word to describe it is *sedate*, almost to the point of boring. Plenty of Birkenstocks, chinos, and hair gel. Favorite question: "Do you want red or white wine?"

9. **Talladega:** Women who agree to men chanting "Show us your boobs" receive Mardi Gras–like beads as a reward.

    **Sonoma:** "Honey, can you put some sunscreen on my back, please?"

8. **Talladega:** Beer—and lots of it (the favorite brand being Budweiser, of course).

    **Sonoma:** A little chardonnay or merlot, perhaps (what would you expect, being in the middle of California's wine country?).

7. **Talladega:** Cops are kept busy with fights and DUIs (of the fans, not the racers).

    **Sonoma:** The biggest call that cops typically get is to help motorists who locked their keys in their cars.

6. **Talladega:** Local anthem is Lynyrd Skynyrd's "Sweet Home Alabama."

   **Sonoma:** Local anthem is Scott McKenzie's "San Francisco (Be Sure to Wear Some Flowers in Your Hair)."

5. **Talladega:** It's hard to find coffee at the concession stands.

   **Sonoma:** Plenty of stands sell lattes and cappuccinos.

4. **Talladega:** Double-wide trailers dot the surrounding area.

   **Sonoma:** Multimillion-dollar homes are just a couple of miles away.

3. **Talladega:** Rednecks and staunch Republicans.

   **Sonoma:** Liberals and steadfast Democrats.

2. **Talladega:** Tornadoes.

   **Sonoma:** Earthquakes.

1. **Talladega:** The Confederate Flag.

   **Sonoma:** The rainbow flag.

## Could a NASCAR Race Ever Be Held Indoors?

The following question was posed by Dusty Duncan of Claremore, Oklahoma (the only reader to get *two* questions included in this book):

> One of the most popular races in midget racing is the annual Chili Bowl Midget Nationals held in Tulsa, Oklahoma, an indoor race. Given the fact that Dallas Cowboys owner Jerry Jones just built a state-of-the-art sports stadium costing in excess of $1 billion, it's not entirely outside of the realm of possibility to think a racetrack big enough to accommodate NASCAR could be built indoors. Would you go watch NASCAR racing "under the roof"?

Logistically, building a completely enclosed racetrack would be possible, but the cost would be astronomical, and there are a number of other drawbacks. The building process itself would be easy: just build a complex like a football stadium, slap a roof on it, install a dirt or an asphalt racing surface inside and, voilà, we're ready to go racing.

Unfortunately, it's not that simple. One of the major concerns would be ventilation. How would you disperse all the carbon monoxide that would build up inside from all the exhaust emissions? How would you keep a steady stream of fresh air drifting throughout the seating area while also keeping out the fumes from the cars, the tires, the gas, and the other materials around the racetrack?

Then there's the sound element. Race cars are loud, period. If you are in an enclosed facility, all that racket goes straight into your ears. We've had indoor events for things like the Chili Bowl or for Monster Truck or motocross racing, but the sound of those pales in comparison to the sound a stock car produces.

Speedway Motorsports chairman and billionaire Bruton Smith has jokingly suggested that he might enclose either Bristol Motor Speedway in eastern Tennessee or Charlotte Motor Speedway (formerly Lowe's Motor Speedway) in suburban Charlotte, North Carolina, but that might be a heady project even for a guy with Smith's deep pockets. If there's anyone who *could* do it, Smith would be the one. But I don't see him doing it anytime soon, if ever.

Around 2000, there was a strong movement to build an indoor race-track in Chip Ganassi's hometown, adjacent to the Pittsburgh airport, but lack of funding kept the project from essentially ever getting off the ground. The grand design of the $300-million project (which would probably be between $750 million and $900 million today) was ambitious. But major sanctioning bodies like NASCAR failed to get behind it, and I can understand why, given the relative uncertainty that it would ever actually be built.

There was an attempt a few years later to resurrect the project in eastern Ohio, but that situation was short-lived, as well, due to residents' complaints about what the track would do their property values, along with the associated problems of traffic congestion, crime, and noise.

Cowboys Stadium, Jerry Jones's new facility in Arlington, Texas (between Dallas and Fort Worth), is without question one of the biggest and most glorious facilities in the world. (But then, what else would you expect from Texas, where everything is supposedly bigger and better?) Because there is a retractable roof on Cowboys Stadium, it would be possible, theoretically, to run a race inside, because much of the noise and sound pollution would be dissipated through the opening in the roof. But given the limited available space around the field, it would be very difficult for teams to get up to any appreciable amount of speed due to the size. The frontstretch and the backstretch would each be only about three hundred feet long. Then you'd have to erect some type of banking to make up the four turns.

At Bristol Motor Speedway, the cars rarely go faster than 110 miles per hour. If NASCAR was to race at Cowboys Stadium, I'm willing to bet that the cars wouldn't reach more than 85 miles per hour, if that. And what kind of race would that be? NASCAR could mandate smaller cars for a facility like that, but it would probably have to downsize all the way to go-carts just to have any semblance of a decent race.

If money were no object, I'd love to see an indoor track. But the sheer cost would likely far eclipse the reported billion-plus dollars that Jones spent on the Cowboys' new mansion. Besides, isn't one of the biggest lures of watching a NASCAR race in person the ability to watch it *outside* in the fresh air and sunshine or under the lights? It doesn't get better than that.

## Who Was the Most Important Man in Shaping Modern-Day NASCAR (and the Only Person Who Could Strike Fear in Bill France Jr.)?

Okay, I admit, this is a trick question. In fact, I'll throw a bit more spice into the mix to make it even harder to answer: Who was the most important man in shaping modern-day NASCAR, yet never raced in the sport; never was a crew chief, a team owner, or a sanctioning body official; and never was a major broadcaster or writer? Despite all this, the sport would probably never have reached the point it's at today if not for him.

It's not Bill France Jr. Nor is it Neal Pilson, who was the executive producer of NASCAR's first national live telecast, the 1979 Daytona 500. For run-of-the-mill NASCAR fans, the name may mean very little. But ask guys like Rusty Wallace, Mike Helton, or Mark Martin, and they'll immediately give him overwhelming credit.

His name is William Ralph Seagraves, otherwise known simply as Ralph. The self-professed "little ol' cigarette salesman from Winston-Salem [North Carolina]" became the most influential man in modern-day stock-car racing when he convinced the mighty R. J. Reynolds Tobacco Company in 1972 to sponsor what became known as the Winston Cup Series. He would later do the same with NHRA and its Winston Drag Racing Series, as well as other sports including boat racing, golf, and tennis, which all utilized various brands in Reynolds's fleet of cigarette divisions.

How Seagraves married RJR and NASCAR is the stuff of legend. In 1971, legendary team owner Junior Johnson came to Seagraves seeking a $250,000 sponsorship to run his team. To Seagraves, that was chump change. Not only was he willing to give Johnson the seed money he sought, he essentially said, "Why stop there? How much would it cost for us to sponsor the whole Grand National Series?"

Johnson was placed in a very unusual position: he didn't know what to say or how to react. He merely told Seagraves that he'd approach Bill France Jr. with the suggestion and see what happened. And the rest, as they say, is history.

When NASCAR was feeling a significant financial burden, Seagraves rode in like an all-American cowboy wearing a white hat. The seemingly unlimited RJR budget not only saved the sport, it also helped to save several racetracks, race teams, and owners in the process, not to mention saving several drivers from calling it a career prematurely.

It was while he was president of the tobacco company's Special Events Operations group that Seagraves saw a golden opportunity to align the Winston cigarette brand with a sport whose fans mirrored Winston's demographics. When government restrictions prevented the company from advertising on television or radio, RJR spent billions of dollars to promote itself through sports. To some, it was a sneaky way to get free and legal advertising, but it worked. Seagraves made Winston, RJR, and NASCAR synonymous with one another, seemingly joined at the hip. Where one ended, the others began.

Stories are legendary of how Seagraves would oversee the distribution of ten or more cartons of cigarettes to anyone who wanted them, and the best part of the deal was they were totally free. Even nonsmokers in the industry willingly took all the smokes they could carry, giving them to thankful friends and relatives and being a big hit in the process.

Seagraves was one of the few people who could put Bill France Jr. in his place. If France objected to something Winston or RJR did, Seagraves would quickly respond, "Well now, Bill, we can always take our ball [money] and go back home with it to Winston-Salem. You wouldn't want that, would you?" Seagraves would say that with a laugh, and France would also crack a smile, but deep down France knew who controlled the purse strings—and it wasn't Bill Jr.

Seagraves would oversee the sport's growth before handing control to his prodigy, T. Wayne Robertson, who continued what his predecessor had begun and took it to even higher levels.

Seagraves was inducted into the International Motorsports Hall of Fame in 2008, ten years after he passed away in 1998. It's sad that it took the Hall of Fame that long to give Seagraves his just due, especially when the National Motorsports Press Association inducted him into its hall of fame in 1992, followed the next year by the International Drag Racing Hall of Fame.

Seagraves died on September 27, 1998. Some say it was from a broken heart, because Robertson, who was like a son to Seagraves, had been killed in a tragic boat crash in the Louisiana bayou eight months earlier.

As the late Paul Harvey loved to say, "Now you know the *rest* of the [NASCAR] story."

# BLACK FLAG

# Things That Should Be (or Finally Were) Changed

# Should Restrictor Plates Be Taken Away from Daytona and Talladega?

NASCAR implemented horsepower-robbing restrictor plates more than twenty years ago, shortly after Bill Elliott flew around Talladega Superspeedway at an incredible speed of more than 212 miles per hour. A restrictor plate is a piece of aluminum that is placed between the carburetor and intake manifold to limit the amount of airflow into the engine, thus restricting horsepower and slowing race cars down so they don't fly into the grandstands.

Up to now, the plates have served their purpose, for the most part. But they also created another set of problems that continues to this day. Because a restrictor plate robs an engine of horsepower and takes away a driver's ability to mash the gas pedal for the type of passing power he has at every track other than Talladega and Daytona, it essentially leaves all cars driving at the same speed.

The only way that a car can make any significant forward movement is through drafting, in which a trailing car gets up on the rear end of the car in front of it and pushes it forward by aerodynamics. In essence, two cars together become significantly faster than the same two cars apart.

But if cars don't draft with each other or try to make solo moves, they typically have little to no extra power to do so. Falling back very quickly because you lost your drafting partners is called "getting out of the draft," and it can cause wrecks—especially when patience wears thin—usually multicar wrecks, which can involve two to as many as two dozen trailing cars.

And some of those wrecks can be incredible spectacles. At the Aaron's 499 race on April 26, 2009, at Talladega, Carl Edwards was on the final lap, heading to the checkered flag with Brad Keselowski locked to his rear bumper. As the finish line grew closer, Keselowski made a last-ditch attempt to get under Edwards's car and challenge him for the lead. Edwards's car slammed against the fence and almost sailed through it, injuring seven fans (including one who suffered a broken jaw from flying debris).

Like everyone else on the racetrack, Edwards had a restrictor plate on his car, making it pretty clear that restrictor plates are now part of the problem they were designed to correct. In a situation like this one, two things are likely to happen:

- Unable to have extra passing power in reserve to pull away, Edwards is going to do his best to block Keselowski's bid to get past.
- Faced with that situation, Keselowski has the choice of lifting up off the gas pedal (not likely) or making contact with the left rear of Edwards's car (most likely).

Keselowski's car spun Edwards's Ford around, right into the path of Ryan Newman, who had nowhere to go. Newman's subsequent contact with Edwards in the left rear end—at roughly 190 miles per hour—caused Edwards's car to lift off the ground. And while normally the rear wings on Sprint Cup cars are supposed to keep them glued to the racetrack, in this instance they acted as airfoils or wings, lifting him upward, while momentum and gravity pushed him sideways into the front-stretch fence, showering nearby fans with debris and causing injuries.

It was not the first time a dramatic crash such as this has occurred at 'Dega, a place that has become synonymous with the phrase "the Big One," a spectacular multicar crash that sends cars flying in virtually every direction: straight ahead, sideways, backward, upside down, and even in an end-over-end barrel roll. Frankly, it's not uncommon to see more than one "Big One" in the same race; it's part of the allure that keeps bringing fans back to Talladega year after year.

Racing legend Bobby Allison had been involved in a similar horrific wreck in 1987, shortly after restrictor plates were introduced to the sport. Allison watched Edwards's crash on TV and told a reporter who called him afterward that it was "almost identical" to his own crash, including almost going through the fence that separated cars from the fans.

If Allison's and Edwards's crashes were anomalies, it would be one thing. But after two nearly identical wrecks roughly twenty-two years apart—not to mention all the other types of wrecks that have occurred in that time—who's to say that the third time something like this happens, it won't result in the deaths of the driver and/or innocent fans in the stands who merely came to the track to watch what they hoped would be an exciting race?

Therefore, isn't it time to consider removing restrictor plates from cars at both 'Dega and 'Tona, once and for all? As I've advocated for the last five years or so, I firmly say yes—but with a caveat.

Not only do restrictor plates take away horsepower, they also prevent drivers from breaking out of the pack on their own. The drivers have to become master drafters, not to mention master tacticians who can see what fellow drivers will draft with them.

In my opinion, the solution is simple: take away the plates but also mandate the use of smaller, less powerful motors in the cars. Instead of a motor that cranks out eight hundred horsepower, for instance, how about a motor that turns six hundred horses on the dynamometer? That way, drivers would once again have full control of their cars, could still pass at will (as they do at other tracks), could still approach 190 miles per hour in the turns, yet would also do all that in a much safer fashion.

I'm no physics professor, but I figure that drafting on the high banks of both tracks would still be a viable option even without plates on the cars. Can someone come up with a better solution? Restrictor plates do slow cars down, but they also make racing similar to the old International Race of Champions series, where cars were equally prepared and typically performed very similarly.

In early January 2007, NASCAR ran an experiment at Daytona, allowing a few cars to run without restrictor plates during a heavily monitored practice session. The result was surprising, particularly with the cars of then–Penske Racing teammates Kurt Busch and Ryan Newman. The cars were able to reach speeds close to 200 miles per hour, but they gripped the racing surface more snugly, they were able to move freely from one side of the track to the other, and, as Busch said, they "drove like real race cars."

Unfortunately, a test was all it was. NASCAR compiled the data from the demonstration and filed it, most likely never to be seen again. It's time to really give consideration to removing restrictor plates. Take away the plates, and I guarantee that there will be more excitement, better racing, and greater fan interest at both Talladega and Daytona—not to mention increased safety. And, quite frankly, isn't that what's racing is all about, anyway?

## Should the Races Be Shortened?

Race length is one of my biggest pet peeves about NASCAR. When I go to a race, I expect to see an exciting, compelling, and nonstop, action-filled event—not a grueling, monotonous, and often boring marathon. Yet we continue to see races that routinely last four hours or more, making NASCAR king of long events among professional sports leagues.

A football game is typically three hours and fifteen minutes, from opening kickoff to the final whistle. You can practically set your watch to it. Go to a major league baseball game, and you're usually out of there in three hours or less—unless, of course, the game goes into extra innings. A basketball game rarely goes longer than two and a half hours (unless it goes into overtime). So why must NASCAR races just go on and on?

I've posed that question several times over the years to fans. Invariably, the response is about 80 percent in favor of shorter races and 20 percent against the idea. The dissenters typically cite two major arguments to bolster their case:

1. If the races are shortened, the ticket prices should be reduced accordingly (and we know that NASCAR isn't going to do that anytime soon).
2. The fans spend great sums of money on traveling to the track, staying at hotels, and buying food and gas. They want their money's worth, and this means as much racing as they can get.

Both are valid and legitimate arguments on the surface. But let's also consider that the attention span and the time availability of the average race fan have continued to constrict in the last decade. We're busier and spread out in so many different directions by so many events and distractions in our lives that our time has become much more precious.

Particularly with the Car of Tomorrow, the longer races have tended to become more boring, regardless of NASCAR's insistence that the race is fostering closer side-by-side racing. That may be the case in the final 20 laps of a race, but if you've got a 500-mile event, things can get pretty dull and tedious from about 50 laps into the race until the last 25 or 30 laps.

Do we *really* need a 500-mile race at Pocono Raceway in Pennsylvania, one of the most boring tracks on the circuit? Even more, do we need *two* boring 500-milers there? *Why?* Frankly, I'd be quite happy to have a 350- or even 400-mile race, tops, at the 2.5-mile tri-oval track in the Keystone State.

Critics who say that shortening a race would take away from the excitement or integrity of a race are obviously not students of the sport. For years, Dover International Speedway held only 500-mile races. But in the fall of 1997, it cut the race length to 400 miles. The result was better and more competitive racing.

Michigan International Speedway held just one 500-mile race, its first Cup event in 1969, before track officials realized that was just too long on the high-banked 2-mile track and far too grueling for the drivers and the fans alike. Ever since, Michigan has held nothing but 400-mile races. That does not include the races that have been shortened by rain or the 1974 spring race won by Richard Petty, which was shortened 40 miles by NASCAR chairman Bill France Jr. to show that the sanctioning body was "doing its part" during the nation's gas crisis.

Daytona International Speedway holds its iconic Daytona 500 in mid-February, but when it's time for the return trip there in the summer, the racers have to go 400 miles, leaving fans with a good balance through the course of the two races.

Even the legendary Indianapolis Motor Speedway, home of the Greatest Spectacle in Racing, the Indianapolis 500, hosts only a 400-mile NASCAR event, the Brickyard 400. I dread to even think of the boredom that would occur if NASCAR and Indianapolis ever decided to lengthen that race (not to mention having to worry if the tires would last the extra length).

Shorter races mean more excitement, closer side-by-side action, drivers willing to take chances earlier in an event, and more competition throughout. I don't care if some fans think they wouldn't be getting their money's worth. To me, a shorter, more exciting race is far more worth its weight in gold than a long, monotonous, drawn-out event that seems to be more about consuming time than enhancing competition.

Cynics will tell you that the difference between 400 miles and 500 miles can be quite lucrative—not so much for the drivers, but for the racetrack concession stand and the souvenir sellers. The longer the race, the more opportunities fans have to spend more of their money shopping for more food, beer, licensed merchandise, and the like. And who owns most of the tracks and concessions? International Speedway Corporation, the speedway arm of NASCAR.

When it comes to shorter races, two tracks that "get it" are Phoenix International Raceway and New Hampshire Motor Speedway. Both flat 1-mile tracks, they almost always put on great displays of racing, due significantly in part to running shorter-than-the-norm races.

Phoenix calls its events 500s and 600s, but that's in name only. The races are actually just 312 laps, equal to five hundred kilometers, or 375 laps, equal to six hundred kilometers, homage to a period about twenty years ago when there was a move to convert the United States to the metric system. Phoenix thought it would do its part for the proposed change; it was a noble gesture, but the rest of the country didn't exactly follow suit. Still, track officials hit upon a perfect formula for short, fast, and competitive races, and the "500" moniker (and length) stuck. To this day, I've yet to hear from a fan who would like to see a longer race there, even though NASCAR increased the length of the April 2010 race at Phoenix to a 600 to accommodate a longer TV broadcast.

Similarly, short-track racing has always been king at New Hampshire, particularly modified and late-model racing, and the track draws a lot of fans of those particular genres with its own 300-lap Cup events around its 1-mile surface.

If I could wave a magic wand and adjust the schedule, here's what things would look like once the fairy dust settled:

- **Pocono Raceway.** Cut both races to 400 miles in length. If the events remain boring after about a three-year trial at the shorter distance, then I'd cut even further and make them 350-mile events. I'd even be willing to cut down to 300 miles, although my top preference would simply be to remove Pocono from the Sprint Cup schedule altogether. At the very least, they should scale back to just one race there per year; a shorter one, of course.
- **Auto Club Speedway.** This track has received so much criticism throughout the years for boring races, events run in triple-digit heat, and a terrible geographic location (Fontana, California) for fans to get to (resulting in numerous empty seats). I think the 500-mile length of both Cup races there each year is the biggest problem. I'd reduce the length to 400 miles and run both races on a Saturday night. Southern California residents have so many options for entertainment that you have to give them a reason to skip trips to the beach, the mountains, to Vegas, or even just hanging around the house. I'm quite confident that a Saturday night race in Fontana, at a shorter distance and perhaps with lower-priced tickets as a promotion for the first two or three events under the new policy, would bring fans out in droves.
- **Atlanta Motor Speedway.** This place is kind of a hybrid between Pocono and Auto Club Speedway. The races are too long, and the track has had a serious problem attracting ticket buyers in the last several years. The solution is to cut both the spring and the fall races to 400 miles, and run the spring race on Sunday afternoon and the fall race on Saturday night. Then you'll have Hot-lanta burning once again for Sprint Cup racing.

On the flip side, here are the tracks that I would keep at 500 or more miles:

- **Daytona 500 and Talladega.** These races should stay at 500 miles primarily because of tradition and the fact that they're among the biggest and most popular races on the circuit.

- **Bristol Motor Speedway and Martinsville Speedway.** Short track racing should also remain at 500 laps because of the always unpredictable nature of the action at both facilities. Each facility is roughly .5 mile, so 500 laps at both places equals only about 250 miles. I can more than live with that—although admittedly, sometimes massive wreckfests can turn races into four-hour-plus affairs.

- **Texas Motor Speedway.** This is arguably the premier 1.5-mile track, and even though races there can occasionally get boring, the size of the crowds (150,000-plus) and the usually exciting action are enough to warrant keeping both its yearly events at 500 miles. But even if one of the two annual races were trimmed to 400 miles, Texas is such a unique facility that fans who have watched closer and quicker racing would probably leave there thinking that they just saw a 500-mile event.

- **Darlington Raceway.** Even though it's held several 400-mile races in its storied fifty-year history, 500 miles just seems a more natural fit for the track that is known as the Lady in Black (for its black asphalt) or the Track Too Tough to Tame (due to having the hardest walls in the sport). There's a historical factor here, much like at Daytona and Talladega, to justify keeping things the way they are.

- **Charlotte Motor Speedway.** The former Lowe's Motor Speedway has perhaps the best combination of races on the circuit, with the 600-mile Coca-Cola 600 on Memorial Day weekend, the Sprint All-Star Race the weekend before that, and the annual 500-mile event in October. This is probably as close to a perfect combination as you will find. Some critics would like to see the fall race cut to 400 miles, but I think that the race would suffer a loss of luster in the end.

## Should a Race Have Fewer Cars in It?

Why do we, or must we, maintain a forty-three-car limit per race? NASCAR keeps telling us that it was the number it settled upon more than a decade ago—1998, to be exact—and whenever the sanctioning body doesn't want to change a rule, it simply says that it doesn't see a need to alter the status quo at the present time.

Part of the logic is money—what else? After all, this *is* NASCAR, where money and keeping sponsors and so-called corporate partners happy seems to be just as important as who wins each race.

Prior to 1998, NASCAR had semistringent yet bendable guidelines of sorts, typically limiting starting fields to thirty-six cars on short tracks and forty to forty-four on larger tracks (although at times that number was slightly higher). But even the sanctioning body itself couldn't seem to make up its mind about what exactly constituted a "standard" field prior to 1998.

Here's what official NASCAR historian Buz McKim of the NASCAR Hall of Fame and Museum had to say when I asked him:

> The starting field numbers were all over the map until 1998. As examples, Daytona had fields of forty to forty-three from 1970 through 1997. Darlington, for years, had a field of forty for the Southern 500 [on Labor Day weekend] and thirty-six for the spring race.
>
> [Charlotte Motor Speedway] had a field of forty-four for many years and then forty or forty-two. Martinsville had as many [in the '60s] and then only thirty or thirty-one through the '70s and '80s. Crazy. I've never found any rhyme or reason for it. But clearly, something had to be done to standardize the field.

NASCAR could surely change the number of cars in a starting field. Even the policy it instituted in 1998 is subject to change if a compelling enough reason is put forth.

The economic recession that began in 2007 would have been the perfect time for NASCAR to reduce its fields from what is often an unwieldy number (trying to squeeze forty-three cars into a .5-mile oval like Bristol Motor Speedway or Martinsville Speedway).

In fact, NASCAR would have gotten some great publicity out of such a move, aligning itself with this country's green movement. Think of all the positive news stories that would have been written or broadcast about NASCAR caring so much for the environment that it did its part to help out by reducing the number of cars, thus reducing the amount of fuel needed, as well as cutting the amount of poisonous gases created by having so many cars on a racetrack at one time. Unfortunately, NASCAR missed the boat on that one—it's yet another mistake the sanctioning body has made when it comes to doing something so obvious that would help the image of the sport in general and NASCAR in particular.

Will we ever see fields of more than forty-three cars? No way. If anything, we might see even smaller fields, perhaps more so by default than by a NASCAR requirement. If the cost of running a typical competitive Sprint Cup team continues to climb past the $20 million mark, where it is today, teams will soon be priced out of the market, unable to be able to afford to compete. The only teams that would be likely to remain are those that belong to the top four organizations whose team owners have deep enough pockets to maintain multicar operations: Rick Hendrick of Hendrick Motorsports, Joe Gibbs of Joe Gibbs Racing, Jack Roush and John Henry of Roush Fenway Racing, and Richard Childress of Richard Childress Racing.

Even if smaller and independent teams—like Yates Racing, Earnhardt Ganassi Racing, Robby Gordon Racing, Michael Waltrip Racing—were able to sustain and continue racing, the economic struggles that NASCAR has gone through in the last few years should be enough to convince it that reducing the number of cars on a race-day field could ultimately provide substantial savings to NASCAR. In addition, it would save money for the racetrack owners, the promoters, and the teams, because they would not have to spend as much money for extra equipment, testing, wind-tunnel testing, and the like.

You are probably thinking to yourself, "Okay, Bonkowski, if you have all the answers, what would be the best field size in a Sprint Cup race?"

I actually like the forty-three-car field and wouldn't mind if it stayed at that number. But if it became necessary to cut the size of a starting field to make a race more competitive, I'd be the first one to support it (particularly if it was coupled with the race being shorter in length). If the field were trimmed to thirty-five and maybe even thirty cars, it would provide much more exciting racing in the long run.

The biggest bane in professional sports over the last forty years or so has been expansion. The more teams that are permitted to join a league, the more the talent level is watered down. No one can tell me that the National Football League (NFL) of today is stronger at thirty-two teams than it was at sixteen or twenty. It's the same with every other major sport, from major league baseball to basketball and hockey.

NASCAR, if it contracted somewhat, would be significantly stronger in the long run, because only the best teams would be able to make races. The overall race field would be closer and more competitive, and there would be greater parity. Instead of having one team or driver run away with things (like Jimmie Johnson and Hendrick Motorsports did in the last few years), smaller race fields would bring out the best in the best. We wouldn't have to worry about things like "mulligans" (do-overs) or talk about having "throwaway" races when a driver has an unusually bad or unfortunate outing—particularly in the Chase for the Sprint Cup.

Rather—and in much the same fashion as Johnson won his four consecutive titles from 2006 to 2009—success would be predicated upon having and striving for the best performance possible in every race.

With only thirty to thirty-five race cars, we could have smaller race fields *and* make each race all the more important. We could then reduce the schedule, thus keeping the best races and the best markets, and get rid of tracks that are marginal, at best. Or we could take away races from lesser performing tracks and award them to new or existing facilities that currently don't have Cup races to call their own, or to tracks that currently host only one annual race (like Las Vegas) and have proven they deserve a second yearly event.

The old expression "the bigger, the better" doesn't necessarily mean the bigger, the best. If we reduce the number of cars on race-day fields, I think you'd see a domino effect of fewer cars but much better racing—and that's the goal, isn't it?

# Who Would Be the Best Replacement If Brian France Stepped Down as Head of NASCAR?

Brian France assumed his role as chairman and CEO of NASCAR in September 2003. Although his tenure has been somewhat controversial, particularly due to the many changes he's made in the sport that have not sat well with loyal, longtime, and diehard fans, France has nepotism on his side.

In other words, the third-generation leader of NASCAR is not likely to go anywhere anytime soon. Although he will turn fifty in 2012, if France is anything like his father and his grandfather, you can expect him to remain at the helm of both the sport of stock car racing and its sanctioning body for at least another fifteen years after reaching his half-century milestone.

Since France ascended to NASCAR's throne, his reign has been marked with rumors that he wasn't long for the sport, that he had other designs. Most notable was a rumor in early 2005, just a little more than a year after he had assumed his new position—that he was actively seeking to become part of a group that would bring an NFL team (via either expansion or relocation) back to Los Angeles, where France had lived for close to a decade. France denied the reports, saying he was 100 percent committed to staying at the helm of NASCAR, and for a long time.

So we'll give Brian the benefit of the doubt. For argument's sake, let's say he stays in place until he's sixty-five or maybe even sixty-seven, the age his father, Bill Jr., was when he gave his only son the keys to the chairman's office. Who would replace Brian France atop the NASCAR hierarchy when the time comes?

- **Jim France.** NASCAR vice chairman and executive vice president, Bill Jr.'s kid brother, and Brian's uncle, Jim is sixty-six years old, an age closer to retiring than taking on the challenge and headache of running NASCAR. Of course, Jim could serve in an interim role, if necessary, but that would most likely be short-lived. Jim's happy with what he's doing with NASCAR and the Grand American Road Racing Association and International Speedway Corporation. Jim has a son, Jamie (known as J. C.), who is a road course racer, but it's unlikely that he would be in the line of succession to replace Brian, particularly since he was arrested for drunk driving and crack cocaine possession in October 2009 (charges were subsequently dismissed in April 2010).
- **Lesa France-Kennedy.** Brian's older sister is president of International Speedway Corporation and is considered the most

powerful woman in U.S. motorsports today. But she also turns fifty in 2011. Because she's a France by birth, Lesa would be the most likely candidate to replace Brian if he left his role prematurely. She has intelligence, moxie, and leadership, and like her brother, she was raised around the sport. Lesa and her late husband, Dr. Bruce Kennedy, who was tragically killed in a plane crash in 2007, have one son, Ben, an aspiring racer (he turns twenty in 2011). It may be a long shot, but given that Bill France Jr. was his grandfather, you can't rule out Ben as a potential leader of NASCAR in twenty to twenty-five years. It may be the only way to keep NASCAR's leadership in the family. That has to be a pretty heady possibility riding on Ben's shoulders, knowing he could potentially be a future leader of NASCAR and stock car racing.

- **Brian's kids.** Brian France has two children of his own, twins born to him and his former wife, Megan, in 2006, but they're only four years old, so we won't see them running the family business anytime soon. France has since remarried; his current wife is Amy, and they have no children together.

- **Mike Helton.** One candidate who is not from the France bloodline is the current NASCAR president. However, Helton turns sixty in a couple of years. Unless France were to step down in the next few years, it appears that Helton has gone as high as he can go on the NASCAR corporate ladder. Of course, if France were to leave in the next year or two or become unable to run the sanctioning body, Helton could be considered as a possible interim chairman, but it's doubtful that he would become the first non-France to run the sport on a permanent basis or for any extended period.

It's possible that NASCAR would go outside the France family— by choice or by necessity, if the fourth France generation either isn't interested or isn't up to the task. After all, Helton became the first non-France to reach the role of the sanctioning body's president.

The current or previous NASCAR officials who could eventually succeed Helton, and possibly even Brian France, are as follows:

- **Robin Pemberton,** vice president of competition (although at fifty-three, he may be long retired before Brian France steps down)

- Former NASCAR vice president **George Pyne**, now president of International Management Group
- **Gary Crotty**, senior counsel
- **Paul Brooks**, senior vice president
- **Robbie Weiss**, vice president of broadcasting
- **Steve O'Donnell**, vice president of racing operations
- **Steve Phelps**, chief marketing officer
- **Grant Lynch**, senior vice president for business operations, International Speedway Corporation (and former president of Helton's old stomping grounds, Talladega Superspeedway)
- **Robin Braig**, Daytona International Speedwar president. He is the biggest dark horse in the mix, in my opinion. He has the intelligence, experience, savvy, and charisma as a leader. If any current track president is to jump up to NASCAR's or International Speedway's front office, I think it will be Braig. (Full disclosure: He was my classmate at Ohio University, where we both earned master's degrees in sports administration.)
- Other track presidents who have an outside shot: **Roger Curtis** (Michigan), **Rick Humphrey** (Talladega), **Doug Fritz** (Richmond), and **Gillian Zucker** (Fontana).

Admittedly, the pickings are a bit slim after that, leading one to wonder whether France's eventual successor might come from outside the sport as well as outside the France family. That's right, an independent commissioner. It's not likely, but there is a precedent of sorts in another sport. Former National Basketball Association (NBA) executive Gary Bettman, who was among those believed to be in line to eventually replace David Stern as NBA commissioner, jumped ship to become the man in charge of the National Hockey League.

It would take an extremely dynamic leader, particularly someone who is a marketing whiz—in other words, a man or a woman who can bring tons of cash into NASCAR's coffers. Gee, President Obama will be looking for a new job in about seven years. He'd cover the parts of being a dynamic leader and a marketing whiz, and he would be a huge plus for NASCAR's diversity efforts.

But given how closely NASCAR has been held to the France family vest for more than sixty years, something tells me that control of the sport and sanctioning body won't be leaving home anytime soon—not even for a former president of the United States.

## What Would I Change If I Ran NASCAR?

I've often been asked what would I do if I had the opportunity to run NASCAR or to fix what longtime fans see as some of its messes and shortcomings. Boy, talk about a loaded question and the potential to open a huge can of worms. But I always tell it like it is, regardless of whether those who control the sport like it.

So if I were NASCAR king for a day, here are some of the things I'd do:

- **Appoint an independent commissioner to oversee the sport and be in charge of everything from top to bottom.** The time is long overdue to get rid of the nepotistic practices of the France family and turn the future and fate of the sport over to an outsider who will shake things up and get rid of NASCAR's longtime business-as-usual modus operandi. For the sport to return to the kind of substantial growth it enjoyed from the early and mid-1990s until 2005 or so, it needs someone along the lines of retired NFL commissioner Paul Tagliabue or NBA chief David Stern. NASCAR is beholden to far too many special interests and "partners," companies that pay multimillions of dollars to have exclusive corporate rights unlike those seen in any other major professional sport. I've heard NASCAR referred to far too many times as "the stock car mafia," and there are more than a few shreds of truth in that. As Tony Stewart once told me, "It's NASCAR's way or the highway." We need to blow up that highway and rebuild it from scratch. If not, the struggles the sport has endured in recent years—a more than 20 percent drop in TV ratings since 2005 and plummeting at-track attendance (who can forget so many empty seats at places like Atlanta, Fontana, and Michigan?)—will continue. The fan and sponsor base will erode in the future, to the point where NASCAR runs the risk of soon no longer being considered one of this country's major sports—if we haven't reached that point already.

- **Thoroughly rewrite the rule book.** The time is *long* overdue to eliminate all the gray areas in the sport's rule book. No more phantom cautions. No more "lucky dog." No more using "actions detrimental to stock car racing" as a catchall punishment. If corporate America can operate successfully with its own rule books and business plans, NASCAR can do the same.

- **Change penalty infractions to make them more consistent.** How many times have we seen NASCAR go easy on some drivers (such as Dale Earnhardt Jr.) for infractions while hammering other drivers seemingly unmercifully? If the sanctioning body would establish a standard set of rules and penalties, it wouldn't get constant complaints from fans about favoritism, nor would we see mysterious calls during the course of a race that suddenly seem to "help" a driver who needs an advantage (Junior again).

- **Break up the strangleholdlike monopoly held by NASCAR and International Speedway Corporation (ISC).** Even though both entities insist they're independent of each other, the two couldn't be connected any closer at the hip if they were Siamese twins. ISC controls twelve Sprint Cup racetracks, which just so happen to host nineteen of the series' thirty-six races each year. If that isn't a monopoly or collusion, I don't know what is. There have been attempts in the past by federal legislators to examine the relationship and business operations of the two, yet NASCAR and ISC always seem to skate away. Another example: If a new track not owned by ISC wanted a new NASCAR event, or a rival like Speedway Motorsports Inc. wanted to bring a race to Kentucky Speedway or add an additional race date to a track it owns (like a second yearly date at Las Vegas Motor Speedway), it's virtually impossible because of ISC's control of tracks and NASCAR's control over awarding race dates.

It's a vicious catch-22 cycle that benefits just NASCAR and ISC. The time has come to break them up. If they refuse to do it, federal legislators most likely will. With so many apparent conflicts of interest, the publicly traded ISC and NASCAR are a Securities and Exchange Commission investigation just waiting to happen.

- **Make some serious changes in the schedule.** I can hypothesize all day over moving races from one track to another and thus opening up the possibility of adding a new race or two to a new track or a second race to an existing track. But if NASCAR is to move forward, here's how I think it should proceed:

  1. **Take one race away from Martinsville Speedway.** Even though it's a racing treasure, it can hold only about sixty-five thousand fans in a facility that needs a major overhaul. It's a quaint place, not to mention the oldest track on the circuit, but it's a place that time has passed by. Unless NASCAR and ISC are willing to put up at least $20 million for renovation and expansion, it's better to let it keep one race (*not* in the Chase) and at least keep its legacy and its legend alive.

  2. **Close Pocono Raceway, lock, stock, and barrel.** Whenever there is talk about taking a race away from a track, Pocono is usually among the first to be mentioned. That's not by happenstance: the racing there is terrible, and the facility is in dire need of an overhaul—which it most likely will never see. Put this place out of its misery once and for all.

  3. **Give Las Vegas Motor Speedway a second race.** With its annual spring sellout, this track and Sin City have more than proven they can host a second annual race date (and definitely put it *in* the Chase). I'd also give a second date to Chicago. And even though there's a huge Hard Rock Hotel and Casino planned for the Kansas Speedway, I would hesitate to give it a second date, simply because I don't think the facility can sell out a second date, regardless of when it would be inserted into the schedule (most likely late spring).

  4. **Explore the possibility of adding a race in Canada, in either Toronto or Vancouver.** Of course, a new racetrack would

have to be built. The perfect type of track I envision would be like Phoenix: a tight, 1-mile oval.

- **Make NASCAR much more open to the fans.** It's an autocracy now; I'd like to see it be more of a democracy. Give more consideration and credence to fan complaints, be more open and honest with the fans, and make goodwill offerings to fans with legitimate complaints. Most important, reduce ticket prices by 10 to 20 percent as a sign of goodwill.

- **Don't let NASCAR be beholden to sponsors.** Open sponsorship up to competition, such as by allowing rival phone companies like AT&T (which already had to pull out of the sport due to NASCAR rules) and Verizon to take part even though Sprint is the series title sponsor. The more competition there is, the better it is for the sport. It allows more teams to have more sponsorship dollars, which is sorely needed in the current economic climate. Let's face it, the sport is really hurting for sponsorship money right now. Tell me how it makes good business sense to turn away companies that are ready and willing to invest millions of dollars in your sport. That's ludicrous, and it's another reason that Brian France is so often criticized.

- **Establish a universal code of conduct for everyone in the sport.** No exceptions and no wiggle room, whether one is a driver, a crew chief, a crew member, a team owner, or one of the sport's officials. The two key areas in the code of conduct would involve substance abuse and intentional cheating:

  1. If anyone involved in the sport other than a driver is found to have used illegal drugs before a race, they would be banned from the sport for one year for the first infraction, with the stipulation that they get significant treatment and counseling. A second infraction, even if it's ten years later, would mean a permanent banning from the sport. If it's a driver, however, it's a one-and-done proposition in my mind: if you're caught using, you're gone forever. No second chances, no appeals, no reinstatement; you're simply history, never to be seen or heard from again. The way I see it—and I'd have a hard time finding anyone to disagree with me—*no* driver

should be allowed to risk the lives of his fellow drivers while competing under the influence of narcotics. A perfect example of this is banned Truck Series driver Aaron Fike, who admittedly competed in at least one event while under the influence of heroin. If drugs are that important to you, then NASCAR isn't—and you have no business being in the sport ever again.

2. As for cheating, I'm not stupid. Cheating exists in every sport, but no other sport has unofficially endorsed cheating as much as NASCAR has. How many times have we heard "If you ain't cheatin', you ain't tryin'"? Or how about working in the infamous "gray area," a locale that Chad Knaus, crew chief for four-time Cup champ Jimmie Johnson, has made a career of being in? For the most part, cheating seems to come mostly from the crew chiefs, although the drivers and the other team members aren't completely without blame, either. All that said, there is no place for cheating in NASCAR, regardless of its history and legacy. I would make a very simple rule: Everyone is given two chances. The first time you're caught, and it's a provable offense that traces directly back to you, you're suspended for half a season. The second time, you're gone for a full year—and that includes working back at the shop in the interim. If you're gone, you're gone from *all* association with the team during your suspension. That's how Knaus got around things; even though he was suspended from being at the racetrack, he could still work six or seven days a week back at the shop at Hendrick Motorsports. Some penalty! If you're caught cheating a third time, you're banned from participating in the sport in any form or fashion forever. Gone, banished, period, end of story. And that's the way it should be—the *only* way it should be. Of course, if that were the norm and the rule of NASCAR already, we wouldn't ever talk about Knaus again, would we?

# Should a Team Owner Be Limited to No More Than Four Teams?

When NASCAR chairman and CEO Brian France decreed in 2005 that team owners would be limited to a maximum of four teams under their corporate umbrella, it obviously didn't sit very well with multicar team owners like Jack Roush, Rick Hendrick, Richard Childress, Joe Gibbs, and Roger Penske.

France claimed that limiting the number of teams an owner may have would increase competition and open up opportunities for more team owners to come into the sport.

Many observers thought that France's edict was a knee-jerk reaction to the fact that Roush had placed all five of his teams in the 2005 Chase for the Nextel Cup (now Chase for the Sprint Cup). This essentially stacked the deck in Roush's favor, particularly since at that time only ten drivers qualified for the Chase (the number was increased to twelve in 2007).

As it turned out, even with half the field wearing Roush colors, no Roush driver—not Matt Kenseth, Mark Martin, Kurt Busch, Greg Biffle, or newcomer Carl Edwards—won the Chase that year. Tony Stewart, driving for Joe Gibbs Racing, emerged as the champion.

At the time of France's edict, Roush was the only team owner who had five or more teams under his umbrella. The debate on whether France was picking on Roush for the success he had in 2005 remains an open topic now, five years later. Due to existing sponsor commitments, France gave Roush until the end of 2009 to rid himself of one of his teams, ultimately leading to the disbanding of the No. 26 Roush Fenway Racing Ford team led by driver Jamie McMurray at the end of that campaign.

As much as France wanted us to believe that his mandate would create more equitable competition and open the door for more owners on the Cup level, that simply has not been the case. The four-team

Hendrick Motorsports organization dominated from 2006 through 2009. The three-car Joe Gibbs Racing operation came on in a big way in 2008, primarily because of Kyle Busch, but it struggled at times in 2009 (when Busch failed to make the Chase for the Sprint Cup). And even though the economy was bad, Richard Childress was still able to lure General Mills and several of its brands from Petty Enterprises to start a brand-new fourth team in 2009 (with Casey Mears as driver), even though all four of his teams struggled miserably. That fourth team, due to lack of sponsorship, lasted just one year and did not return in 2010; driver Mears was ultimately released from the organization.

So, as of 2010, Roush Fenway Racing is down to four teams, like all its peers. And judging from what happened in 2005 and since, having five teams was not a guarantee of superiority or of winning anything. And that, in and of itself, shot down France's original belief that competition would be enhanced and that more owners would be banging on NASCAR's door to let them in.

Red Bull Racing and Michael Waltrip Racing did come into existence after France's edict, but the plans were already in the works for the birth of those teams long before NASCAR announced the four-team limit.

When France issued his mandate, ESPN.com ran a story that included a very poignant observation from Smith College sports economist Andrew Zimbalist, who all but debunked France's rationale and logic.

"I don't think they have any evidence that suggests that this rule is going to make for more balanced competition," Zimbalist said. "And I don't think that limiting the number of cars a team owner can have increases the chances that there will be more new, young drivers coming up through independent owners. It's getting more expensive all the time to field a car; and if there is anyone who is going to be giving young drivers a chance, it's more likely to be guys like Roush and Hendrick."

What we've seen since France's mandate in 2005 has been virtually no change in the competition or in attracting a whole flock of new owners—unless you count Tony Stewart, who was given a 50 percent equity share to rebuild Haas/CNC Racing into Stewart-Haas Racing, which meant that he didn't have to spend a dime of his own money to become a co-owner.

What's more, multicar team owners are having the last laugh on France by partnering with other teams and organizations, creating a de facto farm system of talent. For example: even though Hendrick Motorsports is still a four-team organization, it now has the two-car Stewart-Haas operation as a farm team. In other words, Hendrick is a de facto six-team organization now.

Roush Fenway has Richard Petty Motorsports (which merged with Yates Racing prior to 2010) as its "satellite" operation. Richard Childress Racing has Earnhardt-Ganassi Racing. Joe Gibbs Racing previously had Hall of Fame Racing as a farm team until the latter partnered with Yates in 2009, essentially becoming part of Roush Fenway's farm team.

If France had really wanted to open more doors, he would have reduced the maximum number of teams per owner to three, or maybe even two. But if that were to happen, we might not have enough cars to fill the typical forty-three-car field. It's just another example of the way that France and NASCAR act before thinking. And they wonder where all the fans have gone over the last few years. Duh!

## Why Aren't There More Black Drivers and Participants in NASCAR?

If NASCAR were a country and had to design a flag to best symbolize its sovereignty, the colors would be pretty straightforward: white and green. These hues have been most prevalent throughout the sport's sixty-plus year history: white for Caucasian and green for money. No other colors need apply—and that includes skin color.

Even in today's NASCAR, the sport is still overwhelmingly white and 100 percent green. White skin runs the sport, and green is the fuel that makes it run. Without question, NASCAR stock car racing is one of the most, if not *the* most, segregated professional sports in the United States today. Even the National Hockey League has more diversity.

It's nothing short of an embarrassment that in this era of diversity and multiculturalism, NASCAR still seems like a throwback to the pre-1960s segregated South. "Our sport is not as diverse as it needs to be," Cup driver Jeff Burton readily acknowledges. "To truly be a cross-section of America the way we need it to be, it needs to be more diverse than it is."

In its history, NASCAR's Cup and Grand National series have seen just seven black drivers in sixty-plus years: Elias Bowie, Charlie Scott, and Randy Bethea (1 career Cup start each), George Wiltshire and Bill Lester (2 career Cup starts each), Willy T. Ribbs (3 starts), and the most prolific black driver in Cup history, Wendell Scott (495 career starts from 1960 to 1973 and the only black driver in history to ever win a Cup race).

NASCAR has embarked on several initiatives to reach out to various minority groups, particularly African Americans and Hispanics, and to women. Most notable is the Drive for Diversity, an independent program endorsed (but not funded or operated) by NASCAR. Designed to increase opportunities primarily for the three aforementioned groups, it focuses on developing and placing aspiring drivers, crew chiefs (another area in NASCAR that is all-white), and crew members with existing teams on the Sprint Cup, Nationwide, and Camping World Truck series.

Unfortunately, Drive for Diversity's efforts have produced minimal results throughout the sport. Likewise, although a number of Cup teams like Joe Gibbs Racing and Richard Childress Racing have embraced diversity with their own in-house programs, they remain like all their Cup counterparts: they still have yet to place a woman or a member of a racial or ethnic minority in the sport's premier series. Unfortunately, it appears that this will remain the case for several years.

Chase Austin, a potential candidate for the first full-time black Sprint Cup driver since the late Wendell Scott, remains mired in just occasional runs in the Camping World Truck Series. And that's it. No other drivers of color are even close to making the big jump to NASCAR's top show, I'm sad to say.

It continues a trend in which only two black drivers took part in NASCAR competitions in the last twenty-plus years. First was Ribbs, who added 23 Truck Series starts in 2001 to his brief 3-race Cup career in 1986. More recent was Lester, whose celebrated Cup debut in 2006 lasted just 2 races. He also competed in 142 Truck Series races from 2000 until August 2007 but has not been seen on a NASCAR track since.

"I'm hoping that I'm a small catalyst for change," Lester said prior to his first Cup start in his hometown of Atlanta in 2006. "NASCAR wants this sport more inclusive, and I believe them. They've done a whole lot of things to make it that way. I'm hoping that now [minorities] might tune into NASCAR races and come out here and actually be a part of this excitement."

Because of the nature of the sport, it's likely we'll never see a Tiger Woods–type storm into the sport and make a similar huge impact. One of the sport's most high-profile blacks—and an outspoken critic of the lack of others of his race in the sport—is ESPN and ABC analyst Brad Daugherty. I had a fascinating two-hour interview with Daugherty, a former NBA star, in August 2007 in his hometown of Asheville, North Carolina. We talked extensively about his lifelong love for and involvement in the sport, starting from simply being a fan to becoming a team owner and a broadcaster.

Although he smiled during most of the interview, the look on Daugherty's face changed considerably, growing extremely serious and almost angry when we talked about opportunities for minorities—more precisely, the glaring lack of opportunities for young and aspiring blacks. It's all about the green—the money—and how no one wants to spend it on young black drivers and crew members. Daugherty relayed a keen example that unfortunately keeps being replayed throughout the sport:

A chief financial officer of a company told me one day, "I appreciate what you're doing, and that's great, but this sport is not ready for that, and our company is not ready for that. The reality of it is we want a good-looking, clean-cut Caucasian kid that can run up front, get out, and speak and smile the way we want him to speak and smile, because we want him to move boxes [of product]." It occurred to me after that that it's not about black and white, it's about green. That kind of stuff makes me crazy.

Indeed it should. It sums up the main reason that diversity has failed to make much progress in NASCAR. At the snail-like rate that NASCAR is moving—it took twenty years between Ribbs's last Cup appearance and Lester's first and only two career Cup starts—we'll be lucky if we see the next black Cup driver in another twenty years.

Noted Burton, "I look forward to the day when we're not having to talk about [a person's race] and about what Bill Lester did. That's when we know that we're where we need to be." Sorry, Jeff, but given the climate in the past six decades, excuse me if I don't hold my breath on that happening any time soon—if ever.

# Why Aren't There More Female Drivers in NASCAR?

Only six women have reached the highest echelon of NASCAR racing, Sprint Cup competition, during its modern era (after 1972): Janet Guthrie, Christine Beckers, Lella Lombardi, Robin McCall, Patty Moise, and Shawna Robinson.

Guthrie, who made a name for herself in Indianapolis 500 annals, competed in thirty-three Cup events from 1976 to 1980, until lack of funding ended her stock car racing dream. Most recently, Robinson competed in eight Cup events, the last being in 2002. She ended a nineteen-year absence of women in Cup races when she competed in the Kmart 400 at Michigan International Speedway in 2001. She is now out of racing and works as an interior designer.

Moise had a semisuccessful tenure in the Busch Series and made five Cup starts before moving into semiretirement on her Virginia horse farm. Lombardi and Beckers managed one career Cup start each. This was in the 1977 Firecracker 400 at Daytona International Speedway, arguably one of the most significant races in NASCAR history. It was the only time that three women (Guthrie too) qualified for the same race. McCall had two total career starts, both in 1982.

Let's do the math: six women in fifty career Cup starts in nearly three decades. Subtract Guthrie from the equation, and you wind up with just five women in seventeen career Cup starts in that time. There's a heck of a lot wrong with this picture, and here's why:

- With women making up nearly half of the crowds at NASCAR races—not to mention the millions of diehard female fans who watch Sprint Cup races on TV—how is it possible that other than Danica Patrick, there are no female drivers currently or even on the horizon?
- Why aren't there any female crew chiefs or pit crew members?
- Why are there no female owners other than Teresa Earnhardt in the Cup Series?
- Other than NASCAR board member and International Speedway Corporation president Lesa France Kennedy—who some might argue got her position because she's the daughter of the late Bill France Jr. and the sister of current NASCAR CEO Brian France—why aren't there any women among NASCAR's top executives?

Women are definitely second-class citizens in the NASCAR hierarchy. As with African Americans, who are also trying to make inroads in the sport, the journey is not easy. It seems that most women have given up chasing the dream of being part of the sport—or, to borrow one of its well-worn phrases, one of the boys.

The reasons are simple: no money, no sponsorship support, no desire among team owners to put a woman in the driver's seat, and, perhaps most significant, no other women currently racing with whom to form a support system.

NHRA professional drag racing has been significantly more progressive about female competitors and crew chiefs than NASCAR has. Fourteen-time Funny Car champion John Force, the most dominating and successful driver the sport has ever seen, has watched with pride as his daughter Ashley has become one of the sport's most popular drivers. You sure don't see something like that in NASCAR, though. If a driver is going to be succeeded in the Cup Series, it's going to be by his son, not his daughter.

NASCAR officials certainly have no problem taking money from the female fans who pass through the turnstiles at the racetracks, who buy millions of dollars of souvenirs, and who plop down millions of cold, hard-earned cash at the concession stands. So why doesn't NASCAR treat women as equals to their male counterparts? Why was someone like Robinson so ostracized when she tried to make it on the Winston Cup circuit in 2001 and 2002?

Why has NASCAR thrown its support behind the Drive for Diversity program, which we hope will lead to more minority drivers and crew chiefs, but not formed a similar program exclusively for the development of women in both on- and off-track prominence and responsibility? It seems as though women were added to the Drive for Diversity program almost as an afterthought.

Why didn't Robinson, who proved herself to be a more than capable driver, but who was saddled with inferior equipment most of the time, return to Cup racing after her seven starts in 2002? The reason is best described as NASCAR's culture: it's a male-oriented, male-dominated, and male-controlled sport, and the men seem to be more than willing to keep it that way.

There have been several women who have driven recently in the Busch, Nationwide, and Craftsman Truck series, including Jennifer Jo Cobb, Chrissy Wallace, Tina Gordon, Erin Crocker, Mara Reyes, Kelly Sutton, and Kim Crosby, but none has been able to jump to NASCAR's top level for even one start. And there do not appear to be any women on the immediate horizon who will make that jump anytime soon.

To be quite honest, I am so tired of the almost obligatory camera shots in virtually every televised broadcast of a Cup or a Nationwide series race that show the loyal, hopeful wife or girlfriend in the pits, wishing and praying that her man will take the checkered flag. The camera loves to focus on the women's tears of joy or sadness when things go right or wrong. Is that all a woman is good for, a cheap cheesecake shot for a few seconds of air time? NASCAR needs to take a good long look at itself in the mirror and realize that women need a place in the sport, too (and I don't mean on the sidelines).

This is the twenty-first century, not the Neanderthal age. It's time for NASCAR to give women a chance to show what they can do behind the wheel, in the pits, in the garage, and at the corporate desk. To borrow a phrase from a popular commercial of the 1970s: You've come a long way, baby. However, you've still got a long way to go if you want to be in NASCAR.

## What Existing Tracks or New Markets Most Deserve a Sprint Cup Race?

There are thirty-six points-paying races at twenty-two tracks, so trying to squeeze one or two additional races onto the schedule— is about as easy as driving five cars across at a short track like Bristol or Martinsville.

However, NASCAR is one of the most in-demand sports by both fans and racetrack operators. And it's not just non-NASCAR track owners who want a race. Even NASCAR wants to get into the act more than it already is (it currently owns twelve Cup-level tracks). That's why NASCAR is so intent on widening its reach even more and why it has continued to pursue the possibility of building new tracks in new markets.

First on Brian France and Mike Helton's list is the New York City area. The Big Apple has long been the number one target on NASCAR's dream list. NASCAR's sister company, International Speedway Corporation, purchased land on Staten Island in 2006, but due to large-scale environmental cleanup issues, not to mention almost unanimous opposition from local residents, the project was killed before the first shovel of dirt was even turned.

Even so, NASCAR has not given up on the nation's largest city. The sanctioning body continues to look at a variety of sites, but a bit farther away than Staten Island would have been. NASCAR wants a facility that is .75 mile to 1 mile in length, so the two areas that have the best likelihood of landing a track are across the Hudson River in New Jersey (the Meadowlands) as well as Long Island.

A 1-mile track requires at least eighty acres, plus land for a parking lot. Because land is at such a premium in the New York–New Jersey area, don't be surprised if the Meadowlands ultimately wins out. With the NBA's New Jersey Nets moving to a new home in Brooklyn, all the elements are in place, and there is more than adequate room for a facility.

Number two on NASCAR and the International Speedway Corporation's wish list is the Pacific Northwest, but intense pressure from local residents has already killed several projects in recent years, primarily in Washington state. The third area is the Denver–Colorado Springs corridor, but any track there would probably have to wait until tracks in New York City and the Pacific Northwest become a reality.

The biggest problem NASCAR faces in building a new track or two is the economy. The economic spiral downward that began in 2007 made NASCAR rethink its timetable for building more tracks. With ticket sales across the board having seen significant drops, now is not really the time to add more racetracks.

Here are my candidates for the existing tracks that should get a Sprint Cup race in the near future:

1. **Kentucky Speedway.** With Bruton Smith's purchase of the 66,000-seat facility halfway between Cincinnati and Louisville, you can bet we'll see a great deal of capital improvement and expansion. Smith has already said he plans to increase seating to more than a hundred thousand. But where is he going to get a Cup race date for his newest toy? That remains the big question. Unless he purchases tracks in either Dover or Pocono, each of which has two Cup race dates, and moves one or more of those dates, it's unlikely that NASCAR will give Smith any of International Speedway Corporation's dates. Of course, if he buys a track with two dates, he can give Kentucky one, and the other could be a second yearly event at the Smith-owned Las Vegas Motor Speedway.

2. **Iowa Speedway.** A 30,000-seat facility near Des Moines designed and partly owned by retired Cup great–turned–TV broadcaster Rusty Wallace, this track has received outstanding reviews since it opened in 2006. The .875-mile track already has plans to expand to 40,000 seats, with the potential to grow to 60,000 or more if the demand is there (which it would be if the track receives a Cup race). But because the track is owned by neither International Speedway Corporation or Speedway Motorsports Inc., the odds of a Cup date anytime soon are about as likely as finding a snowball in Des Moines in mid-July.

3. **Gateway International Raceway.** This 65,000-seat facility just across the Mississippi River from St. Louis could be the big dark horse in the bid for an existing track to receive a Cup date. Gateway's schedule, which already includes Nationwide Series and Craftsman Truck Series events, as well as NHRA drag racing in an adjacent facility, is the pride and joy of tiny Madison, Illinois. It's also owned by Dover Motorsports Inc., which owns Dover International Speedway, Memphis Motorsports Park, and Nashville Superspeedway. Gateway has carved out a successful niche for itself, but will it see Cup racing any time soon? Good question. Wish I had an equally good answer.

4. **Nashville Superspeedway.** This 50,000-seat facility just outside Music City U.S.A. hosts Nationwide and Truck events as well as the Indy Racing League. It is a demanding 1.33-mile, D-shaped concrete track. Blueprints have already been drawn up to triple the seating capacity if the track had a Cup event. If Bruton Smith purchases Dover Motorsports Inc., you can bet that Nashville will also get a Cup date, somehow, someday.

5. **Milwaukee Mile.** The oldest operating auto racetrack in the world, the Mile held its first race in 1903 and has been holding races every year since. The 50,000-seat facility is part of the Wisconsin State Fairgrounds in West Allis, a Milwaukee suburb. It's a quaint facility that harkens back to a feel of a local short track, but it is not likely to ever play with the big boys of Sprint Cup racing. Up until 2010, it seemed content in the niche it had held of hosting Nationwide and Craftsman Truck series and Indy

Racing League events each season. Sadly, because an agreement could not be reached between NASCAR, race promoters, and fairgrounds officials, NASCAR will not be represented at the Mile in any form in 2010, but hope remains that it will return in 2011. The Mile also seems to have derailed any chance of hosting a Cup race for the foreseeable future, if NASCAR does come back to Beer Town. If the agreements are indeed reached and you have the chance to go to a race there, don't forget to try the world-famous cream puffs at the concession stands. They're to die for.

## Have Double-File Restarts Been Good for the Sport?

Maybe you can teach an old lucky dog new tricks. That's what happened, in essence, in early June 2009 when NASCAR implemented double-file restarts after all caution periods. It was a move that countless fans had sought for many years. Their major argument was that it would put more excitement into restarts and give the leaders in a race something to race for and against, rather than engaging in meaningless side-by-side racing with drivers whose cars are at least one lap down.

For years, NASCAR was stubborn about making such a significant rule change, even though it's pretty clear that the sanctioning body's own officials could see the logic of such a move and could understand why the fans kept clamoring for it.

With the global economy in turmoil and NASCAR at-track attendance and TV ratings being down substantially, NASCAR had to inject some new excitement to get current and former fans interested in the sport again. When NASCAR made the decision in mid-2009 to adopt double-file restarts, it even gave the driver in the lead at the time the option of starting on either the outside line or the inside line, at his discretion. Major kudos to NASCAR for doing that; it added even more anticipation and drama to the situation, leaving fans to excitedly wonder, "What line is he going to take when the green flag drops again?"

I've yet to find anyone who doesn't like the double-file restart, except for the perennial drivers who are always at the back of the pack. Instead of being able to start on and at the front of the inside row and race to try to get their lap back, as they had been able to in previous years, they're now forced to do it the way most other series do it: make a driver work his way back on his own volition.

In other words, there are no more free passes, which were one of the most boring and wasted parts of a race. How often did we see a lapped car on a restart try to prevent the cars on the lead lap from passing him, fighting hard as if he were on the lead lap when he wasn't?

So long, free pass. It was not a pleasure knowing you. Welcome double-file restarts. May you have a long and successful existence.

## What Should the Nationwide Series Really Be?

When NASCAR decided to form an undercard series to the then Winston Cup Series, it envisioned a true developmental league in which young, aspiring Cup drivers could learn how to race stock cars and pay their dues at the same time. In 1982 NASCAR took what was a long-running sportsman series and morphed it into the Budweiser Late Model Sportsman Series, which was essentially stock car racing's highest rung of minor league competition, similar to Triple-A minor league baseball. It would carry that name for only two years. In 1984 the name changed to the Busch Series; then it changed to the Busch Grand National Series two years later. It began to be the type of league that then NASCAR chairman Bill France Jr. envisioned. Unfortunately, that vision became significantly clouded in the last decade, as the Busch Series (which dropped the Grand National moniker in 2003) became less of a true developmental league and more of a second income or additional practice for the next day's main event for some Sprint Cup regulars who also raced in the Busch circuit, some even on a full-time basis.

For example, the series champions from 2006 through 2009 were full-time Sprint Cup drivers: Kevin Harvick (2006), Carl Edwards (2007), Clint Bowyer (2008) and Kyle Busch (2009).

As the economy began declining in 2007, the Busch Series began to struggle even more. In 2008, when Anheuser-Busch pulled its sponsorship, the name changed again—this time to the Nationwide Series, after the new sponsor, Nationwide Insurance of Columbus, Ohio, which has title rights to the series through 2014.

Young, aspiring drivers quickly became more the exception than the rule, and this trend is likely to continue for the next few years, if the Nationwide Series is even able to survive such a difficult economic period.

NASCAR finds itself in a catch-22. On the one hand, it brags that the Nationwide Series is indeed a developmental series, even though that intent is long gone. On the other hand, having Sprint Cup regulars run at least some (if not all) Nationwide races results in more fans attending the races in person to see their Cup heroes, as well as giving ESPN higher ratings for the same reason.

If NASCAR were to completely ban Cup regulars from the Nationwide Series, many people, including me, wonder how long it would survive. I'd give it two years, tops, before it would go under—and that might be an overly generous prognostication. So you can be pretty sure that such a notion won't happen anytime soon. Ergo, NASCAR continues going with the flow, so to speak. There are still a number of young drivers in the series, like Justin Allgaier, Steve Wallace, Michael Annett, Eric McClure, and Danny O'Quinn Jr. These and others show great promise to someday become stars in the Cup Series.

In 2010 we've also seen renowned Indy Car driver Danica Patrick serve a part-time apprenticeship in the Nationwide Series as a possible precursor to her driving full-time in the Sprint Cup Series in 2012. (Her plans currently call for her to remain in the Nationwide Series in 2011 and add more races to her schedule.)

As costs go up, the teams are going to have much harder times. Unfortunately, the teams that will struggle the most will typically be the smaller, less-sponsored organizations. Cup team owners who have Nationwide Series programs (like Jack Roush, Rick Hendrick, and Richard Childress) can probably manage for the long haul, but that will further reduce the opportunity for young, aspiring drivers to make a name for themselves with smaller teams.

If you were Jack Roush or Richard Childress, and you were pouring several millions of dollars into a Nationwide program, would you rather have a young up-and-comer or a Cup veteran like Carl Edwards or Jeff Burton behind the wheel? How about the winningest driver in Busch and Nationwide history, Mark Martin? There's no question about it, the veterans would win almost every time.

The Nationwide Series has also become somewhat of a test session for future Cup expansion, holding races in venues that are foreign (both literally and figuratively) to the Cup circuit, such as Mexico City (a four-year run from 2005 to 2008) and Montreal (a multiyear run that began in 2007 and continues today).

Even though there are so many Cup veterans who compete in the circuit, the Nationwide Series has also produced a number of young drivers who either have gone on to stardom in the Cup Series or are in the process of making their name in that series. Among these are former Busch Series rookies of the year, including David Ragan (2007), Carl Edwards (2005), Kyle Busch (2004), David Stremme (2003), Scott Riggs (2002), Greg Biffle (2001), Kevin Harvick (2000), Jeff Gordon (1991), Joe Nemechek (1990), and Kenny Wallace (1989).

And even though Cup drivers have maintained a stranglehold on victories and championships in recent years, other Cup regulars earned their first taste of what it takes to win a championship in the Busch or Nationwide series, including Martin Truex Jr. (2004 and 2005), Brian Vickers (2003), Biffle (2002), Harvick (2001), Dale Earnhardt Jr. (1998 and 1999), Nemechek (1992), and Bobby Labonte (1991).

Fixing the Nationwide Series is inevitable if it is to survive in the long run. Fans of young drivers want to see them maximize their time in the series. Although running wheel-to-wheel with Cup vets gives the Nationwide aspirants tremendous experience against the biggest stars in stock car racing, the youngsters are still playing second fiddle, any way you look at it.

I predict that by 2011 or 2012, NASCAR and Nationwide Insurance will radically alter the structure of the so-called minor league series. I expect Cup drivers to still be welcome to race, but they won't be eligible to earn points or compete for the championship. Some might suggest that the number of appearances by Cup drivers should be restricted, but I don't see that happening, because the series definitely needs Cup drivers to maintain some semblance of popularity with the fans. After all, many fans who travel far distances to the tracks for race weekends typically buy tickets for both the Saturday Nationwide race and the Sunday Sprint Cup event. They expect to see big names in both races.

Even if Cup drivers become ineligible to win points or championships, I believe they'll continue to compete, which will make NASCAR and the fans happy and will put the series back to what it was intended to be. The only question is if there will still be enough money to achieve that.

## Does NASCAR Need to Be Franchised?

How many of us have had friends or family members who even after contracting lung cancer kept smoking cigarettes until the day they died? Even though they knew that their filthy, nasty, and expensive habit was killing them, they still needed their regular hits of nicotine and carbon monoxide.

I know my example is extreme, but it's kind of the same way with NASCAR's future. Even when there's something that would be good for the sport and the sanctioning body and ensure continued health, viability, and growth in the next half a century, NASCAR continues being stuck to an old habit that could do irreparable harm if the global economic crisis gets significantly worse.

I'm talking about one of the most controversial propositions in the sport, which NASCAR has thus far successfully kept at bay: franchising. For more than sixty years, NASCAR has not only hosted the biggest poker game for stock car racers and fans, it has also dealt the cards, served as banker, poured the drinks and served the food, parked the cars, and hung up the coats. In other words, NASCAR runs everything associated with top-drawer stock car racing.

Many team owners and drivers, particularly those of the current era, have become wealthy individuals because of their involvement in the sport. But what about equity? What do they have to show for it all? What happens if their sponsors suddenly dry up? What do they have left? If they can't attract new sponsors or don't have enough money in reserve to continue racing, they'll soon go from pit lane to the sidelines.

Look at the great Bud Moore, one of the most prolific owners in the sport. When his sponsorship well dried up in the 1990s, he not only dropped out of the sport (Moore and NASCAR both used the more politically correct term *retired*) and left an uncanny heritage, he also ultimately had to sell most of his racing empire for a mere pittance—certainly nothing near what it was actually worth.

But with no economic savior willing to step forward, Moore did what he had to do to get out as best he could so that he'd have something to show for all his years of racing and something of a nest egg for his actual retirement. It was a sad ending to a tremendous racing legacy, which had included some of the greatest drivers over the years, including the late Dale Earnhardt, Buck Baker, Joe Weatherly (who won two championships for Moore), David Pearson, Cale Yarborough, Darrell Waltrip, Bobby Isaac, Ricky Rudd, and Bobby and Donnie Allison.

Although most of today's owners are likely to scoff at the idea of losing their seat at the NASCAR table anytime soon, in private they sing a totally different song. If sponsorship dries up, so do their organizations. We saw this recently with the venerable Robert Yates. He tried to hold on for as long as he could, but when he lost major sponsors like United Parcel Service and Mars (M&Ms), he simply couldn't afford to keep racing, so he sold the assets of his race team to his son, Doug, who formed Yates Racing. It has not been an easy time for the younger Yates, either. Two years after Robert sold the organization to his son, Doug was forced to merge with Richard Petty Motorsports to keep the Yates legacy alive past 2009.

That's why franchising could be a godsend to current and future team owners. If they were able to pay an entrance, or franchise, fee to NASCAR to ensure that they'd have an equity stake in the sport, they would be part of the decision-making process for the sport's future and have a tangible asset they could sell in order to recoup their original investment (and probably make a profit). Who wouldn't want a more generous system like this than the one that's currently in place?

NASCAR, that's who. The late Bill France Jr. was 110 percent adamantly against franchising. I brought it up to him a couple of times, and he immediately brushed off the suggestion, one time not even letting me finish my sentence. As soon as I got to the word *franchise* in my question, France dismissed the thought immediately.

Some people in the sport believe that Bill Jr.'s son, current NASCAR chairman and CEO Brian France, is more open-minded and amenable to franchising, but there's still been very little movement toward that front in the last few years.

The economy declined, and many workers within the sport lost their jobs; the sponsors departed, and the manufacturing support from Detroit's Big Three and Toyota was drastically cut. Yet the third-generation leader of NASCAR still refuses to consider franchising as a solution to the sport's problems. The reason, of course, is that France and NASCAR don't want to share their wealth or power.

Franchising probably isn't a short-term solution. But in the long run, it would give the owners something tangible to build upon, a value that can be measured not only in dollars but also in the overall worth of the racing empire. For example, if Jack Roush and John Henry were able to convert their co-owned Roush Fenway Racing enterprise into a franchise, they would probably see the overall worth double (at least) in time, and they would also become a more attractive target for potential buyers or investors who want to get involved in something that has long-term meaning and worth.

Currently that's not the case, because team owners are more like renters than home owners in the sport. If NASCAR charged a franchise fee of $100 million, few of today's team owners could afford it. For franchising to work, NASCAR would have to set a relatively low baseline of maybe $20 million, an amount that would essentially be chump change to guys like France and Mike Helton. But there's no way they're going to give up more than sixty years of equity just to give somebody else a little piece of the pie.

Franchising would bring NASCAR more in line with other professional sports leagues. It's my fear that the longer France and the sanctioning body continue to discount the idea, the sooner it could hasten NASCAR's descent into a second-tier sport that would only further diminish the value that everyone currently has, including the team owners, the drivers, and NASCAR itself.

# How Effective Is NASCAR's New Drug-Testing Policy?

When NASCAR announced in September 2007 that it was going to implement a sweeping overhaul of its substance-abuse policy, many observers were a bit nonplussed, because they didn't even know that a policy of that type even existed.

In the past, NASCAR had either caught or presented evidence of repeated drug use that led to the permanent banishment of drivers like Shane Hmiel and Aaron Fike. (The latter had competed in at least one race under the influence of heroin.)

But NASCAR's new policy was a 180-degree turn—with several rocky twists in between. One complication was that the sanctioning body refused to present a comprehensive list of all the substances that were supposed to be banned; instead, it preferred to leave the list open-ended so that other substances could be added later or as new drugs surfaced.

Even though NASCAR chairman and CEO Brian France called the new policy the toughest in all of sports, nothing could be further from the truth. But give it big points for being one of the most confusing policies in all of sports! The NFL, major league baseball, and the NBA all had clearly defined rules and restrictions on types of substances, but NASCAR seemed to make up the rules as it went along.

That's why the May 2009 suspension of Sprint Cup driver Jeremy Mayfield for alleged substance abuse put the new policy to test and found many holes in it. Mayfield claimed that a combination of Claritin D and Adderall, a prescribed medication for the treatment of attention deficit disorder, caused him to test positive in a urine sample that was required as part of NASCAR's new get-tough policy. When NASCAR revealed several weeks later that Mayfield had tested positive for methamphetamine, he vehemently denied having any contact with such a dangerous drug.

As the Mayfield saga played out in federal court, he eventually received permission to return to racing, much to NASCAR's chagrin, though the court ultimately reversed its decision. NASCAR also made itself look like a horse's ass with what was nothing short of a PR disaster in the way it handled the Mayfield affair: it kept certain things quiet, invoking privacy concerns (even though Mayfield wanted everything out in the open), repeated comments from others, and trotted forward so-called witnesses who essentially tore at the fabric of Mayfield's character and credibility. It all should have been reserved for a court trial, not tried in the court of public opinion.

NASCAR is to be commended for finally getting with the times and invoking its first true substance-abuse program, but you can't make such a radical swing from virtually nothing to extremely harsh without some overzealousness or mistakes along the way, such as in Mayfield's case. I'm 100 percent in support of NASCAR taking the big step forward to establish a testing policy, but it should also consider itself fortunate not to have anywhere near as big a drug problem as some of the other sports leagues have had throughout the years.

Still, NASCAR's drug policy has a long way to go. It needs provisions for appeals, provisions for expedient reinstatement, and a process whereby an individual who tests positive either has the ability to retest or has access to a mechanism that ensures fair treatment.

NASCAR's new substance-abuse policy is a good step in the right direction, but it has many more steps to go before it can be the optimal policy that NASCAR wants us to believe it is. The only question is who will be the next driver or official to be either wrongly accused or not given the benefit of the doubt and due process. This is America, where you're presumed innocent until you're proven guilty—except when it comes to NASCAR. Hopefully, that will change before the sanctioning body makes a fool out of itself again, as it did with Mayfield.

## What Changes Could Improve Pit Road?

Thanks to Beth Beutler of Fountain Inn, South Carolina, for this question—with a little embellishment on my part.

> In the interest of safety for pit crew members, should NASCAR impose standardized dimensions for pit road/pit stalls/space between boxes that would be consistent at all tracks? Rationale: it seems some tracks are known for tight pit roads while others have more space, yet a similar type of work is done in the pits at all tracks (with some modification I realize, but overall, gassing, tires, wedge adjustments, are done at all tracks on the same size cars).

The problem, Beth, is the layout of the tracks. You only have so much space at some places. For example, there's plenty of room on pit road at places like Daytona International Speedway, Talladega Superspeedway, Texas Motor Speedway, and Charlotte Motor Speedway. You can very comfortably fit forty-three cars on pit road and still have room left over. That's typically the case with the bigger tracks.

The problem is with the smaller tracks like Bristol, Martinsville, Richmond, and even places like Phoenix and New Hampshire. Because those tracks are so short and small, pit road space is obviously at a big premium. Without question, Bristol Motor Speedway is the tightest, just because of its high-banked layout and short, 650-foot straight-aways. Teams are not only crammed next to each other in the infield, they're cramped even more so on pit road. As a result, Bristol used to have *two* pit roads to accommodate all forty-three race cars, one on the frontstretch and another on the backstretch (which was typically reserved for the slowest qualifying cars).

In 2002, Bristol Motor Speedway officials reconfigured pit road so that it became one long path around the track. While doing so brought some semblance of order and uniformity, it also created confusion for the first couple of years because of logistics: some drivers came onto pit road at the wrong place.

Instead of entering pit road in the way that is conventional at almost every other oval track—coming in off turn four (or turn three on a tri-oval)—the drivers at Bristol who need work on their cars during a caution period must enter pit road off turn two, then drive around the circumference of pit road, often making close to a full lap around the track before reaching their pit stalls.

If that isn't confusing enough, it gets worse. If a driver makes a green flag pit stop, he can enter the pits off turn four if his pit stall is on the frontstretch. If his pit stall is on the backstretch, he can enter from turn two and make a quick exit from turn three—provided he doesn't collide with anyone who is slowing down to enter pit road on the other side of the track. If a driver's pit stall is on the frontstretch, and he pits under green, he enters pit road off turn four and exits off turn one.

Several drivers throughout the years have lost precious spots on the running grid in a race by entering at the wrong spot, including Jeff Gordon, Carl Edwards, Matt Kenseth, and Kevin Harvick. It's no wonder that ingress and egress on pit road is one of the most discussed topics at prerace drivers' meetings at those particular short tracks.

Thanks, Beth, for your question. Now please allow me to add a whole other spin on it.

We know that space is limited at short tracks like Bristol, Martinsville, and Richmond. But on tracks 1.5 miles or longer, and even at places like Daytona and Talladega, which are 2.5 miles or longer, we still see collisions on pit road. Cars that are leaving their pit stall might not see another car coming in. Sometimes a car must dodge out of the way to avoid another car exiting its pit stall, only to slam into the side of another car that is trying to get by on the outside. It's not uncommon to see three and even four cars across on some pit roads. Just like regular drivers on the freeway, everybody's in a hurry!

So let me propose a radical idea. Given that there's more than enough room to widen pit road at most medium to large tracks on the circuit, what about having pit stalls on *both* sides of pit road? The idea might sound ludicrous to many of you. I was chastised quite a bit when I first proposed it in a column several years ago. But really, is there any good reason not to have cars pit on the right side of pit road in addition to the left side of pit road?

By doing so, we would be expanding pit road to twice its size, the cars would have a much easier time getting into and out of their pit stalls, and I'm willing to bet that we'd see fewer pit road collisions, because the drivers' line of vision would be wider, so they would see the cars on both sides ahead of them.

Having crew chiefs and crew war wagons on the other side of pit road might impede the vision of the crews on the left side of pit road. There's also the necessity to build a high and strong retaining wall on the right side of pit road to protect the pit crew members from a wayward car that might come flying off the track and through the grass after a spin or a wreck. But in the whole scheme of things, these are not insurmountable obstacles.

Having stalls on both sides of pit road would allow NASCAR to let those stalls be much closer to the exit, rather than trailing all the way down to the entrance coming off turn four (or turn three on a tri-oval). This would also be likely to cut down on cars trying to squeeze onto pit road two and three across.

Finally, we already have cars on the opposite side of pit road at Watkins Glen International, and the teams are easily able to service their cars, as they do at every other Sprint Cup track. Argue that with me.

# Are Driver Contracts Hurting NASCAR's Financial Situation, and Should They Be Reduced?

The cost of operating a competitive NASCAR Sprint Cup team has all but doubled in the last ten years. Whereas we were talking about $10-million team budgets in 1999 and 2000, we're now talking about $20 million or more for the average Cup team.

Even with supposed cost-saving measures like the one-engine rule, the impound rule, and the implementation of the Car of Tomorrow, the fact remains that even when teams save money in one area, they wind up spending more in other areas.

If you're a Cup team with a budget of between $10 million and $15 million today, good luck. You're relegated to second-class status. If you manage to pull off one or two top-ten finishes in a season, that's about the best you can expect. Fans have told me for years (either in person or in e-mails) that a big part of the problem is driver salaries; if they were cut substantially, the cost of operating a team would also take a big whack. I disagree.

There are drivers who fall into some of the highest tax brackets around—guys like Jeff Gordon and Dale Earnhardt Jr., who are both rumored to make roughly $10 million per year just to race (not including the additional tens of millions they make through endorsements and sponsorships). Take away that much cash, and suddenly it theoretically costs only $10 million to operate the Nos. 24 and 88 teams. But let's be realistic. Drivers like Gordon and Earnhardt are worth their weight in gold because they sell tickets—lots of them. They also have become virtual money machines, with all the licensed merchandise, memorabilia, and souvenirs that bear their names, their likenesses, their car numbers, or all three. And don't think that their team owners don't get a healthy cut of the take; they do.

As NASCAR's most popular driver, Earnhardt, by some reports, makes an estimated $40 million in endorsements and sponsorships, which is 400 percent more than he's making from his driver salary. Meanwhile, most other top drivers make between $3 million and $7 million. But like Gordon and Earnhardt, they can make even more money through endorsements and merchandise sales—online, in their at-track souvenir trailers, and even at retail giants like Kmart and Wal-Mart.

If Rick Hendrick hit his head one day and suddenly decided that Gordon and Earnhardt were ridiculously overpaid and fired them both, he could certainly find a couple of other drivers who would fill their seats for a much cheaper price. But he wouldn't get the residual payout from souvenirs, sponsorships, and advertisements. He would also still have to spend tens of millions of dollars for parts, equipment, testing, travel expenses, and payroll for more than five hundred employees.

So stop blaming the drivers for all the high costs associated with racing. Given the risks they take each time they climb behind the wheel, I
would consider many grossly underpaid for what they do, particularly
when you compare their salaries to athletes in other sports. The real
culprit of out-of-control costs is the number of races. For each race, the
biggest teams spend at least $50,000 and often top $100,000 for things
such as jet fuel for team planes, airline tickets (for team employees who
fly commercially), diesel fuel for transporters, hotel rooms, rental cars,
food, and the ever present payroll.

Just sending a big team to Daytona for the 500 and Speedweeks
can cost close to $250,000. Because a team wants to stay as close as
possible to the track, the hotel bill can run $399 to $599 per night
per room, and that does not include taxes. Multiply that by fifty or
more employees, and you can see how costly it is, even if some of those
employees (like crew members) double up in a room.

If NASCAR really wanted to save a lot of money, it would do away
with the marginal races, like those at Pocono, Martinsville, and Watkins
Glen. Just these three tracks alone represent five races out of thirty-six.
The savings would be significant.

Let me leave you with another key thought on this subject. Because
larger teams and racing organizations like Hendrick, Gibbs, Childress,
and Roush can sustain themselves longer than smaller operations can,
they attract the best talent with better pay and, most important, the
best drivers who attract the bigger sponsors.

Yet even with such deep pockets, those teams cannot continue
to spend money like a drunken sailor, ad infinitum. If the economy,
as well as NASCAR, continues to struggle, I predict that you will
start seeing a shift away from high-priced drivers to good, talented
drivers who can be had for a far more reasonable paycheck. Now
that might contradict what I said earlier, but team owners are very
much a follow-the-leader kind of bunch and will do some crazy
things, even if conventional wisdom tells them they're making a
huge mistake.

If, for example, Hendrick decides to dump Earnhardt, even with
all the residual income his name and popularity bring in, for a young
and hungry driver, he'll most likely think he's making a smart business
decision by dropping millions of dollars in high-priced overhead. But

in the long run, the monetary savings may be short-lived, and letting a high-priced driver go may eventually cost a team much more money, particularly in sponsorship, because companies want to align themselves with Earnhardt, Gordon, Tony Stewart, Jimmie Johnson, and others among the crème de la crème.

It's a catch-22. Then, if a young driver takes off and starts winning races and potentially championships, he's going to take his talent to the highest bidder, and we will have the same vicious cycle.

Then there's the Car of Tomorrow, which was supposed to bring an interchangeable, inexpensive car to NASCAR Sprint Cup racing that would save millions of dollars. At least, that's how NASCAR chairman Brian France explained it when it was first introduced. Unfortunately, that hasn't been the case. Although the Car of Tomorrow may have saved money, on the one hand, the other hand has remained out, requiring even more money for other areas, particularly fluid expenses for things like transportation and lodging on the road.

It's a vicious cycle that shows no sign of changing anytime soon. But it's quite clear we can't blame the drivers. Heck, if any race car fan were offered $5 to $10 million a year to drive a race car, we'd jump at the chance. The drivers aren't the problem; they're simply using the problem and the current system to their advantage.

And that, dear readers, shows why drivers have to be not only good racers but also very, very shrewd businessmen. What are they going to do, tell the team owner they work for, "Hey, instead of paying me five million dollars a year, I'll settle for one million to make things easier on you economically"? Like that's ever going to happen.

## What Are Five Rules That NASCAR Should Have?

Okay, let's do some hypothesizing. Let's say that this is a perfect world and that NASCAR listens to everything we tell it. We want something done; snap, two minutes later, it is. I could only wish for that kind of scenario.

But let's play this out for what it's worth. If we could implement or change five rules in NASCAR stock car racing to make the racing and the overall sport better, what would they be? Here are my picks, from fifth to first:

5. **Points, points, and more points.** Give 10 points for earning the pole and 25 extra points for winning a race. In the past, I've advocated a system that would give 5 points for the pole and as many as 50 points for the win, but I've changed my thinking somewhat. Qualifying has become a blow-off type of exercise for many teams. They know they're typically not good qualifiers, so why bother, particularly if they have an automatic seed in the race, courtesy of NASCAR's top-thirty-five rule (which I address later in this list)? This way, qualifying has a very important prize associated with it, and it forces teams and drivers whose forte is not qualifying to dig deep and try to find a way to become good qualifiers. In a sense, I'm actually trying to help poor qualifiers by implementing this rule. But perhaps more than anything, I am thinking about guys like Kasey Kahne, Ryan Newman, and Jeff Gordon, who are among the top qualifiers in the sport. Why shouldn't they be given a slight bonus for having worked at their craft and perfected it to the point where they have a good chance of sitting atop the pole in every race they compete in?

4. **Win two races in the first twenty-six (the Race to the Chase), earn an automatic berth in the Chase for the Sprint Cup.** But if the driver drops at least 200 points behind the series leader at the halfway point of the Chase, he's automatically eliminated. Some people might say that this is a bit harsh, but there's been no driver thus far in the Chase who has come back from such a deficit in the final half of the ten-race play-off. Let's forget about the also-rans and focus on only the guys who have a legitimate shot at winning in the final five races.

3. **Limit Sprint Cup drivers to fifteen starts per season in Nationwide Series races.** I admit this is risky, because lots of fans want to see their favorite drivers, and sometimes they can afford a ticket to a Nationwide event but not to the pricier

Cup event the next day. The Nationwide Series is for developing new and young drivers, so let's get back to what it was originally designed for. If we truly see more development, I'd even be willing to eventually cut the number of Nationwide races that Cup drivers can compete in to ten—and eventually, I hope, to zero if the undercard series can prove that it can stand on its own without any help from its Cup brethren.

2. **Eliminate the rule that guarantees a starting spot to teams that are in the top thirty-five in owner points.** If a driver is going to compete in a race, make him earn his way in and qualify for it. As the old saying among race fans goes, "Run what ya brung" and see if it's good enough against everyone else. We don't see automatic berths in other motorsports series, so why must NASCAR cling to this archaic system of rewarding sponsors and advertisers? Companies and sponsors already know what they're getting into when they start signing checks to support a team. Just as in regular business, there are risks to take and rewards to reap. Don't turn it around the way NASCAR has, into giving rewards and taking no risks.

1. **Eliminate cheating altogether.** No more working in the "gray area" or "outside the box." For too long, NASCAR has had a "boys will be boys" mentality. Some of its top administrators today or in recent years were some of the biggest and best cheaters in the business. I'm sorry, but cheating has no business in *any* sport. And don't give me the "It's cheating only if you get caught" bull. There's right and wrong, black and white, positive and negative. Some former fans might very well still be following the sport if there wasn't such cheating or if NASCAR wasn't so begrudging in its enforcement of some rules. I have numerous e-mails from fans in the last few years pointing to guys like Chad Knaus and Todd Berrier, who have been among the most penalized crew chiefs in the game (translation: they've been caught the most), and this has directly led to fans losing interest in the sport, firmly believing that only cheaters win races and, ultimately, championships. I can't say I disagree.

The penalties should be that if you're caught once, it's an automatic six-month suspension, not just for the offender but also for the driver and the team owner, even if they both had no direct knowledge of the cheating. So if Knaus were to get caught again, that means that Johnson and Rick Hendrick would also be forced to sit out for the same amount of time. A second infraction is a year off for the driver, the owner, and the offender. A third time means permanent banishment from the sport for the offender (I wouldn't banish the driver or the owner in this instance, because I think they'd have gotten the message by this point). Oh yes, one other thing that in the past has made NASCAR look like a horse's ass: when a crew chief is suspended, he should *not* be allowed to have any involvement with the team during the course of that suspension. That means no working on cars at the team's shop Monday through Friday and then off for the weekend to serve the "suspension." If anything, it's more of a vacation when crew chiefs get the weekends off for being bad. Not a bad punishment, is it? Instead, if you're caught cheating, you don't work, you don't get paid, and you have no involvement with the team, period. Monitor it with independent private detectives if you have to. In these trying economic times, sponsors pay good money to put their names on the sides of race cars. Many companies pay big money just to be linked with that particular driver (and secondarily with the crew chief, in most cases). If the driver and the crew chief are suspended for underhanded activities, do you think a big sponsor will want to stick around, giving the impression that it's condoning cheating, at the risk of losing customers in its regular world? Not a chance. If NASCAR worked to clean up all the underhandedness in the sport, I guarantee you'd see a big influx of new and former fans. Who needs the Car of Tomorrow or the Chase or bigger purses? All you really need is a fair and level playing field for everyone.

# The Final Lap

# Which Is the Better Race: the Daytona 500 or the Indianapolis 500?

This has been one of the biggest arguments among racing fans for more than half a century. There are certainly a lot of similarities between the two greatest races on American soil. Here are three:

- **Both are 500 miles long.** The Indianapolis 500—originally known as the International 500-Mile Sweepstakes Race—set the standard a century ago, in 1911, when it was decided that the ultimate test of man and machine would last five hundred miles, with the earlier races at Indianapolis taking the better part of a day to complete. The Daytona 500 debuted in 1959 to coincide with the opening of NASCAR's first true superspeedway, the 2.5-mile, high-banked Daytona International Speedway (which, not coincidentally, was the same length as its rival 975 miles to the north, Indianapolis Motor Speedway).
- **Both had long preludes to the main event.** For years, Indianapolis had two weeks of practice and two weekends of qualifying. The first weekend set the majority of the field, and the second included "bump day," when there were last-second efforts to make the field as the 6 P.M. closing time approached on the Sunday before the big race. This changed in 2010, when qualifying was reduced to just one weekend to reduce costs for teams. But prior to 2010, for the most part, the month of May meant one thing to race fans: Indianapolis. NASCAR, meanwhile, starts its season in Daytona in early February with what has become known as Speedweeks, roughly two weeks of events that include the Budweiser Shootout exhibition race, pole qualifying (for only the first two spots on the race-day starting grid) and the subsequent qualifying races known

as the Gatorade Twin 150s (also known as the Twin 150 Duels) for the 41 other remaining starting spots.

- **Both are the hottest ticket in motorsports in the country.** Each is a mecca for its style of racing: Indianapolis for open-wheel Indy cars and Daytona for the top level of stock cars. Prime seating at both venues can go for as high as the market can bear: I've heard of tickets going for a thousand dollars or more for the seats that are right near the start-finish line. In a sense, both races are the Super Bowl for their respective racing genres. For years NASCAR has referred to the season-opening Daytona 500 as its Super Bowl, complete with pomp and circumstance, festivities and events both on and off the track, akin to what the NFL does for its yearly championship-deciding event. Indianapolis is the same way, even though its answer to the Super Bowl actually comes early in the annual Indy Racing League season. That's one thing many fans still wonder about: How can either Daytona or Indianapolis be considered the Super Bowl of its race genre if the event isn't held at the end of the season?

Indianapolis ruled the overall racing world from its debut in 1911 until 1996, when the celebrated split between the then Championship Auto Racing Teams (CART) and the upstart Indy Racing League (IRL) occurred. Because Indianapolis had long been touted as the place where the best of the best in the world come to race, the split between the two sanctioning bodies kept many of the so-called best in CART away from Indianapolis for many years, and hard feelings arose from the split. Reunification of the two series finally occurred in 2008 under the IRL umbrella (CART had gone through a couple of name changes in the interim).

This is a NASCAR book, so why am I writing so much about the Indianapolis 500 and the IRL? Simple. It was the 1996 separation in the open-wheel Indy car world that allowed Daytona to grow significantly in popularity, media exposure, and commercial success. During the split, Indianapolis still filled (or came close to filling) the roughly 250,000 seats that ring the Indianapolis Motor Speedway layout.

(Some estimates have attendance as high as 400,000 on race day, due to temporary infield seats, the crew members and other employees associated with individual teams, and a large media contingent that annually reaches 2,500 or more.)

But when drivers like Michael Andretti and others from the CART world were essentially locked out of the Indianapolis 500 for several years, NASCAR pounced. That's partly why the sport grew so much beginning around 1993, when Jeff Gordon came onto the scene full-time, until 2006, when TV ratings and at-track attendance began to decline appreciably.

Speaking of TV ratings: From 2002 to 2004, before the open-wheel world reclaimed its title as the most watched racing event in the country, NASCAR actually drew more viewers for the Daytona 500 than the telecasts for the Indianapolis 500.

Before I answer which race I consider to be better, let me point out a couple of sidelights. Never to be undone, NASCAR has had two other events that were strongly influenced by the Indianapolis 500.

First, there was Darlington Raceway and the Southern 500, a Labor Day weekend tradition that lasted fifty years before NASCAR moved that race date to the Auto Club Speedway in Fontana, California. Darlington Raceway founder and longtime sportsman racer Harold Brasington had ventured to Indianapolis in 1933, in the middle of the Great Depression, to see what all the fuss was about over the Indianapolis 500. Brasington was blown away by everything he saw, particularly the huge crowds. He returned to Darlington determined to build a track that, even though half the size of Indianapolis, would host a similar five-hundred-mile event on another major holiday weekend. With Daytona International Speedway having racing rights to the July 4 weekend, Brasington chose Labor Day, and the rest is history.

Although the track lost its annual Labor Day event in 2003, the legendary name of the Southern 500 returned in 2009 to mark what has become a new tradition at Darlington: the Mother's Day weekend Cup event. It is expected to remain there for years to come. For the record, six years after the Labor Day weekend race was moved to Fontana, it was again shifted to Atlanta, in 2009. Why couldn't they have just brought it back to where many people think it still rightfully belongs, Darlington Raceway?

Second, there was what NASCAR called the ultimate test of man and machine, which would make Indianapolis look paltry by comparison: the World 600 (which would eventually be renamed the Coke 600 and then the Coca-Cola 600). The event was unequivocally the longest and arguably the hardest race on a racetrack (not including events like the Baja 1000 or marathon road racing rallies).

Okay, decision time: Which is a better race and overall experience, Indianapolis or Daytona?

I love the Daytona 500. I get goose bumps just thinking about the track, its history, and some of the greatest races the world of stock car racing has ever seen. But there's just a magical vibe of sorts at Indianapolis that cannot be denied. From the minute you drive in from 16th Street or Georgetown Road and enter the track through its tunnels, this massive behemoth springs forward before your very eyes. This is where legends have been built—like four titles each for Rick Mears, Al Unser, and A. J. Foyt—and where several drivers were killed while trying to win racing's biggest prize.

The racing action at Indianapolis is faster and more thrilling, giving fans more of an edge-of-the-seat, fingernail-biting experience that just isn't quite found in the Daytona 500. NASCAR fans who may be angry with me have to experience the vastness of Indianapolis Motor Speedway in person, as well as all the events that go on for more than two weeks before the green flag drops to start the actual race. Then they should fully understand and appreciate why I give the edge *this* time to the Indianapolis car world.

At the same time, Daytona has nothing to be ashamed of. It still is the best of the best in the stock car racing world. No other NASCAR track or event can even hold a candle to the Daytona 500, so both it and the Indianapolis 500 remain in classes of their own.

## Are Race Car Drivers Really Athletes?

On the surface, most observers are likely to believe that the only physical exertion a NASCAR driver undergoes during the course of a race is mashing the gas pedal to the floor, hitting the brake, and turning the steering wheel. If you look at many old pictures from NASCAR's formative years, particularly in the 1950s, when beach racing was popular, you can readily see a number of drivers hauling ass around a racetrack with cigarettes or cigars prominently sticking out of their mouths. Yep, that's a healthy workout for you.

It's also no secret that many drivers of years gone by would party hardy the night before a race, then come back the next day and race with a hangover or a splitting headache from too much imbibing at what were once legendary get-togethers heavy on drinking, eating, and romancing. More often than not, these drivers weren't exactly, shall we say, svelte. In fact, it was not unusual for some of the biggest big men to be nicknamed "Tiny."

Guys like Richard Petty, Darrell Waltrip, Junior Johnson, David Pearson, Bobby and Donnie Allison, Dale Earnhardt, and others of their era rarely, if ever, visited a gym for a workout. Rather, the extent of exercise for many would be lifting twelve-ounce cans of their favorite beer.

If you asked me whether a race car driver of the 1950s, the 1960s, the 1970s and even the 1980s was a true athlete, compared to other sports, I would have said no. But over the last twenty years or so, the drivers have come to realize just how much being in top physical condition correlates with success on the racetrack. That's why so many of today's drivers, both young and old, have become fitness fiends.

Check out Carl Edwards. He is perhaps the most dedicated fitness buff of the twentysomething drivers in NASCAR today, and he has the abs to prove it. Edwards maintains a grueling daily routine that includes running, weight lifting, and bicycling. It's not unusual on off weekends for Edwards to bike a couple hundred miles and hardly break a sweat. The Columbia, Missouri, native attributes much of his racing success to his physical condition. Perhaps that's why he makes it look so easy when he emerges from a race car after winning a grueling four-hundred- or five-hundred-mile event, does his infamous celebratory backflip, and doesn't have a drop of sweat anywhere or a misplaced strand of hair on his head. That's true conditioning for you.

And then there's aging Mark Martin. At the half-century mark, Martin has religiously followed the same extensive exercise program for more than ten years, and he is in such excellent shape that he puts drivers who are ten or twenty years younger to shame with his conditioning, strength, endurance, and overall feeling of well-being. "There's no way I could do the things today I do in a race car if I didn't work hard at keeping myself in shape," Martin said. "Racing keeps me young, but it's staying fit and in shape that also helps keep me young, as well."

Martin's former teammate at Roush Racing, Jeff Burton, admires his longtime friend's dedication to fitness and has borrowed heavily to devise his own stay-in-shape routine. One of the benefits is the ability to remain competitive as a driver past forty years old.

"I think if you're going to be treated and compensated and want to act like a professional athlete, then you need to behave like one," Burton said. "This is a serious business. Anything you can bring to the table to make you and your team better, you need to bring it. Anything you can do to eliminate the rate at which you can't be successful, you need to eliminate them.

"Fitness is very important. When a fifty-year-old man like Mark Martin is in better shape than you are, and you're thirty, then you need to get to work. I think it's a vital part of being successful. I know that through a pretty hard training program I feel a lot better. . . . It's a long year and it grinds on you, and then on top of that you add all the physical stuff of driving the car and the mental stuff of driving the car, and it makes for a long year. I think fitness is hugely important."

Even portly Tony Stewart has been bitten by the exercise bug, although he keeps falling off the wagon. In 2006, Stewart embarked on an extensive workout program that produced outstanding results, including the loss of more than thirty-five pounds. He hired a personal trainer, purchased more than $20,000 in exercise equipment, and proved to be dedicated to losing weight and improving his overall strength and stamina. Unfortunately, Stewart's noted penchant for food (both good and bad) got the better of him, and he started packing on some of the pounds he had lost. One of his chief sponsors in 2009 and 2010 is Burger King, which is one of Stewart's favorite culinary establishments.

But even with his iffy diet, there's a bright spot: even though Stewart has regained some of the weight he lost, he still likes to work out fairly regularly. He may not be in optimal shape, but it could be worse, right?

Jeff Gordon is a latecomer to the benefits of exercise, but he's quickly becoming an avowed and enthusiastic convert. When Gordon failed in 2008 to win even one race for the first time since his rookie season in 1993, and was constantly struggling with trying to control his race car, it was pretty apparent that something was wrong, even though Gordon continually denied it.

It wasn't until early in 2009 that the four-time Cup champion finally admitted that there was indeed something wrong the previous season: he had experienced some of the worst back spasms of his life. At the behest of his wife, Ingrid Vandebosch, Gordon consulted with a physical therapist and trainer during the off-season. He was put on an extensive regimen to strengthen his back and to gain mobility and flexibility. The results were almost immediate and positive. Here's Gordon's take on his reformed ways:

> I have had some back issues, and even on our good days, I'd walk away from the track really in a lot of pain. This year [2009], working with a trainer . . . I have been doing more things than I ever have, and just physically I feel so much better as well. Better prepared, I am stronger. My muscles are stretched and looser and just doing a lot more from my aspect, from a driver's standpoint.
>
> It is really my wife that I owe the credit to. I have been telling her I wanted to put some time on my calendar to work out and go to the gym. She said, "You're wasting your time. You're not going to do it; you're not going to be committed. The only way you are going to do it is to get with a trainer." We have known this individual that she has done some training with in the past and others that we know. So, she said, you have to get with him. If you don't get with him, then you are just wasting your time.
>
> I finally bit the bullet and I did it, and this guy is kicking my butt. I mean, I don't know why I keep going back, but I feel the best I have felt in a long time. I am following that up with some back specialists and also an individual at [several racetracks on the circuit] that is stretching me. The combination of those things has made me a whole new person. When I come to the racetrack, I'm ready to go. I feel good, I feel stronger. . . . I feel like I am in the best shape that I have been in in a long, long time.

Yes, race car drivers *are* athletes. You may scoff at such a bold statement and ask me to give you just one reason that this can be true. Well, I'll give you ten reasons, and I'll back each one up with examples gleaned from other sports:

1. **Cardiovascular condition.** Drivers need strong lung-function ability in order to breathe deeply, control their blood pressure and breathing capacity during the most stressful times in a race, and to deal with issues like carbon monoxide (to be discussed later), burning rubber from a tire blowout, and the stench of flames when an engine catches fire. Perhaps this is the best example of why so few Cup drivers smoke cigarettes—which I find quite ironic, given that the sport was sponsored for thirty-two years by a tobacco giant that not only produced billions of cigarettes each year but would also drop off tens of thousands of free packs and cartons to fans, drivers, and crew chiefs after every race. The main reason more don't smoke (or don't smoke any longer, thanks to programs like Nicorette's Quit Crew), is that they don't want to do any more damage to their lungs than what they're already doing by inhaling fumes and heat from the race cars.
   **Best example:** A NASCAR driver best compares in this category to a track and field sprinter, who has remarkable bursts of energy fueled by outstanding lung capacity and unimpeded inhalation and exhalation. Let's face it, you have to have a great cardiovascular system going for you if you want to survive in race car driving; when was the last time you saw a driver get into his car wearing a mask and toting a portable oxygen bottle around with him?

2. **Hand-to-eye coordination.** Although most athletes have to make split-second decisions in their sports, NASCAR drivers have one of the most difficult tasks of all: to process what's going on and to react in literally a millisecond. That is particularly pertinent for avoiding a wreck in front of them (if they can) at 190 miles per hour, for quickly switching lanes to try to get a run on the car in front of them, and when even one-thousandth of a second is the difference between finishing first and finishing fifteenth. The drivers' eyes have to keep moving as much as their hands

move on the steering wheel. They have to check what's ahead of them, what's alongside them (which is made much more difficult with the head-and-neck restraint devices that severely hamper peripheral and lateral vision), and what's in the rearview mirror (traffic gaining on them rather quickly). For the most part, drivers either have excellent vision or wear strong contact lenses that give them twenty-twenty vision.

**Best example:** A baseball player, particularly a batter at the plate, has to keep his eye on the ball from the second it leaves the pitcher's hand to the time it hits the catcher's glove (unless the batter takes a swing at it first).

3. **Muscle tone.** When was the last time you saw a fat race car driver in NASCAR, Tony Stewart not withstanding? Butterballs simply have no place in the sport, and if they try to compete, they're typically weeded out fairly quickly. Team owners and sponsors want drivers who are in decent shape and have little body fat. That's why 99 percent of the drivers you currently see on the circuit are lean and light, with remarkable body definition and low body fat. Most drivers (like Carl Edwards, Jimmie Johnson, and Jeff Gordon) are also very conscious of what they eat. More often than not, it's chicken and fish, lots of salad, very little (if any) red meat, and limited amounts of soda pop and alcoholic beverages, particularly beer, which put on pounds quickly. I have already discussed Stewart's weight struggle. As Tony once said, "I'm telling you, there's a skinny guy somewhere deep inside of this body. I just have to find him."

   **Best example:** Basketball and hockey players tie for this one. With the exception of the burly enforcer types in the National Hockey League, most basketball and hockey players are full of vim and vigor, not extra poundage.

4. **Tolerance for the elements.** Football games are played with perhaps the greatest range in the elements, from subzero to 100-plus degrees, from blistering sun to blizzardlike snow and torrential rain. Typically, the only thing that will stop a football game is the imminent threat of lightning. NASCAR drivers are

also forced to compete under some very harsh elements, from chilly fifty-degree night races to days when the temperature is 100 degrees outside and 140 or 150 degrees inside the race car. That's why air conditioning, particularly within a driver's helmet, is so important. Unfortunately, like anything mechanical, air conditioning can fail at times. When that happens, the drivers become almost like baked potatoes within the cockpit, having to endure the heat that emits from the metal plating inside the car and that comes through the firewall from the engine. Another side effect of broken air conditioning is heat exhaustion, which can cause the drivers severe cramps, shortness of breath, elevated body temperature, and passing out (which, fortunately, rarely happens in a race car). The drivers also have to battle carbon monoxide fumes at times. Former Sprint Cup and Nationwide series driver Rick Mast was so overcome by such fumes that he was forced to retire early because of severe carbon monoxide poisoning. Another key thing the drivers must do for themselves to successfully battle the elements is to stay hydrated. That's why you see most drivers being handed drinks like water or Gatorade on pit stops, or they keep bottles inside their car and take occasional sips. "One of the most important things you can do as a driver is to always remember to stay hydrated," veteran Cup driver Mark Martin says. Of course, that leads to the question of where all that fluid goes after drivers ingest it, since there are no time-outs or potty breaks. But that's a question we'll leave unanswered until the next debates book.

Best example: A triathlete must have physical endurance, but he or she also has to endure climate and elevation changes while running or biking and temperature differences while swimming.

5. **Strength.** If you think it's easy to drive a thirty-six-hundred-pound stock car at 190 miles per hour or faster with limited power steering capability, guess again. Stock cars, especially those in the premier Sprint Cup Series, are nothing short of monsters or beasts to handle. What's more, a driver is forced to almost constantly "saw" at the wheel, which means that he can't let up on the pressure he's exerting to turn the wheel, lest he go directly into a wall or another competitor. Arm strength comes into

substantial play even more as changing track and car conditions eventually make a race car loose (steering too easily) or tight (steering too hard). Although constant steering back and forth may not necessarily pump up arm muscles as weight lifting does, the upper-body strength of race car drivers is utilized more often than not because of the amount of exertion that is required in the actual turning of the car. That same task becomes even more difficult when the series takes to the two twisting, serpentine road courses on the Cup schedule each year at Watkins Glen International (New York) and Infineon Raceway (California). Here's one thing I've noticed about a driver's strength: I can't recall ever receiving a limp-wristed handshake from a driver. Rather, virtually every driver I have ever shaken hands with has offered up a strong, firm, often painful grasp, which is indicative of significant upper-body strength.

**Best example:** Although football players need huge biceps and triceps, baseball players and golfers too must have good upper-body strength and strong arms to swing a baseball bat or a golf club with power and finesse.

6. **Ability to withstand hard impacts.** No athlete in any other sport is forced to take and attempt to absorb more brutal and punishing impacts. This goes not only for NASCAR drivers but also for drivers in other high-speed motorsports, including the Indy Racing League, the Formula One open-wheel series, NHRA drag racing, and the International Hot Boat Association, which holds drag races on water. The NHRA, in particular, takes things more to the max than its open-wheel or stock car counterparts. The drivers sometimes crash well in excess of 300 miles per hour; they are typically encased in either a fiberglass Funny Car body, with a minimal roll cage to protect them, or an elongated Top Fuel dragster that has an open roll cage and a flexible but durable chassis that is designed to break away and absorb most of the impact of a crash. Still, unfortunately, NHRA has not caught up with NASCAR; it has lost several drivers in crashes in recent years, including Funny Car driver (and former two-time Top Fuel champion) Scott Kalitta in 2008

and Funny Car driver Eric Medlen in 2007. NASCAR has been at the forefront of safety developments and enhancements that have all but stopped what from 1999 to 2001 was a sickening regularity of drivers being killed, and this has motivated other racing series to adopt some of NASCAR's stringent measures.

**Best example:** Football players and boxers both sustain a lot of blows. Yet even though the impact from helmet butting or a blindside punch to the head is fierce, how many could sustain a wreck into another car or head-on into a retaining wall at 190 miles per hour and walk away with only bumps and bruises, if that?

7. **Tolerance for pain.** This comes from the often spectacular wrecks in which drivers are involved. Yet few drivers have been seriously injured in recent years. It's a testament not only to the physical condition they're in but also to the strides in safety that NASCAR has made in the last decade. The latter was due primarily to the fatal tragic wreck of Dale Earnhardt.

   **Best example:** Football players and boxers routinely shake off cuts, blood, and serious pain to continue on the football field and inside the boxing ring, respectively. It's the same with race car drivers, who try to display their machismo and bravado even when they're in a world of hurt after climbing out of a mangled race car. But as three-time Cup champion Darrell Waltrip likes to say, "It only hurts for a little while."

8. **Physical condition.** Even if they're not fanatics about working out with weights, running, or biking, most of today's drivers in the Sprint Cup, Nationwide, and Camping World Truck series still maintain somewhat regular physical activity. Only instead of doing bench presses or squats, they typically do more urbane things like playing golf, fishing, hunting, and working on cars. The key is that they're not being couch potatoes, with a beer in one hand and a TV remote in the other. They are doing something they enjoy and getting some type of stimulating physical workout that gets the lungs huffing and the blood pumping.

   **Best example:** Bowlers and golfers aren't exactly sterling examples of athletes in tip-top shape (bowlers often compete with a can of beer by their seat, and golfer John Daly is a well-known party animal who smokes and drinks), yet they're still considered athletes. Why not NASCAR drivers?

9.  **Mental and physical endurance.** The NASCAR schedule is arguably one of the most grueling of any major professional sport. What other sport begins in January with preparations, kicks off competition in mid-February, lasts through most of November, and has only five to six weeks off before it starts the whole cycle again? Some critics say that NASCAR drivers are nothing more than part-time workers, because they have a three-day workweek on a race weekend (or a two-day one at places like Richmond), but the grind of covering five hundred miles in about three hours can be very physically and mentally demanding. How often do we agonize over making long-distance driving trips of hundreds of miles in five hours? Not only do race car drivers have to maintain triple-digit speeds, they also have to stay mentally alert every second to avoid causing a wreck or being caught up in someone else's wreck.
    **Best example:** Marathon runners, triathletes, and competitive bicycle racers have to keep it all together for long periods. They know that while being in good physical shape is important, being in good mental shape is even more often the key to winning—just as in NASCAR racing.

10.  **Competitive spirit.** This is the essence of every athlete. NASCAR drivers are some of the fiercest competitors in all sports. I liken them to a combination of football and hockey players, who not only try to outwit the opposing defense but also bang into their opponents (body parts rather than car fenders). Drivers who bang into their opponents' fenders, of course, run the risk of being penalized by NASCAR, but usually that penalty is a slap on the wrist. What would happen if drivers on our local freeways tried some of the things that NASCAR drivers get away with? Besides causing lots of accidents and injuries, it would make our insurance rates go through the roof.
     **Best example:** All athletes, regardless of the sport, are competitive. Competition is the lifeblood of any sport, and NASCAR is no different.

If all these things don't make a NASCAR driver an athlete, nothing does. So the next time you hear someone say that race car drivers aren't athletes—that it's nothing for them to lose ten or more pounds during a race due to 130-degree heat in the driver's cockpit, or that they don't need precision hand-to-eye coordination to keep themselves off the wall and out of wrecks with others—tell the nonbelievers to try to replicate workouts like Martin's, Edwards's, and Gordon's. They'll be out of breath before they even reach the first turn.

## Should NASCAR Run Races on Other Days of the Week?

Forty years ago, the NFL broke with the tradition of having games only on Sundays, first adding Monday night games and then occasional Thursday night games. One must wonder why NASCAR remains locked into its routine of Sunday first, Saturday night second, and that's it. Why not a midweek race, televised nationally during prime time? Can you just imagine the strong ratings and the viewership? Or how about embarking on the equivalent of Monday Night Football: Monday Night NASCAR, anyone?

Granted, Sunday afternoon and Saturday night races are already "races of the week," but holding a race on any other day of the week would lend the sport a bit more meaning and publicity, rather than just being another in a string of thirty-six races.

Think I'm wrong? Football exploded in popularity when Monday Night Football joined the schedule in 1970. It became *the* game of the week, the one that both the fans and the players anxiously looked forward to. Even though that game carried the same weight as a Sunday contest, there was a special feeling if teams were chosen to play on Monday night, because in most cases it was the best of the best who played each other on that night. Of course there have been some snoozers over the years on Monday night, but it still wound up being a must-see game for many football fans.

When ESPN was negotiating its part of the current eight-year Sprint Cup television package, along with Fox and TNT, it brought up the idea of having races during the week in prime-time hours, particularly during the Chase for the Sprint Cup, on either ESPN or (even better) ABC. The idea was unique yet a no-brainer. According to one ESPN source, the company pushed the issue until it became quite clear that NASCAR was not going to budge. Then the idea ultimately died, which is too bad, because I firmly believe it would have greatly helped the sport.

Even though TV ratings have been dropping from 2006 to the present, including during each of the last four Chases, NASCAR still doesn't see the benefit of taking a Sunday afternoon or a Saturday evening race and turning it into a Wednesday or Thursday night prime-time event.

The perfect situation, in my opinion, would be to schedule a Sunday afternoon Chase race in Martinsville, then follow it up on Thursday night with a prime-time televised race at Charlotte. It makes sense: Martinsville is only two hours from Charlotte, and most drivers and teams are based in the Charlotte metro area. Or how about racing at Michigan on Sunday afternoon and at Bristol on Thursday night? Now that would be a heck of a show, just like Bristol's August Saturday night race.

While I don't necessarily agree with his weekends-or-nothing viewpoint, I asked Ramsey Poston, managing director of corporate communications for NASCAR, his thoughts about the possibility of midweek races.

"Most of our fans work during the week and look forward toward to relaxing and watching NASCAR on the weekends," he said. "Many of our fans travel several [hundred] miles by car or RV to get to the track, so having a race in the middle of the week would affect their ability to attend. Additionally, our events are typically two- to three-day shows that include qualifying and practice time (not to mention [the] travel time it requires officials to get from track to track), making the weekend the best suitable time for the fans."

I've recommended elsewhere in this book that race weekends should be shortened to two-day shows—and indeed NASCAR has done that with several races on the 2010 schedule. A midweek show with practice and qualifying on Wednesday and the race on Thursday would be a winner, particularly if the race was held during the summer to accommodate the fans who want to combine it with their vacations.

It might be a bit more tricky to schedule Sunday/Thursday races during the Chase, but it certainly would add to the allure and put a unique spin on the Chase.

# Was Teresa Earnhardt Right to Let Dale Earnhardt Jr. Leave Dale Earnhardt Inc.?

I have never had a more volatile issue arise in my entire quarter-century of covering motorsports than the rift between Dale Earnhardt Jr. and his stepmother, Teresa Earnhardt, the widow of Dale's late father who helped the late Intimidator build Dale Earnhardt Inc. (DEI).

From December 2006 to May 2007, the battle for the control of DEI was front-page news. Teresa Earnhardt was quoted in the *Wall Street Journal* as questioning Junior's dedication to the sport and his team, and Junior announced that he was leaving DEI. (He'd name Hendrick Motorsports as his new home just 33 days later.)

Hundreds of stories flew across the newswires in that period describing how Junior demanded controlling interest of DEI from his stepmother, who steadfastly refused. Some stories said he wanted full ownership, whereas others indicated that he would be happy with a 51 percent controlling interest.

The Junior Nation became more incensed than it ever has been. Thousands of e-mails streamed to my Yahoo e-mail box, with roughly 80 percent in Junior's favor (why is that not surprising?). You can't believe some of the vile notes I received; no derogatory adjectives were spared to describe Teresa.

The writers in the minority believed that Junior had no right to demand something that his father and the latter's third wife had built together. There were reports of plans having been drawn up so that one day the deed of DEI would pass on to the elder Earnhardt's four children: his oldest son, Kerry, from his first marriage; his daughter, Kelley, and his younger son, Dale Jr., from his second marriage; and Taylor, the daughter he had with Teresa.

Junior's outright demand that DEI be given to him and Kelley (who serves as his business manager), with seemingly little concern for his half-brother and half-sister, left a bad taste in a lot of people's mouths, both Junior fans and non-fans.

The drama gripped the NASCAR world like a cheap soap opera. In mid-January 2007, during a stop on NASCAR's annual preseason media tour of shops and teams, I happened upon Richard Childress Racing driver Kevin Harvick. I asked him what his thoughts were about how Teresa Earnhardt rarely came to the racetrack to watch her stepson compete. Harvick's comments set off a firestorm that was picked up around the world.

"I think it's hard when you have what I call a deadbeat owner that doesn't come to the racetrack," Harvick said. "You always see Rick Hendrick, Richard Childress, Chip Ganassi, and all these other owners, and they all come to the racetrack. It's not just a money bit, where someone says, 'Well, I can make money off Dale Jr. or off Dale Earnhardt.' You can't run these race teams away from the racetrack. You have to be at the racetrack, you have to play the politics of the sport, you have to be part of your team, and you have to understand what's going on. [To] me, from the outside looking in, it just doesn't look like that's happening."

Coincidentally, later that same evening, Teresa Earnhardt held a dinner for reporters prior to a screening at a nearby theater of the movie *Dale*, a tribute to her late husband. Dale Jr. was also in attendance, but he kept his distance from his stepmother, who gave brief welcoming remarks and then quickly departed without answering questions. When it was Junior's turn to talk, I raised my hand to ask a question. After giving him a quick recap of what Harvick had said, I asked Junior for his reaction.

"Man, you're killing me," Earnhardt replied, saying about Harvick's comments, "That's ridiculous. I don't really think there's a comment for Kevin's remarks."

I then asked Junior whether he would like his stepmother at races to support him, as the owners of other Cup teams do for their drivers. Despite the battle that was raging between him and his stepmother for control of the company, Junior was quite diplomatic in his response.

"With everything that's happened, not just to the company but to the family over the last five years, she's had a full plate," Junior said. "The things she's been responsible for willingly and openly are very important for a long time, the battle over the autopsy photos [of her late husband], all these things. That's just the tip of the iceberg of the stuff that she's been responsible for and had to take care of and had to deal with. That's probably been the sole reason she hasn't been as visible at the racetrack and whatnot. But she's taken [care of] things that are much important when it comes to the family."

Two weeks later, prior to the start of Speedweeks in Daytona, Junior stoked the fire even more by revealing that he had asked Teresa to turn over control of the DEI—anywhere from 100 percent of DEI to a 51 percent controlling interest to him. Teresa declined.

Four months later, Junior announced that after a great deal of soul-searching—actually, it was probably more because he couldn't get his stepmother to budge—that he would be leaving DEI when his contract expired at the end of the 2007 season and was declaring himself a free agent.

He would take a publicized "tour" of several race team shops, including Richard Childress Racing, Joe Gibbs Racing, and others, but ultimately, on June 13, 2007, announced that his future would be at Hendrick Motorsports.

The feud between Teresa and Junior did not appear to end with his departure from DEI. When the following year's preseason media tour visited DEI in January 2008, virtually everything related to Dale Jr. had been removed from view. There were no old cars, no uniforms, no souvenirs, no banners (including those for his two Busch Series championships)—absolutely nothing. It was as if his time and tenure at DEI had never existed.

Junior was ecstatic about moving to Hendrick Motorsports. He truly believed that joining the best organization in the sport would ultimately bring him many more race wins. More important, he thought it would bring him something that DEI never did (or would, if he had stayed): one or more Sprint Cup championships.

Let's review how far Junior and DEI have come since their famous divorce.

2008: Junior made the Chase for the Sprint Cup in his first season with Hendrick Motorsports, but he ended up last in the twelve-driver field. He also won his first race since 2006, breaking a span of 76 winless starts, but he was unable to build upon the momentum of that victory.

2009: Junior suffered through his worst season ever in Cup competition. Not only did he record his lowest finish (25th, whereas his previous low, in 2005, was 19th), he did not reach victory lane, and he had another career low of just two top-five finishes for the entire season. In addition, longtime crew chief Tony Eury Jr. was reassigned within Hendrick Motorsports and replaced at the end of May by Lance McGrew. Unfortunately, the McGrew-Earnhardt pairing just could not do much of anything, which led Junior to remark in mid-October that he was "at the end of my rope" with all the frustration and disappointment he had undergone in the last two years.

It remains to be seen whether 2010 will be any better for Junior, but as this book was going to press, lots of rumors had begun flying that he might even ask to leave Hendrick before his five-year contract expired in 2012. Some reports had Earnhardt starting his own Cup team with Hendrick support; others had him moving to Richard Childress Racing and potentially driving the black No. 3 Chevrolet his father made famous. Only time will tell if any of these reports are true.

As for DEI, it struggled miserably once Junior left. Even though then DEI president of global operations, Max Siegal, said the organization would be fine without Junior, that's not exactly how things turned out. In fact, Siegal and his right-hand man, John Story, left the organization during 2008, both moving to run the Drive for Diversity initiative.

In terms of competition, Martin Truex Jr. made the Chase in 2007; Junior didn't, but finished 16th in his DEI swan-song season. The third member of the DEI stable, Paul Menard, finished a lowly 34th. DEI acquired the assets of Ginn Racing in mid-2007, the most notable asset being Mark Martin, who raced part-time for DEI for the remainder of 2007 and during the 2008 season before joining Earnhardt at Hendrick Motorsports for the 2009 season.

Once Junior left, DEI admittedly struggled in 2008. Truex, who inherited the No. 1 position as the top star on the team—to match the No. 1 of his car, by pure coincidence—failed to return to the Chase, ultimately finishing 15th. Menard improved slightly, finishing 26th. Newcomer Regan Smith, who would win Rookie of the Year honors, finished 34th, only to promptly lose his place on the team altogether when the sponsorship dried up and DEI let him go at season's end.

Around the same time, partly out of desperation from a lack of sponsorship for both teams, DEI merged with Chip Ganassi Racing to form Earnhardt Ganassi Racing. This was solely for the Cup Series; DEI remained a separate entity for the Nationwide Series.

It was that merger that began DEI's turnaround in 2009. Truex slipped to his worst season performance in the Cup Series, finishing 23rd (just two spots ahead of Dale Jr.), but Juan Pablo Montoya raced strongly and consistently all season, qualifying for the Chase for the first time in his three-year tenure in NASCAR and ultimately finishing a very respectable 5th. Unfortunately, Aric Almirola, who had taken over driving duties on a part-time basis in the No. 8 (Junior's old number) car, was eventually released when sponsorship disappeared. He ultimately sued Earnhardt Ganassi Racing for breach of contract, which ended his brief tenure there. Meanwhile, Truex finished the season with Earnhardt Ganassi before moving to Michael Waltrip Racing for 2010, where he would team with David Reutimann and drive the No. 56, essentially replacing Waltrip, who had scaled back to part-time driving status.

That brings us to the present. As this book is going to press, I'm willing to bet that in the summer of 2010 Montoya will once again be among the top drivers in the sport. I picked Earnhardt to have a major rebound and to make the Chase, but if he doesn't, I would not be surprised to see him leave the Hendrick camp after 2010 or 2011 if things don't markedly improve.

Now let's get back to the original question: Was Teresa Earnhardt right to stick to her guns, not cave in to Dale Jr.'s demands, and retain control of DEI (even with the eventual merger with the Ganassi organization)?

In my opinion, yes, without question. She and her late husband built DEI; Dale Jr. didn't. And even though DEI was built to eventually be passed on to the Earnhardt children, the power grab that Junior and Kelley attempted to make in 2007 backfired miserably. Junior should have put his tail (his ego) between his legs, stayed at DEI, and worked his way back into Teresa's good graces. She was 100 percent right to question his commitment to the team and to the sport. He had too many nonracing interests, including making commercials, opening a new bar in downtown Charlotte, and being involved in several other enterprises that took away from his ability to concentrate and make racing his sole priority.

In the biggest twist of irony of all, however, less than two years after Junior attempted his power play to wrest control of DEI away from her, Teresa actually seeded significant control of the company to Ganassi, which freed her up to spend more time with her daughter, Taylor, a budding equestrian.

If Junior would have just kept quiet, I believe he'd be in a much better situation now with DEI than he is at Hendrick. What's more, had he not left, several dozen smart minds like Max Siegal, John Story, Steve Hmiel, and others would likely still be at DEI, and Junior would have prospered as a result.

Junior might never win a Cup championship in his career, and it doesn't matter whether he's racing for DEI, Hendrick, Richard Childress Racing, or himself. It's pretty clear that Teresa won a battle that could have been avoided. Had Junior not thought that it was his divine providence to assume control of DEI and show Teresa how to really build a winning organization, he very well might have eventually achieved that goal just by staying put.

Life can be funny in that way. Don't be surprised if history ultimately proves me right and Junior wrong when I say that his future would have ultimately been brighter at DEI than anywhere else. Score: Teresa Earnhardt, 1; Dale Earnhardt Jr., 0.

# Are Crashes Good for NASCAR?

Face it, NASCAR fans, many of you are sadists of sorts, a throwback to the time of the Roman empire, in which the citizens would congregate to watch Christians be fed to the lions. Even though we come to the racetrack week after week to see daring moves, great passing, and exciting and unpredictable finishes, it's a pretty safe bet that most of us also come to watch the cars go boom.

Crashes catch our attention immediately. We crane our necks to see where and how the wreck is unfolding, and we hold our breath at the almost artful and graceful dance that is being executed when race cars collide. The more cars that are involved, the more aesthetically pleasing and thrilling it becomes. We ooh and aah as though we're watching a beautiful fireworks display as the multicolored race cars bounce off one another in virtually every direction.

Crashes are the by-product of, as many drivers often say, their peers "running out of talent." Far too often, the drivers become square pegs trying to squeeze into round holes, and they simply can't do it. Instead, physics takes over, and before you know it, they're spinning, twisting, crashing, and bashing.

We love to watch the cars bash fenders—or, as many of us like to call it, "trade paint"—as they bounce off one another in an almost choreographed and rhythmic display. We've even come to greatly anticipate certain races in which we *know* that wrecks are likely going to happen early and often.

No place exemplifies this better than Talladega Superspeedway, the largest oval track on the circuit. Throughout the years, Talladega has been the site of some of the most spectacular crashes the sport has ever seen. The track even has its own lexicon for crashes. We love to hear about, anticipate, and watch the so-called big one, in which an almost pinball-like symphony plays out, with cars running into some cars but missing others, only to be crashed in from the rear or the side, or simply running out of room and being unable to avoid a wrecked car in front of them.

Ask the fans who go to Talladega; I guarantee you that the majority are not happy if they leave the track and at least one big one hasn't occurred.

Most big ones involve six or more cars. I've been at races where close to two dozen cars were involved in and torn up in one pileup. I've also been at races where one big one occurs, followed shortly by another. Like songs on the radio in the 1960s and early 1970s, the hits just keep on coming—particularly at places like Talladega and its sister track, Daytona.

Yet even though watching crashes can be thrilling and exciting, each wreck also serves as a constant reminder of the strides in the safety equipment that NASCAR has mandated, which allows most drivers to get out of their wrecked vehicles with few, if any, injuries as a result.

The death of Dale Earnhardt in February 2001 at the Daytona 500 changed crashes, particularly the big ones, forever. In most races for the remainder of that year, the fans held their breath each time a wreck occurred on the racetrack, fearing that the fate that befell Earnhardt would befall another unfortunate driver. Earnhardt's death has been a freak occurrence so far. Still, his passing shook the sport to its core, and everything from a fender bender to the multicar big ones can leave fans anxious and on the edge of their seats, filled with angst about whether their favorite driver is going to be okay.

There's another unfortunate by-product of crashes. If you are watching the Sunday evening sportscast on TV, what are you more likely to see, highlights of the winning driver crossing the finish line, or a video of a huge wreck at some point in the race? More often than not, the wreck (especially if it's spectacular) will trump the win. If there's enough airtime, however, you might see both the wreck and the winner taking the checkered flag.

NASCAR can't buy better publicity than that, even though the best story should really be the guy who won, not the guys who wrecked. Still, it is what it is, and NASCAR enjoys having its highlights aired locally, nationally, and internationally. And if big wrecks attract a few new fans to the sport, so be it.

In the closing laps at Talladega in April 2009, Carl Edwards's car went airborne and almost landed in the stands. Had it not been for the fence around the racetrack, Edwards and many fans would have been seriously injured, if not killed. Yet I guarantee you that the wild ride Carl took was on virtually every TV sportscast in the country. It was that wild, that crazy, and that awesome, even though we could very easily be talking about it in a much darker and sadder way.

Let me throw some statistics your way that both confirm and deny some long-held preconceptions. Between 2006, when the tracks began keeping records of the number of accident-related delays, and 2009, at the start of the Chase at New Hampshire, the top ten tracks in terms of the number of crashes that brought out the caution flag were the following:

1. Martinsville, 65
2. Richmond, 62
3. Daytona, 47
4. Bristol, 43
5. Charlotte, 41
6. Atlanta, 34
7, 8, 9. TIE: Talladega, Las Vegas, and Dover, 27 each
10. Loudon, 26

If one looks at the numbers of accidents from 1999 (rather than from 2006) through the start of the 2009 Chase, however, the numbers are much different. These figures include the number of cars that had *accident* written under their official finishing place; that is, their day was done after a wreck. These figures do not include the cars that wrecked, were repaired in the garage, and returned to the track to finish the race. The top ten are as follows:

1. Talladega, 151
2. Daytona, 113
3. Bristol, 107
4. Dover, 100
5. Charlotte, 98

   6.  Richmond, 86
   7.  Loudon, 69
   8.  Pocono, 67
   9.  Atlanta, 61
  10.  TIE: Darlington and Texas, 53 each

The tracks with the fewest finishes due to accidents in the same period (1999–2009) were the two road courses, which have narrower racing surfaces and tighter turns: Watkins Glen (26) and Infineon (22). Go figure.

Crashes bring about the best and the worst in people. We want to see destruction and mayhem, but at the same time we don't want to see anyone get hurt. That's just the way it is and the way it always will be. Now, what about that wreck the other day? Did you see it? Boy, how did he walk away from that?

# Which Track Is Currently in the Direst Need of Reconfiguration?

NASCAR doesn't like to get rid of racetracks, particularly those that its sister company, International Speedway Corporation (ISC), owns. There's probably only one ISC-owned facility that could lose one of its events, and that's Martinsville Speedway. Even that's a long shot, given who owns the place.

Yet if NASCAR and ISC had an opportunity to host a new race at a new facility—for instance, at one with a seating capacity of 100,000 rather than Martinsville's paltry 65,000—wouldn't it make sense for them to go bigger and better, rather than sticking with the old and staid?

The following tracks have been reconfigured in an effort to make the racing more competitive:

  ■ **Darlington Raceway.** This track has gone through several con-
    figurations in its more than fifty years. The most notable was in

1997 when the egg-shaped oval was essentially reversed, with the frontstretch becoming the backstretch and vice-versa. Then, in 2007, the track underwent a multimillion-dollar resurfacing that only added to the improvements from the configuration change ten years earlier. The result was a big success.

- **Atlanta Motor Speedway.** This track too saw its frontstretch and backstretch reversed in 1997, and two slight doglegs were added on the newly christened frontstretch. The result was that this track became the fastest non–restrictor plate track on the circuit, so its changeover was a huge success.

- **Charlotte Motor Speedway.** Formerly Lowe's Motor Speedway, this track went back to its original name in 2010 after the Lowe's Home Improvement chain decided not to renew its decade-long naming rights with the racetrack. The track has one of the most unique stories in NASCAR. Although it has undergone several changes throughout the years, the most notable and notorious was in 2005, when the track was resurfaced for its marquee event, the Coca-Cola 600. The only problem was that the track was "levigated"—diamond cutters were used to grind away at the top surface of the asphalt to, in theory, make the track faster and have more grip. The initial levigation proved to be a mistake for that May's 600, however, prompting further work on the surface in the next five months to prepare for the race in October. It turns out that the "fix" failed to do that, so the officials had to spend another $3.5 million to resurface the 1.5-mile track yet a third time. Result: If at first you don't succeed, try, try again. Many drivers wish that the old racing surface was still intact. So much for "progress."

- **Las Vegas Motor Speedway and Texas Motor Speedway.** These sister tracks have undergone several changes to their respective facilities. In 2006, Las Vegas had its banking increased and its track entirely resurfaced to a smooth veneer. Texas has done extensive changes since 1997, including installing new drainage systems, fixing dips in two of the corners, and widening the track. The result was significant improvements for both.

Looking at today's tracks, other than Martinsville, what other ISC-owned venue (that is not expendable) is in need of a major makeover? Forget Daytona, Darlington, Talladega, Kansas, Chicagoland, and even Watkins Glen. They're not going anywhere, nor are they going to change appreciably much in the next few years.

However, there is one ISC-owned facility that stands out: Auto Club Speedway, formerly known as California Speedway, in the eastern Los Angeles suburb of Fontana. The fans want it, the media want it, and the drivers definitely want it. How much more evidence does ISC and NASCAR need to realize that they have a severely broken facility that is in serious need of a major fix?

This is the second worst track on the circuit, in my opinion, but it's the worst track among ISC-owned facilities, hands down. Although track president Gillian Zucker has done a tremendous job of trying to attract fans and has gone the extra mile to increase the facility's significance among Southern California sports fans, she's ultimately been fighting a losing battle. The fans simply don't want to sit in a facility that is two miles around, bake in often triple-digit heat, and watch racing that is for the most part, uninspiring.

Frankly, little Irwindale Speedway (which seats between 6,500 and 15,000 with temporary seats installed) usually draws better crowds per capita than its 91,200-seat counterpart in Fontana, and it's just thirty miles down the road.

So how do you fix Auto Club Speedway? If I had to make that decision, I'd simply blow up the place and start from scratch. Although its 2-mile counterpart and model, Michigan International Speedway, is a good fit for its location in the Midwest, Auto Club is not a good fit for Southern California. Southern Californians can probably be considered the largest ADHD-type crowd of sports fans in the country. Their attention span is so short that it's dreaming the impossible dream to expect them to sit in the broiling sun for five or six hours, watch an event that is typically pretty boring until the final laps, and fight hours of traffic to and from the speedway.

Southern California sports fans need to be challenged, intrigued, and wined and dined, so to speak, if you want to get and keep their attention. And with all the longtime stalwarts in Los Angeles sports teams, like the multiple-champion Lakers, the Dodgers, the Angels, the Clippers, the Kings, the Ducks, and various college teams, stock car racing sits pretty far down on a typical Southern California sports fan's list of priorities.

Ideally, if I could wave a magic wand and move Las Vegas Motor Speedway—owned by ISC's main rival, Speedway Motorsports Inc.—to Fontana, I'd have a winning formula: a 1.5-mile track with its Neon Garage infield, which would allow fans to be up close and personal with the drivers and the teams; great food and entertainment; and simply a much more enjoyable, all-encompassing experience for everyone.

Obviously, this is not possible. Nor do I want to build a duplicate copy of Las Vegas Motor Speedway less than three hundred miles southwest of it in Fontana. So what's the best solution?

Again I say blow up the place and rebuild it. I mean it. Sell off parts of the current facility to souvenir hounds. Even though the track is surrounded by a large industrial park of factories, warehouses, and a waste-management facility (no, I'm *not* kidding), there are a number of things that could be done to improve its aesthetics.

First, cut the track's size from 2 miles to about .75-mile, roughly the same size as Richmond International Raceway. Second, add high banking, similar to that found at Bristol Motor Speedway, so the action is fast and tight. Granted, that negates some of the need for better passing, but I'm willing to forego that. If the banks were built wider than Bristol's, the new track would seem somewhat like a bicycle-racing velodrome.

Third, build a major hotel, entertainment, shopping, and eating complex around it, much like Westgate City Center, which encompasses Jobing.com Arena (formerly Glendale Arena) and the University of Phoenix Stadium. In other words, make the track more than a track; make it a destination people want to go to, where they can not only enjoy an exciting race but can also stick around to enjoy great food, shopping, and entertainment.

Just a couple miles to the west, there's Ontario Mills Outlet Mall, which has spawned a massive building project of hotels, restaurants, stores, and various attractions that draw tens of thousands of folks to the area every day—and many, many more on race weekends.

I can envision a four- or five-story complex, complete with suites, several restaurants, private dining and meeting facilities, and things like babysitting and pet-sitting services—anything that would make a fan's experience more comfortable and enjoyable. Adjacent to the complex would be a hotel (preferably abutting the track so that the guests can see the race action from their rooms, much like the hotel at Dover Speedway).

What's more, build the track in such a way that it can be multipurpose, such as serving as a venue for concerts. Also, add some type of shading element that sticks out from the top of the grandstands to cool large sections of fans (much like Cowboys Stadium in Arlington, Texas); install lights so that races can be held at night, when it's cooler; open the track to more smaller racing series (perhaps in conjunction with sister events at Irwindale); and make the facility much more community oriented.

Only then will both Southern California and NASCAR have a gem of a place where race (and other sports) fans can go—where they will *want* to go—to enjoy some great race action and have fun before and after at a club, a restaurant, or a store. Short of a beach in the mix, what more could a Southern Californian want?

# Which Three Drivers Woulda, Coulda, Shoulda Been Huge Successes but Were Tragically Stopped by Fate?

It's easy to pick the greatest athlete in a sport. All you have to do is look at who has the most career championships, the most wins, or some other category in which they stand head and shoulders above everyone else. But picking someone who seemed destined for greatness, only to be taken prematurely from this earth and the sport, is a far more challenging task.

Picking the top three drivers from NASCAR's modern era who were most likely to join the sport's all-time greats but whose careers were tragically cut short (not even on the racetrack, ironically) is pretty easy. The following drivers unquestionably stood out far above any others:

1. **Tim Richmond.** Richmond died August 13, 1989, at the far too young age of thirty-four. Although he passed away at such an early age, he still had an outstanding career, with 13 Cup victories, including 7 wins in 29 starts in 1986. Even after he was diagnosed with AIDS, Richmond won 2 races and had two other top-ten finishes in 8 starts in 1987, before he became too ill to drive. His last race was on August 16, 1987, at Michigan International Speedway; he finished 29th due to engine failure. Almost to the day two years later, Richmond passed away quietly. Even though he had only one season with more than 2 wins, he had five consecutive seasons of incredible top-ten marks: twelve of 26 starts in 1984, fifteen of 30 in 1983, eleven of 30 in 1984, thirteen of 28 in 1985, and seventeen of 29 in 1986 (including the 7 wins).

2. **Davey Allison.** Allison was just entering the prime of his racing career when he died on July 13, 1993, at the age of thirty-two. Unlike Richmond, who died an agonizingly slow death, Allison was taken from the NASCAR community in the blink of an eye: he was killed while attempting to land his new helicopter at Talladega Superspeedway. Davey's death was even more devastating to the Allison family, and to NASCAR families in general, because it followed exactly eleven months to the day his younger brother, Clifford, had been killed at Michigan International Speedway on August 13, 1992, while practicing for a Busch Series race. Davey Allison made 191 career Cup starts, winning 19 and finishing in the top ten in an incredible 92 of those races. Many observers believed that Davey had the talent and the potential to win as many races as his father, Bobby, did in his illustrious career (84 wins), which had Bobby tied with Darrell Waltrip for the third most wins in the NASCAR annals. Unfortunately, we'll never know.

3. **Alan Kulwicki.** NASCAR's much-beloved Polish Prince was able to enjoy his first Winston Cup championship for only four

and a half months—the shortest reign of any modern-era champion—before he was tragically killed at age thirty-eight in a plane crash while attempting to land at Blountville, Tennessee, near Bristol Motor Speedway, on April 1, 1993. The crash was found to be caused by both pilot error and ice on the plane's wings. The tragedy deprived NASCAR of watching Special K (another of Kulwicki's nicknames) add more chapters to one of the most inspiring rags-to-riches stories in the sport's history. A native of the Milwaukee suburb of Greenfield, Wisconsin, Kulwicki went to North Carolina in 1985 with a borrowed pickup truck and a race car to earn his fame and fortune. The owner and driver of an independent one-car operation, Kulwicki was the first college graduate (University of Wisconsin–Milwaukee, mechanical engineering, 1977) and the first Midwest native in NASCAR history to win a Cup championship, defeating Bill Elliott by a scant 10 points for the 1992 Winston Cup title. That held the record for the closest championship-winning margin until Kurt Busch defeated Jimmie Johnson by 8 points to win the 2004 Nextel Cup title. Even though Kulwicki earned just 5 Cup wins in his career, he overcame monumental odds and will be forever known in NASCAR history as the little engine that could—and did.

## Should There Be Do-Overs in NASCAR Racing?

Thanks to Dusty Duncan of Claremore, Oklahoma, for this question about "mulligans":

> In golf, players sometimes get "mulligans" (in essence, do-overs). What if NASCAR gave mulligans? If you could change one race in the history of the Chase for the Championship [Chase race only] thereby affecting the outcome of the Championship, what race would that be?

Let's start with the second question first. My personal pick would be the 2004 Chase opener at New Hampshire International

Speedway, when Robby Gordon lost his cool and crashed into Jeremy Mayfield while collecting and taking out Greg Biffle and Tony Stewart in the process. Both Biffle and Stewart were unable to come back from that race; Kurt Busch not only won the race but went on to win the first Chase for the Nextel Cup (now Sprint Cup) championship. Stewart had come into the first Chase race at New Hampshire as the fourth seed (just 15 points out of first place), so had he not been caught up in the Gordon-caused wreck (falling 124 points behind the points-leading Busch afterward), Busch might not have been the eventual champ that year. In a sense, Stewart redeemed himself the following year when he did win the championship.

Now, as for the question about mulligans. Plenty of readers over the years have asked the same question. They'd like to see the implementation of a mulligan play-off system in which a driver can throw out his worst performance of the Chase, thus making him still eligible to win the championship.

I'm sorry, but I'm not a fan of the mulligan at all. I think it's a contrived gimmick that only cheapens the outcome of an event and the credibility of the sanctioning body that allows it. It also puts Chase drivers in a fairly biased position. If they're doing well in the Chase overall, their tendency is to vote against having mulligans, but if they have at least one really bad performance in the Chase, suddenly they seem a lot warmer to the do-over idea.

In 2008, Carl Edwards led all the drivers with 9 wins and ultimately finished second to Jimmie Johnson in the championship. Had it not been for a bad finish at Talladega—or if that score had been thrown out under a mulligan-type system—Edwards would have had a fighting chance of overtaking Johnson for the championship.

It's no wonder that Edwards's team owner, Jack Roush, became a mulligan proponent at the time. "It would be my suggestion, as NASCAR looks at how to make this thing more exciting, [that it would be good] if we had an opportunity, every team had an opportunity, to throw out one race and be able to just count nine of the ten," he said. "That means you could have a mulligan and you could be able to come back from it."

Some drivers have taken the mulligan concept one step further and have suggested the idea of throwing out both the worst and the best performances of each driver in the ten-race Chase. That doesn't make any sense to me. What happens if your best finish is a win, but your worst finish is 20th and many of your opponents' worst finishes are 35th or lower? How is that fair, I ask?

Jimmie Johnson, for one, agrees with me. "I wouldn't be thinking now we need a mulligan in this series, or we need this or that to try and make it even," Johnson said. "We all show up for the 10 races, and the points were there, and you go earn it. That's what you do."

The Chase is a ten-race play-off format, and that's the way it should remain. It's not a ten-race play-off format that morphs into a de facto nine- or eight-race format that allows one or two do-overs along the way. If NASCAR ever agreed to allow mulligans, it would make the sanctioning body look even more like World Wrestling Entertainment, with contrived and scripted story lines and predetermined outcomes.

Mulligans have no place in professional sports. We don't see them allowed in football, baseball, basketball, hockey, or any other major pro sport. Ergo, there's no legitimate reason to ever consider implementing a mulligan system in NASCAR, unless you want to alienate fans and make a mockery of the sport.

I mean, if we allowed mulligans in NASCAR, what's next? Legalized cheating? Oh wait, Chad Knaus already perfected that system—just kidding, Chad!

# Are Some Drivers and Owners Just Not Destined to Win Championships?

NASCAR is a sport of competitiveness and outsmarting the next guy. Whoever can do that on a regular basis will ultimately enjoy success, both on a race-to-race basis and in winning championships. But there's another intangible element that no one can explain, let alone understand. It's luck—or the lack thereof. Although hard work typically accounts for most of the success of an individual, a team, or organization, having luck on one's side can often be the difference between being good and being great.

Look at Hendrick Motorsports. It's won nine championships since Rick Hendrick opened his racing operation in 1984 with just one driver (Geoff Bodine) and little more but a dream and a fiery internal drive to become the best.

The same applies to Richard Childress Racing. Its namesake decided to retire from racing as a competitive racer to make room for a fledgling young driver by the name of Dale Earnhardt. Earnhardt won the 1980 Winston Cup championship for team owner Rod Osterlund, but Earnhardt did not become a household name until he joined forces with Childress. They became one of the most successful driver-owner partnerships in the sport, winning six additional Cup championships before Earnhardt was killed in 2001.

Granted, Earnhardt had a tremendous amount of talent, but he and Childress together also seemed to have a Midaslike touch that made everything they set their minds to turn to gold. On the track, it was race wins and championships. Off the track, it was multimillions of dollars in souvenir sales, commercials, and sponsorships. Luck seemed to have a hand in their success.

There are also drivers, teams, and organizations that seem to forever be under a dark cloud, unable to catch a good break or forced to toil for years or decades in less than fortuitous circumstances. Some people might call it being cursed or jinxed or say that a team or a driver simply "ran out of talent" when it mattered the most.

Here's my list of NASCAR's most vexed teams or drivers:

1. **Jack Roush.** Roush came into Cup racing in 1988 after a long and very successful career in other forms of racing, primarily sports-car competition, as both a driver and an owner. Roush may have been cursed from the start, because the first driver he hired was Mark Martin, who would become one of the sport's biggest tough-luck stories in terms of winning championships. In nearly two decades with Roush, Martin came close to winning a title four times, finishing second each time (plus four other third-place finishes), yet he was never able to get over the hump to win a championship. Of particular note was 1990, when NASCAR assessed a 46-point penalty against Martin late in the season, which ultimately cost him the championship by 26 points to the

late Dale Earnhardt. Martin, who left Roush after 2005, has yet
to win his first title. But finally the Roush organization broke
through: Matt Kenseth won the last Winston Cup title in 2003,
and Kurt Busch won the first Nextel Cup championship the following year. Unfortunately for Roush, the organization has failed
to win another Cup title since.

2. **Richard Petty.** Petty's 200 career wins and seven Cup championships led Petty Enterprises (now Richard Petty Motorsports)
to become the winningest organization in stock car racing history. But ever since Petty's last Cup title in 1979, his team has
not even come close to winning one again. Some people have
called it the "Petty curse," because when Petty Enterprises was
winning, it was winning big. But when it began losing, it fell
into such a downward spiral that it still hasn't found a way to get
out (Kasey Kahne's appearance in the 2009 Chase for the Sprint
Cup notwithstanding). Some have likened the Petty curse to
the infamous jinx of the Chicago Cubs, when restaurateur Sam
Sianis brought a goat to Wrigley Field in 1945 and it was denied
admission. As a result, Sianis put a curse on the Cubs, and they
have not been in the World Series ever since. (The last time the
Cubs *won* the World Series was more than a century ago). Every
year, hope springs eternal among millions of longtime diehard
fans that the Petty name will return to success and prominence,
but some higher power seems totally opposed to that. Talk about
going from the penthouse to the outhouse; that's been the legacy
of Petty Enterprises and Richard Petty Motorsports.

3. **Roger Penske.** Penske is the most successful team owner in
open-wheel, Indy car racing, hands down. His drivers have won
the biggest race in motorsports, the Indianapolis 500, a record
15 times through 2009. Penske drivers have also won a combined
11 Indy car championships, 10 in the now defunct CART racing
series, and 1 in the current Indy Racing League series. But that
kind of enviable success has never been able to translate into
stock-car racing for Penske. To date, the closest Penske has come
to a Cup championship was Rusty Wallace's runner-up finish in
1993 and third-place finish the following season. (Wallace had

won the Cup title for former Cup team owner Raymond Beadle in 1989 before being lured over to join the Penske camp in 1991.) Kurt Busch competed in the 2007 and 2009 editions of the Chase for the Sprint Cup but didn't win the championship either season, so Penske is still searching for his first Cup championship as a NASCAR team owner since converting his part-time organization (formed in 1972) into a full-time effort in 1991. Most of Penske's stock car drivers have been incredible over the years, including Wallace, Busch, Ryan Newman, and Sam Hornish Jr., who won an Indy Racing League title for the Captain (Penske's nickname) in 2006 and who would like to do the same for his boss in NASCAR. Penske Racing's biggest accomplishment in NASCAR has been Newman's 2008 Daytona 500 victory, with Busch right behind him as they crossed the finish line. Unfortunately, Newman was unable to capitalize on that Daytona success and left the team at the end of the season, moving to the Stewart Haas Racing organization for 2009.

4. **Richard Childress Racing.** For all its success with the late Dale Earnhardt behind the wheel, Richard Childress Racing has struggled terribly at times since The Intimidator's death, particularly in 2009. In 2008 its top three drivers finished fourth through sixth, in the Chase, but in 2009 not one of them even came close to winning. Neither did newcomer Casey Mears, who came to Childress when the organization expanded to four Cup teams. Could the Earnhardt tragedy have brought about some type of curse or jinx for the Childress camp that might not be broken for a long time?

5. **Dale Earnhardt Inc.** Speaking of Earnhardt, the racing organization he formed with wife Teresa, DEI, can also have a case made for it being cursed since its cofounder's death at Daytona. DEI won two Busch Series championships with Dale Earnhardt Jr. in 1998 and 1999, but it never won a Cup championship during Junior's ten-year tenure there—and it still hasn't, since he left after 2007 (even though Juan Pablo Montoya made the Chase in 2009).

HONORABLE MENTION: **Wood Brothers**, the pride and joy of Stuart, Virginia, may be nearly as famous and fabled as the former Petty

Enterprises was, but other than one third-place finish with David Pearson in 1974, it has never come any closer to winning a Cup championship. Of course, a big part of that reason is Wood Brothers has primarily been a part-time racing organization on the Cup level for most of its fifty-seven-year existence. One can only wonder what might have been if Wood Brothers could have been a full-time operation. If that were the case, we wouldn't be including it in this chapter but would be listing it as one of the most successful teams ever. Unfortunately, the truth is what it is.

## How Has Money Changed Stock Car Racing?

We've talked a lot in this book about how the sport of stock car racing has changed throughout the years. Without question, one of the biggest changes has come not in how drivers perform on the racetrack but in what is waiting for them when they pull into victory lane. I'm talking about money here, folks—green, cold, hard cash. As the sport has grown over the years, so too has the prize money, to almost ridiculous amounts.

Perhaps the best example is The King, Richard Petty. During his illustrious career, Petty won a record 200 Cup-level races from 1958 to 1992, earning a grand total of $8,541,210 in prize money. He earned, on average, $7,214 in each of the 1,184 Cup races he competed in. Or, if you want to simply break the numbers down to how much each win was worth (including all the races he competed in), this would be an average of $42,706 per win. The most money Petty won in any one season was $561,933 in 1979, the year he won his seventh and last Cup championship.

In contrast, from 2001 through 2009, Jimmie Johnson earned nearly $90 *million*. What's more, from 2006 through 2009, when he won the Cup championship, he earned more than $15 million *each* season.

From his first start in 2001 through the end of 2009, Johnson earned $305,898 *per race*. The California native had won 47 races through

2009. If you add up all the money he earned up to then (including bonuses) and divide it by the number of wins, each triumph was worth a cool $1,893,964. In other words, Johnson earned more than three times as much money *per win* as Petty did for an *entire season*.

But prize money isn't the only thing that has skyrocketed over the years. As NASCAR became more popular, particularly when it climbed to its peak, from the mid-1990s to around 2005, the sport seemed to go from one that was based on competitive racing to one in which everyone was out for every dollar he could get.

As more fans came into the sport, more money flowed into everyone's pockets. We're talking billions of dollars. With multibillion-dollar TV rights packages, prize money, sponsorship money, driver contracts, the sale of licensed merchandise, and the like, the money flowed like water through a tap.

In the midst of all that newfound wealth, the sport began its transition from who was the most competitive to who had the most dollars. It's no wonder that the most well-financed teams prospered the most at the racetrack and at the bank. Teams like Hendrick Motorsports and Joe Gibbs Racing became monolithic organizations worth eight and even nine figures.

The more prosperity increased and the more the fan base grew, the more money it took just to stay competitive. For example, in the mid-1990s, when NASCAR was climbing at perhaps its fastest, the cost of running a typical Cup team averaged between $5 and $10 million.

By 2000 the price tag had jumped up to between $10 and $15 million, and by 2005 you could tack on another $5 to $10 million per year—all just to stay competitive. It was a financial house of cards that stood ready to collapse not if but when NASCAR took a dive. And when the overall global economy as a whole started taking a plunge in 2007 that continued into 2010, NASCAR's fortunes fell drastically.

Teams could simply not afford to spend $20 to $25 million without heavy-duty sponsorship. Unfortunately, as the economy got worse, the sponsors became more tight-fisted with their money. Sponsors used to want exclusive rights to all the races in a year, but now they suddenly wanted to have their logos and their names on the side of the race cars for a certain number of races. That began the era we see today, in which some drivers seemingly have new sponsors every three or four races (and some actually do).

As sponsorship became tighter, the teams simply could not survive on their own, which prompted numerous mergers or outside partnerships to take some of the weighty burden off their financial backs.

NASCAR, the sanctioning body, spent money aggressively in its heyday because it wanted to prove that it belonged among the big boys of other sports—namely, the NFL, the NBA, and Major League Baseball. Unfortunately, those leagues did not suffer as much as NASCAR from the economic downturn. Ultimately, NASCAR had to stop spending money like a drunken sailor. Its sister company, International Speedway Corporation, was forced to lay off dozens of employees, both in the Daytona Beach corporate offices and at many of its racetracks.

Success and the heretofore nonstop flow of money helped NASCAR to make a lot of people millionaires. When the house of cards collapsed, industry experts estimated that more than a thousand people—some say even as many as three thousand—within the sport (public relations directors, body fabricators, engine specialists, and crew members) were summarily laid off. Some found jobs with other teams, but many have not returned to the sport and might never do so.

NASCAR lived the high life for a long time, and I'm not faulting it for that. It had a product that became wildly successful, and it deserved the rewards that came with it. But the NASCAR of today is a far cry from the NASCAR of the past sixty years. During the sport's golden era, cash was important, but it wasn't the be-all and end-all. It helped in putting events together, and the payoff in victory lane or at the championship banquet was just a reward for a job well done, but there was never an obsession for the green stuff. As NASCAR grew bigger and bigger, the corresponding increase in money was nice, but it never seemed to be enough.

NASCAR was like an active alcoholic: the more it had, the more it wanted. Whereas once racing had been king, cash became king, controlling virtually everything about the sport. This role continues today, only now the free-spending days are over, and everyone has to be more concerned because the shrinking dollar has shrunk the sport.

I doubt that we'll ever see things return to the way they used to be. And as NASCAR prepares to negotiate a new TV deal in 2014, it's a pretty good bet that the multibillion-dollar contracts of 2001 and 2006 will be substantially reduced. At the very least, if the numbers remain the same in the next broadcast package, the overall value will be less, due to inflation and the economic troubles that are likely to continue.

A lot of jaded fans began to refer to NASCAR as "CASHCAR," because money was put ahead of the racing and even dictated what kind of racing we'd have (such as the implementation of the Car of Tomorrow, the ban on testing at Cup-sanctioned tracks, and the one-motor-per-weekend rule). Although I can understand that kind of sentiment, I don't necessarily agree with it. It has become nearly cost-prohibitive to remain in the sport, let alone try to enter the sport, which is why we have seen few new teams debut in the last couple of years, and none on a full-time basis. However, if the money isn't there, the racing isn't going to be there, either. It's a catch-22.

The economic downturn has taught NASCAR and its teams to learn how to do a lot of things for a lot less. But in the end, if you don't have the cash to pay, you simply won't have a chance to play. It's a matter of supply and demand: If you've got the money, the sport has its arms open for you. But if you don't, NASCAR will be like the pretty girl at the bar: it won't even look at you, no matter how nice a guy you might be.

How money has changed NASCAR isn't just limited to the modern day, either. The sad thing for former drivers like Richard Petty and those of his generation (the drivers who stopped competing before NASCAR really began to hit it big in the early-to-mid 1990s) is that NASCAR failed to do what its peers in other pro-sports leagues did: take care of its own, including establishing a pension program for its participants. It's a shortcoming that continues today.

It's not that the drivers of today really need help, given the often outlandish amounts of money they're earning per race and per season. But many of the old-timers could sure use a helping hand financially in their golden years, and they deserve it, for all that they gave to the sport.

Is it any wonder that some of the greatest drivers in the sport's history, like Bobby Allison, still have to sell autographs at fan conventions or T-shirts and other memorabilia online, from trailers, or at race sites? Long after they stopped competing as active drivers, they're doing this just to make ends meet.

Even the late great Dale Earnhardt, who earned $42 million in his Cup racing career, still maintains a significant presence with several souvenir trailers at virtually every Cup race from Loudon to Fontana. Every dollar generated helps to keep the company he founded in business and his legacy alive.

So the next time someone tells you that money hasn't changed NASCAR as much as it has changed other professional sports, tell him or her to read this section of the book. It might just open a few eyes.

# What Are the Most Coveted and Most Unique Trophies in NASCAR?

Winning a race is always first and foremost in a driver's mind. But taking the checkered flag also brings with it two extra benefits: a very sizable winner's check and a unique first-place trophy. The trophy is "one of the main reasons we do this," says four-time Cup champion Jeff Gordon. "Even after nearly thirty years of doing this, going after the trophy never gets old for me."

Some trophies bring with them greater bragging rights or more excitement than others about putting something unique in a driver's trophy room or on his living room mantel. The reason might be the significance of the victory, like winning the Daytona 500, or just the unique fashion or shape of the trophy. Either way, trophies have been and probably always will be coveted remembrances of a job well done and a victory well deserved.

The unfortunate thing is that some trophies are short-lived, often because of the quirks and desires of the race sponsors. If the sponsorship changes, the trophy usually changes, as well.

Picking a best or a worst trophy is difficult, because each trophy has a significant meaning to the race winner or to the track that awards it. That's why I've worded the question as I have: the most coveted and the most unique trophies in stock car racing today.

Some of these trophies have been around for many years, whereas others are relatively new. Because so many trophies have changed throughout the years, I'm focusing only on those that are still being handed out or have been awarded until recently. I admit that such a list is completely subjective. The ones I pick as most coveted and most unique could be exactly the opposite ones that would be picked by someone else. Maybe none of mine would make your own list. But I tried to use as broad a judging scale as possible, with heavy emphasis on the uniqueness of the trophy. So without further ado, here are my picks, in no particular order:

## Most Coveted Trophies

**Daytona International Speedway's Harley J. Earl Trophy.** Next to the Sprint Cup championship trophy, this is arguably the most coveted trophy in NASCAR, because it proves that you won NASCAR's biggest race, the Daytona 500. Named after its noted General Motors designer, the trophy features a miniature 1954 Firebird One rocket, a concept car that Earl designed. Three-time 500 winner Bobby Allison said to me a few years ago, "To win at Daytona, to get your name on that trophy, once you do that you will always be known as a Daytona champion, and no one can ever take that away from you. Even if you never win another race in your career, you'll still always be called a Daytona champion."

**Goodyear Gold Car Award Trophy.** It may have a simple name, but this is one of the most beautiful trophies you'll ever see. Unfortunately, very few folks do get to see this in person, because it's presented annually to the Cup champion at NASCAR's postseason awards banquet. Made by noted model maker Michael Dunlap, the trophy is an identical replica of the manufacturer's car that was driven by the champion that season (for example, Jimmie Johnson's four championship trophies were all Chevrolets). All the parts, from the steering wheel to the tires, are plated with twenty-four-karat gold, and the trophy is worth $25,000. "This is by far one of the coolest trophies and awards you can ever win," a beaming Johnson said after receiving his first trophy in 2006.

**Martinsville Speedway's Independence Grandfather Clock.** This tradition was started by track founder H. Clay Earles in 1964. The winners of every Sprint Cup, Nationwide, and Camping World Truck series races that are held each year at this little half-mile bullring take home one of the coolest grandfather clocks you'll ever see. Produced by Ridgeway Clock Company of Martinsville, these stately timekeepers are reportedly worth $11,000 each and play "God Bless America" and "America the Beautiful." Richard Petty won the most: fifteen clocks. The only problem with them is that they're so big, they can't fit on anyone's mantel. Jeff Gordon, who has won seven grandfather clocks at Martinsville, gives them away to close friends or associates, like former crew chief Robbie Loomis and current crew chief Steve Letarte.

**Texas Motor Speedway's Cowboy Boots, Hat, and Six-Shooters.** One of the most coveted as well as unique trophies in all sports are the framed and hand-carved cowboy boots, a genuine Charlie 1 Horse cowboy hat, and a pair of Beretta six-shooter handguns given to the winner of each Cup race at Texas Motor Speedway. (The winners even get to pop off a few blank rounds in victory lane in celebration.) Another trophy here is the twelve-gauge Beretta Jubilee shotgun, reportedly worth $65,000, which is awarded for the pole position winner.

**Richmond International Raceway's and Nashville Superspeedway's Electric Guitars.** Richmond presents the winner of the Chevy Rock & Roll 400 each September with a Paul Reed Smith guitar that is shrouded in aluminum flames. The guitar can be removed from the trophy and played. The trophy stands more than four feet tall and weighs nearly seventy-five pounds. At Nashville Superspeedway, the winners of the Nationwide Series and the Camping World Truck Series races receive what I consider slightly better than the Richmond trophy: a custom Gibson Trophy Guitar designed by noted motorsports artist Sam Bass and tabbed by *Sports Illustrated* as one of the ten coolest-looking trophies in sports. Kyle Busch made headlines in 2009 when he smashed his guitar trophy in rock star–like fashion after winning a Nationwide race at Nashville. Given that he had already won more than fifty NASCAR trophies, I guess he won't miss one more, no matter how coveted it is.

**Las Vegas Motor Speedway's Champion's Belt.** The winning driver of the spring Sprint Cup race at Las Vegas takes home one of the most prized trophies in the sport: a replica prizefighter's championship belt that can actually be worn. The belt is encrusted in gold, diamonds, and rubies and is worth more than $3,000. It sure as heck beats Richard Petty's noted cowboy belt buckles.

HONORABLE MENTION: **Bristol Motor Speedway's Bristol Cup.** Weighing fifty pounds (the original, in 1983, weighed eighty pounds), this trophy was featured in Will Ferrell's movie *Talladega Nights*. It is too big (four feet high), too heavy, and too outdated (a winged woman on top of a cup), yet it remains one of the most prized artifacts a driver can claim in his racing career.

## Most Unique Trophies

**Dover International Speedway's Monster Trophy.** This is definitely one of the most unique trophies, not just in racing but all sports. It's a miniature replica of the forty-six-foot monster statue outside the racetrack. As much as I like the folks at Dover, I still get the willies each time I see this thirty-inch, white sandstone trophy that looks suspiciously like a cross among King Kong, the Michelin Man, and the Pillsbury Dough Boy. Still, there is one really cool aspect of the trophy: a diecast model of the race winner's car is placed into the trophy prior to the victory lane celebration.

**Atlanta Motor Speedway's Bass Pro Shops' Wildlife Trophy.** Unfortunately, this trophy is now defunct because the company no longer sponsors any races at Atlanta. But when it did, it awarded some of the most attention-getting and talked-about trophies in the world, with stuffed and mounted wildlife placed upon a large block of wood. The types of animals have included a pair of eagles and a largemouth bass. Perhaps the most notable was a life-sized grizzly bear. It dwarfed every other trophy and provided one of the most hysterical moments in the history of the trophy in 2006 when Tony Stewart won it. Standing ten feet tall and weighing eight hundred pounds, it was far too large to place in Stewart's private plane, so it had to be sent back to North Carolina in the team's transporter.

**Atlanta Motor Speedway's Pep Boys Auto 500.** Pep Boys was one of the sponsors that replaced Bass Pro Shops at Atlanta, and its trophy falls far short of the trophies produced by Bass Pro Shops. I understand that the sponsor foots the bill for the naming-rights honors of a race and should be allowed to design whatever trophy it wants to give out. But the Pep Boys' trophy looks like the Three Stooges holding a tire, a battery, and a trophy in victory lane. File this not so much under unique, but under "needs a lot of work."

**Kansas Speedway's "Soaring" Trophy.** Derisively called "the can opener" by some, this abstract-looking trophy is produced by a Canadian sculptor. Aren't there any local sculptors in the Jayhawk state who can bring a little homegrown touch to the victory lane? I mean, what's next—do we start singing "Oh Canada" to the race winner? I wouldn't be surprised if this trophy fails to make most winners' mantels, but it would probably make a nifty doorstop. In one word, this trophy is *ugly*.

**Indianapolis Motor Speedway's Brickyard Trophy.** This is one of the most simplistic yet effective designs of first-place trophies. A single brick sits atop a base of gold, aluminum alloy, and sterling silver. Kansas Speedway could learn a few things from this uniquely smart design when it comes to trophies: sometimes abstract and obtuse are *not* the way to go.

**Infineon Raceway's Toyota/Save Mart 350 Trophy.** This trophy is made of a three-liter wine bottle (which you can actually fill up and drink from in victory lane) and five small wooden casks, surrounded by a landscape of the Sonoma Valley hills. The winner also receives a foot-tall wine goblet mounted on a marble base. Infineon is probably the only track on the circuit where instead of beer or champagne, wine is the drink of choice for celebrating in victory lane. That includes spraying it all over the winning team, your family, your friends, and the reporters.

**Memphis Motorsports Park's Elvis Trophy.** Even though the King (Elvis, not Richard Petty) died in 1977, he continues to live on in NASCAR circles, because the winner of the Truck Series race at Memphis receives a gold statue of a swivel-hipped Elvis playing the guitar. Weighing sixty pounds and standing twenty-seven inches high, it's a replica of the nine-foot statue of Presley that stands on Beale Street in downtown Memphis.

**The Sprint Cup Trophy.** To the winner go the spoils. In addition to getting the championship-winning check, which is typically $5 to $10 million, the seasonal champ in the Sprint Cup competition also receives the aptly named Sprint Cup Trophy, a sterling silver centerpiece reportedly worth more than $50,000 and produced by the world-famous Tiffany jewelry company.

# Which Drivers Stayed Around Too Long Before Retiring?

Even at the young age of twenty-two, just as he was beginning his emergence into NASCAR superstardom, Kyle Busch was asked by reporters, "How long do you expect to race before you retire?" That might seem like an odd question for a driver whose racing career was just starting to take off. But it also shows the importance that the media, the fans, the team owners, and even fellow drivers place upon a driver's ability to still be productive and successful as he starts to get up in years.

People are already asking that of guys in their thirties and forties such as Dale Earnhardt Jr., Tony Stewart, Jimmie Johnson, Jeff

Gordon, Matt Kenseth, Greg Biffle, Elliott Sadler, and Jeff Burton. The last thing anyone should want to do is to have a successful career become significantly affected by sticking around the sport longer than their talents allow.

There are exceptions to the rule, like Mark Martin, who turned fifty in 2009 yet continues to compete on a high level, comparable to the performance of a driver in his late twenties or early thirties. But for the most part, when a driver hits forty, he should have a retirement plan in place and an exit strategy ready. Unfortunately, it doesn't always happen that way.

There's a racing adage that you're remembered more for your last race or last season than your greatest race or season. In the last twenty-five years, we've seen a number of drivers stick around far too long, to the point where the glory days of their racing prime have become somewhat foggy because they don't know when to call it quits.

Some guys got out at the right time, and they knew it—like Dale Jarrett and Rusty Wallace. Others, like Bill Elliott and Terry Labonte, keep coming back even though they're in their mid-fifties and their performances indicate that they might be better off staying away. All it seems they're trying to do is capitalize on past fame so that they can sell more shirts and hats at their souvenir trailers.

More recently, another fiftysomething driver, Sterling Marlin, became part of the bunch who should have quit while he was ahead. A good but not great racer in his time, Marlin hung on far too long. After finishing third in 2001, he led the points in 2002 before becoming seriously injured in a wreck. This kept him out of the final seven races of the season, so he lost his chance at the title and finished 18th. The wreck did serious damage to Marlin's neck and back and effectively ended his career as a productive driver. There was even speculation that another bad wreck might cause permanent damage, including the possibility of paralysis, but Marlin waved off that concern.

Marlin continued to drive into his fifties. In 2003, at age forty-six, he finished 18th; in 2004, he finished 21st; in 2005, he finished 30th; in 2006, he finished 34th; and in 2007, he finished 40th, after being released from Bobby Ginn Racing barely two-thirds of the way through the season and competing in just twenty-one of that year's thirty-six races. Of course, the folding of Bobby Ginn Racing shortly afterward was a significant part of Marlin's release, as well.

In the last quarter-century or so of NASCAR, two of the sport's greatest drivers were also two of its most stubborn players: they practically had to be dragged kicking and screaming from the racetracks. This may indeed be a lousy way to treat two of the sport's all-time greats. But Michael Jordan has conceded several times that he should have hung it up for good once he left the Chicago Bulls after six championships, instead of trying to relive old glory and perform his old magic with a mediocre Washington Wizards organization. NASCAR drivers should do the same, in my opinion.

Here are my picks for the sport's two most stubborn players:

First is The King, Richard Petty. Although he was one of the nicest and among my favorite people in the sport, Petty overstayed his time in NASCAR by at least five to seven years. Petty's seventh and final championship came in 1979. He raced thirteen more seasons. But using the 1979 season as somewhat of a demarcation line, consider these facts:

- Of his 200 career wins on the Cup level, Petty won just 10 from 1980 until his last in 1984, and then he went winless in the final eight seasons of his career.
- After his final championship in 1979, Petty finished 4th, 8th, 5th, 4th, 10th, 14th, 14th, and 8th from 1980 to 1987, respectively. In his final five seasons, from 1988 to 1992, he finished 22nd, 29th, 26th, and 24th, respectively. This is not exactly the way the greatest driver in the sport's history should be remembered, don't you agree?
- Petty's average starting and finishing position per race during the final five seasons was no higher than 22nd.
- After dominating NASCAR for much of his first thirty years as a Cup driver, Petty embarrassingly watched the number of laps he and the fabled No. 43 led in a season drop from an all-time high of 5,537 laps to just 69 laps in his final six seasons. In 1991, he led just one lap the entire season.

My second pick for NASCAR's most stubborn driver is Darrell Waltrip. If Petty was The King, Waltrip was The Crown Prince—although the driving he did in the final years of his career made him more like The Court Jester. Waltrip won 84 races and three Cup championships in five years in his storied career. In my mind, there's no question he's a cinch to be a second- or third-year selection for induction to the NASCAR Hall of Fame (opened May 2010). Many of his friends, including the late Dale Earnhardt, encouraged Waltrip to start thinking of retirement in the waning years of his racing career, but he was thinking everything but that.

Waltrip's last good year was 1989, when he finished fourth (at the age of forty-two). He missed six races in 1990 due to injuries, which relegated him to a 20th-place finish. Once he was back to full health in 1991, he managed to rebound to respectable finishes of 8th, 9th, 13th, and 9th in the next four seasons. That's when he should have made a clean break and called it a career, in my opinion. Unfortunately, Waltrip went downhill from there faster than a roller coaster at an amusement park. His fans won't forget the 84 wins he earned in competition, but they also won't forget the following:

- He failed to reach victory lane even once from 1993 until he called it quits after 2000.
- His final season finishes in his Cup career were 19th, 29th, 26th, 24th, 37th, and 36th He competed in just twenty-seven of thirty-four races in 1999 and twenty-nine of thirty-four in 2000, his final year of racing.
- In his final five seasons, his best yearly starting average was 25th in 1997, and his best yearly finishing average was 23rd, also in 1997. His worst starting average was 35th in 1998, and his worst finishing average was almost 32nd in his final season.
- Waltrip led a total of just 45 laps in his final five seasons, with an all-time low of just 2 in 1996 and 3 in 1999.

If Waltrip had quit after either 1994 (when he finished 9th) or 1995 (when he finished 19th), that would have been fine with me. But to extend his career another five years, ultimately retiring from racing in 2000 at age fifty-three as a mere shell of his former greatness, he became the derisive target of critics and non-fans who laughed at how he tried to hang on when he should have just let it go.

I hope that guys like Tony Stewart, Jeff Gordon, Jimmie Johnson, Dale Earnhardt Jr., Matt Kenseth, and the like will heed what happens to guys they idolized as kids. There should be a rule that you quit driving when you're at the top, or at least in the middle of your career, and not at or near the bottom.

# How Can You Not Feel Sympathy for Mark Martin?

Virtually every professional sport has at least one athlete who epitomizes greatness, gives it his all every day and during every event, and has earned almost universal respect throughout his sport for his demeanor, personality, and character. Baseball had Hall of Famer Ernie Banks of the Chicago Cubs, who never played in the World Series. Football Hall of Famers Dick Butkus and Gale Sayers gave the Chicago Bears fans great memories, but they never saw a Super Bowl.

NASCAR has its own version of Banks, Butkus, and Sayers, rolled into one. He is without question a future Hall of Famer, is arguably the most respected man in the garage, has been racing on all levels for more than thirty years, and remains fiercely competitive to this day. Still, one thing continues to weigh around his neck like an albatross: Mark Anthony Martin, the pride and joy of Batesville, Arkansas, has never won a NASCAR Cup championship in his career.

Other drivers have never won Cup titles, as well. But how many of them have competed in nearly 800 races, have 40 career wins, have more than 400 top-ten finishes and nearly 50 poles and have earned more than $75 million in prize money in twenty-eight years of Cup racing?

No one. That's why Martin is my pick as the driver who deserves the most sympathy from his fans, fellow drivers, and anyone who has ever been associated with the sport. Even though he is one of the most consistent drivers the Cup level has ever seen, the struggles the fifty-one-year-old Martin has gone through in his nearly three-decade career might otherwise be maddening to someone else. He finished runner-up in five different seasons (including 2009), more times as No. 2 than any of his current peers on the Cup level (and four other times in third place). Yet he is still searching for that elusive first Cup championship nearly thirty years after he left the American Speed Association circuit (where he won four titles from 1978 to 1986) for NASCAR.

As a result, it's not surprising that Martin has so often been referred to as "always the best man but never the groom."

To this day, Martin can't forget the most difficult season of all for him, 1990, when he seemed certain to win the title only to be assessed a 46-point penalty by NASCAR late in the season for using an illegal—but not a performance-enhancing—carburetor spacer. He ultimately lost the best chance he might ever have had at the title by a heartbreaking 20 points to the late Dale Earnhardt.

Off the track, Martin deserves significant sympathy as well: his father, his stepmother, and his half sister were tragically killed in August 1998 in a crash of their private plane in Nevada. To his credit, Martin has soldiered on with admirable internal toughness and for-titude despite all his setbacks. For example, even though his father was piloting the plane that crashed on that fateful day, it did not stop Mark from continuing to fly his own private plane to virtually every NASCAR event.

He came so close to winning so many times that even though he once publicly stated, "I'm all right with not ever winning even one Cup championship," when he announced his semiretirement to part-time status after 2005, Martin couldn't stay away for long. Team owner Rick Hendrick convinced him to return in 2009 and 2010 for two more attempts. As of this writing, Martin plans on coming back in 2011, as well, but it's anyone's guess if he'll continue racing past that season.

When he agreed to race for Hendrick again, Martin finally gave a hint that he still had the Cup trophy as his ultimate goal. "If I didn't do it [come back to race full-time for Hendrick], I would always ask myself, 'What would have happened if I did?' I couldn't live with myself if I did that—so here I am, giving it another go-round." How can you not feel sympathy for a guy like that?

## Should There Be Minimum Requirements to Compete in the Sprint Cup?

Let me pose a hypothetical question to you: If your eighteen-year-old son asked to drive your pristine, mint-condition 1969 Chevrolet Corvette that was worth $100,000, and you knew he'd be tempted to push the car to its 160-mile-per-hour limit, would you give him the keys? Of course not. But that's what NASCAR does—and even encourages doing—in racing today.

In recent years, we've seen young drivers jump to the Cup level at an age when they're not even legally able to drink and they're just barely old enough to vote. Drivers like Kyle Busch and Brian Vickers began their Busch or Nationwide series careers at the precocious age of eighteen, then moved up to the Cup level a year or two later.

Then there's Joey Logano, who set a whole new standard for NASCAR's teenybopper set. Logano was promoted to a full-time Sprint Cup ride while he was still eighteen years old. In his first full season, 2009, he became the youngest winner in Cup history at nineteen years, one month, and four days old (it was at New Hampshire Motor Speedway on June 28, 2009 and was a rain-shortened event that was won on fuel mileage rather than through a dominating performance by Logano). The previous record holder, Kyle Busch, won his first Cup race in 2005 (at Auto Club Speedway in Southern California) at the age of twenty years, four months, and two days.

For every teen phenomenon, there seems to be a teen washout. In 2001, Casey Atwood was labeled as "the next Jeff Gordon" at the age of nineteen. Less than two years later, Atwood was essentially on his way out of Cup racing for good. He'd have a few subsequent one-off starts here and there, but it's unlikely that he'll ever return to prominence, especially since he's now closing in on thirty years old.

So many young drivers come and go, particularly in the Nationwide and Camping World Truck series, that they seem to be around one day and gone the next, never to be seen or heard from again. Although NASCAR takes pride in its "young guns," frequently bragging about them as the "future of the sport," many fans and reporters (myself included) think that some type of graduated promotional system would serve the sport better. Essentially, a young up-and-coming driver, whether he's eighteen or twenty-eight, would have to serve an apprenticeship of sorts, with considerable time in both the Nationwide and/or the Camping World Truck series, before being allowed to be "promoted" to the Sprint Cup.

"Too many young kids, these so-called young guns, come up through the ranks too fast and too soon," Richard Petty told me in 2006, "and when they get here, they can't handle the competition. It doesn't do the sport any good, it doesn't do their teams any good, and it definitely doesn't do the young drivers any good, either. What they need to do is log some time in the Busch or Craftsman [now Camping World] Series before moving up to Cup."

Some drivers have partly paid their dues before making the big jump upward, sometimes in an unconventional way. Kurt Busch, who won the 2004 Nextel (now Sprint) Cup championship and the first Chase for the Cup, jumped directly from what was then known as the Craftsman Truck Series to the Sprint Cup, completely bypassing the Busch Series, which was designed to be a developmental circuit for young drivers.

"I would have liked to have had the opportunity to experience racing in the Busch Series," Busch told me during his 2004 Cup championship-winning season, "but when you're called to move up to the Cup level, you can't tell them no. I think racing Busch would only have served to make me an even better driver, but you go when and where you're called."

Regardless of a driver's age, NASCAR should mandate that new professional drivers spend a minimum of one year full-time in the

Truck Series and two years full-time in the Nationwide Series—or at least two years full-time on the Nationwide circuit without any time in a truck—before moving to the Sprint Cup competition. Although it's hard not to bring up prodigies like KyBusch (a nickname I gave him in 2007) or Logano as examples of drivers who shouldn't be excluded from the highest level of racing, most drivers need to learn the sport at a much slower pace. I firmly believe that this will only serve to make them better racers in the long run. If guys like KyBusch or Logano are truly as good as people say, is it really going to hurt anything to make them wait a few years before making it in the big time?

I'd even be willing to make a compromise of sorts for those who think that young drivers should have an unimpeded route straight to the Cup, no matter what their age or previous racing experience. If, for example, a driver finishes in the top ten in the Truck Series in his first year and in the top ten in the Nationwide Series the next season, I'd be willing to waive his second year in Nationwide and make him eligible to jump to the Cup.

In addition to giving more drivers much-needed seat time, my system will also help to decrease today's dearth of young drivers. Even if their talent level isn't necessarily up to par, so many young drivers are being pushed through the pipeline so quickly for reasons like good looks (for sponsorship opportunities) or their ability to bring considerable sponsorship money to the table that they're not getting the full NASCAR experience. At the very least, they're not paying their dues like most of their fellow racers.

Logano is a perfect example. He was already in the developmental pipeline for Joe Gibbs Racing, which intended to slowly bring along his development and progress to the Cup Series. But when Tony Stewart announced that he was leaving Gibbs to become co-owner of another team after 2008, Gibbs decided to take its lumps and give Logano an ordeal in 2009 that it thought would make him a better driver in the long run. That may be true, but I still don't think that the Sprint Cup Series is a training ground where a kid should earn his stripes. By the time a driver gets to the Sprint Cup, he should have already earned those stripes—and then some.

# CHECKERED FLAG

## NASCAR's Future

# How Did Dale Earnhardt's Death Change NASCAR Forever?

There are few dates in NASCAR history more memorable and more tragic than February 18, 2001, the day that changed the sport forever. On the final lap of the Daytona 500, with the finish line just a few hundred feet away, one of the greatest drivers in stock car racing history lost his life in a wreck that seemed fairly mundane and routine, by NASCAR crash standards.

Dozens, if not hundreds, of drivers had walked away from similar wrecks over the years. But not this time; the sport's then biggest star, Ralph Dale Earnhardt, lost his life just two months before his fiftieth birthday while driving his No. 3 Goodwrench Chevrolet. NASCAR's Superman, the larger-than-life superstar both beloved and reviled for a driving style that earned him one of the most powerful nicknames in all of sports—The Intimidator—was gone.

Fighting back tears and looking somber, NASCAR president Mike Helton shocked the world when he announced in a hastily called press conference less than two hours after the wreck, "We've lost Dale Earnhardt." It was a day that would go down in NASCAR's annals as the darkest day ever. Other drivers had tragically lost their lives in the past, but none of them had ever come even close to Earnhardt's stature.

To NASCAR fans, this event produced the same kind of stunned reaction and lingering fallout as the 1977 death of the king of rock 'n' roll, Elvis Presley. Public mourning occurred throughout the country, but most notably at Daytona and Earnhardt's Garage Majal, the Mooresville, North Carolina, headquarters of Dale Earnhardt Inc. Thousands of floral arrangements and gifts adorned makeshift altars built to memorialize Earnhardt. Fans flock there to this very day to commiserate, bond, and remember Earnhardt and his legacy.

Earnhardt was the fourth driver to be killed in a span of nine months. Busch Grand National rookie Adam Petty (the grandson of Richard Petty and the son of Kyle Petty), veteran Cup driver Kenny Irwin, and Craftsman Truck Series driver Tony Roper all perished in wrecks not long before Earnhardt's. Yet NASCAR failed to act over these deaths. With Earnhardt's death, however, it went into crisis mode, determined not to let something like that happen again.

Why did Earnhardt's death prompt action from the sanctioning body, but the others that preceded him prompted little else than sympathy? Petty, Irwin, and Roper were part of the NASCAR racing community, yet they were unlike Earnhardt in one key way: they weren't superstars, and he was the biggest superstar in the game.

Granted, Earnhardt was no longer in his prime as a driver, but he still had a lot of gas left in his tank. In fact, he finished second in the 2000 Cup season final standings at age forty-nine. He could have become the first eight-time champion in Cup history that season, rather than Bobby Labonte winning the title.

Since his first full-time season in the Winston Cup Series in 1979, Earnhardt finished outside the top ten just twice in his Cup career, and he never finished a season lower than 12th. Earnhardt was the Babe Ruth, the Johnny Unitas, the Wilt Chamberlain, and the Wayne Gretzky of his sport. He was NASCAR's most valuable player, so to speak. He was in a class of his own: he had more impact and influence over the sport and its leader (Bill France Jr.) than anyone else (even more than Richard Petty had over Bill France Sr. at the height of his popularity).

Earnhardt was one of the first to realize the multimillions of dollars to be made in licensed memorabilia from places like Action Performance Inc., which manufactured a number of products, most notably fine and precise diecast models of cars that typically sold for fifty dollars or more. Earnhardt once joked that he could make more money by retiring from racing and living on the proceeds of his souvenirs because he was that popular.

Earnhardt's death not only shook the sport of race car driving, it shook the world of sports as a whole. It also confirmed that NASCAR truly had a star system of sorts, which can be quite detracting to less talented or less successful drivers in the long run.

Furthermore, if Earnhardt had not perished in his fateful wreck, what do you think are the chances that NASCAR would have made all the safety innovations that followed Earnhardt's death? I bet zero or, at most, very little. This is just another illustration of what Earnhardt's bigger-than-life personality and significance to the sport meant. NASCAR saw that there truly was a huge flaw in its safety composition, and the sanctioning body followed through with serious action.

The biggest change since Earnhardt's death has been a nearly fanatical approach to safety, including the implementation of SAFER (steel and foam energy reduction) barriers—impact-absorbing material that cushions and reduces the blow and crushing of a car into a wall—and the mandating of head-and-neck restraint (HANS) devices.

NASCAR began using data recorders, similar to the black boxes installed in airplanes, to record information within a race car and then be able to study the data to make further safety advances. There has also been the implementation of the Car of Tomorrow, the most state-of-the-art, high-tech stock car ever designed with driver safety in mind.

But even beyond inspiring these safety precautions, the loss of Earnhardt changed the dynamic of the sport. NASCAR's biggest star and leader was forever silenced, and no other driver has stepped to the fore to be the sport's leader and number one advocate, with the possible exception of young Kyle Busch. No other driver, except for Busch and maybe Tony Stewart, has the character and villainesque persona that Earnhardt had. Perhaps even more important, no driver had NASCAR's ear as Earnhardt did. If something didn't seem right with the sport, Earnhardt made damn sure that Bill France Jr. got a piece of his mind. Even though NASCAR has never had a drivers' union, Earnhardt was perhaps the closest thing to a labor leader for the rank-and-file drivers.

Unfortunately, although many of Earnhardt's fans eventually fell into lockstep and began cheering for his son, Dale Jr., other longtime fans seemed lost or disenchanted with the sport, to the point that they eventually began to lose interest. That can readily be seen in the way that TV ratings and attendance have steadily declined more than 20 percent since 2006.

An indirect result of Earnhardt's death has been the transition from Bill France Jr. to his son, Brian, who took over as chairman and CEO in October 2003. The youngest France has incurred the wrath of fans more in his first six years of leadership than his father did in over thirty years at the helm of the sanctioning body. Brian France has changed so much in the sport in the name of "progress" that it's no wonder so many fans have left under his watch. They like familiarity and feel comfortable with the routine. They don't like to have new formats, gimmicks, and nearly constant change. This fact seems to be lost on France, who always seems to have yet another trick up his sleeve.

Perhaps the best analogy I can offer is something Jeff Burton said a few years ago. When asked what would Earnhardt think of the current state of NASCAR, Burton, as he often does, succinctly summed things up, saying, "Things wouldn't be this way if Earnhardt were still here, I can promise you that." Truer words were never spoken.

# What Will NASCAR Look Like in Five to Ten Years?

NASCAR, 2015 to 2020. I predict that the sport will look significantly different from a number of angles, including geography, driver makeup, and particularly the front office. Here are the ten things that I think will happen:

1. Brian France will be long gone as chairman and CEO (he'll most likely be running an NFL team somewhere, especially if Los Angeles ever gets a team again), and current president Mike Helton will be retired. So who will wind up leading NASCAR? The first female CEO and commissioner of any professional sports league: Brian's kid sister, current International Speedway Corporation chairwoman and CEO, Lesa France Kennedy. She's got the intelligence, the business acumen, and, perhaps most

important, the genes to be the next France in line to run the family business.

2. Dale Earnhardt Jr. will finally give up as a competitive driver around 2015 and will segue into a full-time Sprint Cup team owner, having previously upgraded his JR Motorsports organization from a Nationwide Series operation to a Sprint Cup team in 2012. Whether Junior leaves Hendrick Motorsports to drive for himself remains to be seen. In a sense, Earnhardt will follow in the footsteps of his late father's former boss, Richard Childress, who gave up competitive driving to have the elder Earnhardt drive for him, a pairing that eventually led to six Cup championships. Unfortunately, Dale Jr. the owner will continue to struggle for success from atop the pit box as much as he struggled behind the wheel for most of his driving career.

3. The road courses in Watkins Glen, New York, and Sonoma, California, will be gone from the Sprint Cup schedule by 2015, to be replaced by a second yearly race at Kansas Speedway and a race in the either the New York or the Denver area. Don't be surprised if Las Vegas also gets a second yearly race at that point, with a race date potentially coming from an existing track like Atlanta, Pocono, or Martinsville. Although road courses have some allure, the fan base at a bigger track means more fans, more media attention, and, ultimately, more money in NASCAR's coffers.

4. NASCAR will finally realize its dream of having a racetrack in the New York City area. It is likely to be a .75-mile or a .875-mile track, very similar to Richmond International Raceway. We've talked about this topic at length earlier in this book.

5. Fox TV, TNT, ESPN, and ABC will continue to split the majority of telecasting duties, but probably at an equal or lower price tag. When the current eight-year, $4.8 billion broadcast contract ends in 2014, the rights fees paid to NASCAR will most likely stay level or even be reduced, since NASCAR in 2014 will be nowhere near the popularity level that it was in 2006, before the severe recession and when the most recent TV contract went into effect. You'll also probably see shorter term lengths

for future broadcast contracts, perhaps only four or five years rather than the previous contract of eight years, as TV networks become more reluctant to sign long-term deals with pro sports leagues due to the economic commitment and shrinking profits. NASCAR still sells, it has just become a much harder sell.

6. After retiring as a driver in 2015, Tony Stewart will become the premier team owner in the sport, earning two more Cup titles while still a driver and two others as a team owner. One will come from Ryan Newman, and the other from a driver like Kasey Kahne or Kevin Harvick, if they eventually defect to Stewart Haas Racing. Rick Hendrick's multicar organization will go through a severe drought after 2011, despite Jimmie Johnson remaining in the fold and Jeff Gordon postponing retirement until closer to 2020, followed by Dale Earnhardt Jr. leaving the organization to start his own Cup team in 2012. And Richard Childress will retire and leave the sport somewhere around 2016 to go hunting and fishing on a full-time basis.

7. Sprint will leave the sport after its ten-year contract as series title rights holder expires at the end of 2013. Verizon will be among the companies that look to succeed Sprint, but don't be surprised if Toyota significantly ups its game and becomes the series' number one sponsor. Unfortunately, the *Verizon Cup* and the *Toyota Cup* just don't have such a great ring to them. It would mean that in less than twenty years, NASCAR will have gone from Winston Cup to Nextel Cup to Sprint Cup to some other Cup.

8. If the Chase for the Sprint Cup continues to have the reduced fan interest that we saw from 2006 to 2009, it could eventually see some significant revisions, if not outright elimination. We already saw one change in 2009, when Atlanta, one of the original cities for the Chase in its first five years, gave up its date in the play-offs to Auto Club Speedway of Southern California, which had not been in the Chase previously. The move was designed to prop up sagging attendance for both. If the Chase continues to have ebbs and flows in the next few years, don't be surprised if we once again see the format revamped. Although the Chase was a unique and innovative idea when it was first

announced, and it played out perfectly in its first year, it will forever be judged against that first edition. Also, if Sprint does not renew its sponsorship of the series in 2014, a new series sponsor could dictate other changes in the Chase format, including its eventual demise.

9. As the economy slowly begins to recover and fans start coming back to the racetracks and watching the races on TV, NASCAR remains far from its heyday of the late 1990s until 2005. Its eight-year TV deal with Fox, ESPN, ABC, and Turner expires at the end of 2014, and even though race dates have been moved to more popular venues, a movement is building to shrink the schedule to give races more meaning and significance. In other words, quantity would be replaced by quality. Don't be surprised if the new TV deal in 2015 consists of a thirty-two race season rather than the current thirty-six. One other thing to look for is the shrinking of most race weekends from three to two days, thus giving the fans more bang for their buck, saving them money on travel, hotel rooms, and the like. That movement actually began to take place in 2010 and should likely continue to expand to almost all races on the schedule in the coming years.

10. Somewhere in the next ten years, don't be surprised if either the Nationwide or the Camping World Truck series is eliminated for financial reasons. While having three different series was a boon to the sport in its most popular era, the reality of reduced sponsorship and the constriction and merging of existing ownership groups will make it nearly impossible for small teams to survive or for new ownership groups to come into the sport, particularly in the lower-tier series. Sooner or later, something is going to have to give, and one of those two series is likely to fall by the wayside. In addition, watch for NASCAR to form a link with the Indy Racing League to have doubleheader weekends at selected venues, with Indy essentially taking over as the undercard in several Sprint Cup races to fill the void after the demise of either the Nationwide or the Truck series.

# What Track Was NASCAR's Best Save?

Had it not been for a concerted effort by veteran NASCAR officials and the community as a whole, South Carolina's Darlington Raceway would have become the latest member of the extinct racetracks club. When NASCAR moved the annual Labor Day race that had been the providence of Darlington's legendary Southern 500 to California Speedway in 2005, it set off a firestorm of protests from longtime fans as well as from the Darlington and Florence, South Carolina, communities.

Darlington was still left with one race date, which NASCAR promptly moved to what was typically the worst weekend of the race season: Mother's Day weekend. It was adding insult to injury. Getting rid of the Labor Day event was one thing, but to be saddled with the worst weekend of the year only served to further incense race fans.

But you know what? Darlington has turned lemons into lemonade. It sold out its first five Mother's Day weekend races through 2009, which are held on Saturday night. In addition, more than $20 million in improvements has been pumped into the track, creating 6,000 new seats (2005), an extensive repaving job, a new infield tunnel, and enhanced amenities (all in 2007).

"Looking at the monies that ISC [International Speedway Corporation] has put into that track, I don't think they're going to go away until they get their money back," Richard Petty said with a laugh. "It's not a deal where they're going to improve it and then go away next week. It cements in my mind that it means they're going to have a race there of some kind for a long time, and I feel good about that part of it. It's been part of NASCAR's history and part of the Petty history. Hopefully, it continues for a long time."

Darlington is arguably the most unique track on the circuit. The 1.366-mile facility, known as both the Lady in Black and the Track Too Tough to Tame, is a throwback to NASCAR's origins. Darlington not only was NASCAR's first superspeedway, it was the first paved racetrack to join the Grand National Series shortly after it opened in 1950. Only Martinsville Speedway, the shortest track in NASCAR (.526-mile) is older, having opened one year earlier.

The story of Darlington is yet another example of great NASCAR lore. Local Darlington businessman Harold Brasington attended the Indianapolis 500 in 1933, then returned to rural Darlington intent upon building a Dixie version of Indianapolis.

It took him sixteen years and lots of dreaming, but Brasington was a determined man. The local people called his idea for a racetrack in the middle of cotton fields "Harold's folly." In 1949, he borrowed some bulldozers and earthmovers, recruited some friends and family members, and proceeded to carve out a 1.25-mile oval of sorts. The only problem was that Brasington's vision—his eyesight, that is, not his outlook on what the track should be—wasn't the greatest. Instead of working from blueprints, he worked from sight lines. Compounding the problem was that he had to squeeze his track into an odd-shaped seventy-five-acre parcel of land that he had purchased from an adjacent farm.

The sightlines and the necessity to shoehorn the track into place caused Brasington to come up with an odd, egg-shaped oval, where none of its four turns are the same. As a result, since it opened in 1950, Darlington has proven to be the most confounding track for drivers and crew chiefs. Even with several subsequent repavings and the eventual lengthening of the track to its current 1.366-mile circumference, Darlington truly is still the Track Too Tough to Tame.

It's the only track in NASCAR where drivers who *don't* hit the wall are the exception rather than the rule. Darlington's odd shape and unusual degree in the turns have led to yet another legacy, that of the "Darlington stripe," in which drivers invariably sideswipe the Lady in Black's white walls at least once, if not several times, in a race. In fact, Darlington's maintenance office is forced to repaint the white walls after each race—and sometimes even after an especially grueling practice session before race day—to hide the paint and tire transfers that rub off when the cars skim along its walls.

"Of all the racetracks I've ever run, it's probably the most unpredictable because of the surface, the time of day, and the weather," Richard Petty said. "It's just been a very, very demanding racetrack. It's probably the toughest track to run on a consistent basis, and it was also a very frustrating racetrack. No matter how much you thought you had it figured out, it wasn't always that way."

Darlington may have lost its signature Labor Day weekend event after more than half a century, but I'm telling you that the Lady in Black still looks pretty damn good, even with a face-lift. She's got a new lease on what I hope will be a very long life.

## Are Today's Young Guns Not as Good as Young Drivers from Past Eras?

During NASCAR's first fifty years, the true gauge of whether a young, promising driver was ready for the sport's highest level, the Cup Series, was based almost exclusively on his amount of talent and his past competitiveness in smaller racing series. But for much of the last decade, the sport has settled into a new era of young drivers, complete with a new and different set of "rules" on who, how, and what to be.

Talent is still an element, but you might be surprised at how much the level of expertise has dropped since about 1999 and has been replaced by intangibles that don't necessarily have a lot to do with racing per se: good looks, marketability for potential sponsors (and ad campaigns that can be built around a good-looking, intelligent-sounding young driver), and, in some instances, how much sponsorship money a driver can bring with him to his new Cup home and team.

Gillette went so far as to create a wildly popular promotion called "the Gillette Young Guns," which featured several young and budding superstars, including Ryan Newman, Kasey Kahne, Dale Earnhardt Jr., Clint Bowyer, Carl Edwards, Denny Hamlin, Matt Kenseth, and Kurt and Kyle Busch. The crop of Young Guns has changed since the promotion began in 2004, but the concept is still the same: to feature good-looking, successful, young drivers persuading impressionable consumers to buy Gillette products.

Unfortunately, many of today's "young guns" (in the generic sense, rather than the Gillette campaign participants) are a different breed. They seem more concerned about themselves alone and their accomplishments rather than being part of a team concept.

During my four-and-a-half-year tenure (July 2004 to January 2009) with Yahoo! Sports as its national NASCAR columnist, I wrote extensively about the various young guns in the sport. In particular was one column I wrote on March 29, 2005, which generated some of the largest amount of feedback (thousands of e-mails) that I have ever received for anything I've written. It was about young Cup drivers and how they perceive the sport today, where they fit in, and how they are different from their predecessors.

I thought I'd include that piece in this section, because it illustrates what some of NASCAR's young guns were like in 2005 and what many of them were still like in 2010:

### Respecting NASCAR

NASCAR's so-called young guns have taken the Cup series by storm in recent years. It's the arrival of a new generation in the sport, a generation which many believe doesn't have the same grasp of NASCAR's history and culture as do the sport's retired stars or older veterans.

Today, young drivers often hit the pavement running. Just barely removed from racing sprint cars or midgets or trucks, they are given strong cars and are expected to make an immediate impact—and often they do.

But with the allure of fast cars, fast speeds, and fast money, many of these young drivers quickly fall prey to critics if they become outspoken or don't show respect toward the more than five decades of NASCAR history and tradition that has preceded them.

"I don't know if they really realize the opportunity that this is, to run in this series," veteran driver Terry Labonte said.

All too often, young drivers bring criticism upon themselves with their swagger and aloofness. Instead of wondering how they can make the sport better, many often display a "what's in it for me?" attitude.

One recent instance was the feud that began late last season at Martinsville between teammates Rusty Wallace and Ryan Newman. Wallace was going for the win and Newman wasn't going to give an inch, teammate or not, which immediately drew Wallace's ire. The ill feelings lasted through the off-season.

Some critics said Newman wasn't respecting his elder or the tradition of the sport, where young drivers are supposed to be subservient to their older and more experienced counterparts. Others castigated the South Bend, Ind., native for disrespecting one of the drivers upon which NASCAR's unprecedented success was built.

Even Wallace, never one to mince words, couldn't believe how a driver he helped bring into Cup racing would try to bite the hand that feeds him.

"I just don't understand some of the young kids today in racing," Wallace said. "It's almost like they've got no respect for teammates or other drivers who've been here for 15 or 20 years."

The feud between the aging veteran and one of NASCAR's budding young superstars eventually died down. But it also raised the issue about whether today's young guns truly realize and value NASCAR's roots.

"There are some young kids who come in and don't really realize what this sport means or where it came from," legendary driver Richard Petty said. "They don't appreciate the history of NASCAR and stock car racing."

But many of today's young drivers actually have become students of the sport and its rich history.

"As you come into a sport, I think you have an obligation to learn about your sport, and especially as you become more defined in a sport and a champion, you need to understand what went around before your time and respect that," Jimmie Johnson said.

Even Newman pays homage to NASCAR's past, his battle with Wallace notwithstanding.

"Petty Enterprises, the Wood Brothers, David Pearson had something like 17 straight poles—there's a lot of respect that goes into thinking about somebody like that, as well as what they've done," Newman said. "Leonard Wood comes up to me and talks about old cars sometimes, Richard Petty and I talk about certain situations.

"I appreciate so much being able to have those people around still and respect what they've done and where they've made this sport and the respect the fans have for this sport because of them. It's not just those two guys or those two teams, it's all of what NASCAR used to be, and I think it's important to continue that outlook from the fans as well as everybody else involved with NASCAR."

### Friends and Mentors

Even though there is nearly 40 years between them, Newman, 27, has developed a strong friendship with legendary driver Buddy Baker, 64. Not only are they neighbors, but Baker also has become a mentor to Newman and is one of the first individuals Newman seeks out when he needs advice or guidance.

"Buddy has been a great part of my NASCAR career," Newman said. "I'm not afraid to go ask him about a shock or spring or racetrack or person or how to approach the fans, anything like that. He's a great go-to person for me, just like Rusty is and a lot of other people about what's the right thing to do and what's the wrong thing to do."

Tony Stewart has a similar relationship with another NASCAR legend—Red Farmer, one of the original members of the so-called "Alabama Gang." Stewart, 33, calls Farmer, 72, "my old fishing buddy," as the two spend several days a year together just enjoying each other's company.

"Red's a neat guy," Stewart said. "A lot of times, we don't even talk about racing. But he's also a big connection to NASCAR's past, and I try to learn as much as I can from him, not only about the sport but life in general, too. How can you not want to learn from or respect a guy like that?"

Veteran drivers like Ricky Rudd, who has been racing a Cup car for nearly 30 years, envy today's young drivers because they come into the sport and generally do just what they're hired to do: drive. It was different in Rudd's early days, when a young driver also had to be a mechanic—or learn real fast on the job—because there were no organizations that had 200 or 300 employees like those found today in the monolithic Roush, Hendrick, and Childress camps.

"It was a different time when I came into it," Rudd said. "There were many guys with talent that didn't make it, because back when I got going in the mid '70s, I wasn't a mechanic by trade, but I had to learn to be a mechanic. The small part of your job was learning how to drive cars; the big part was learning how to work on them and set them up so they could be competitive. It's not like that today."

Some young drivers like defending Nextel Cup champion Kurt Busch, 26, actually were raised in an environment that valued NASCAR's heritage.

"I have a very nostalgic father who has helped me understand what this sport means," Busch said. "Things like Richard Petty's championships, or to see some of the nicknames like David Pearson's 'The Silver Fox' and to see what Cale Yarborough did to win the championship in '76, '77, and '78, to win the championship three years in a row—that's never been done before."

Busch's younger brother, Kyle, 19, wasn't even around for much of NASCAR's golden era of racing, namely the period from the early 1960s through the mid '80s. Still, he collects old tapes of TV broadcasts and other memorabilia to educate himself on the significance of the past.

"I've always enjoyed the past with David Pearson and Richard Petty against each other, Cale Yarborough, all the greats like that, Dale Earnhardt and Darrell Waltrip getting into it with each other, Geoff Bodine the first driver for Hendrick Motorsports," Kyle Busch said. "There's a tremendous amount of history out there that's great to remember and great to see. Now, we're making the next chapter of that history in the 2000-plus era."

There are young drivers like Casey Mears who come into NASCAR with a less than lengthy stock car racing resume. Having been raised in a family of open wheel drivers, including his four-time Indy 500-winning uncle Rick Mears, the younger Mears was a bit taken aback when he entered the world of Cup racing in 2003.

"When I stepped in my first year, I probably didn't appreciate what stock cars had been like in the past and all the history and what guys have done, because I was more focused on the open wheel kind of thing," Mears said. "I've grown to appreciate it more and learn and understand because it's been fun. I've had an opportunity to hang out and talk to guys like Richard Petty and Benny Parsons, and you just learn from being around them. Richard's right about needing to know about NASCAR's history and tradition."

One of the things Mears—as well as many of his contemporaries—enjoy most is listening to war stories told by old timers. It gives young drivers a first-person account of what NASCAR used to be and how it developed into the mega-sport it is today.

"It's cool to sit around with some of the older drivers talking about the way it used to be," Mears said. "I could sit and listen to those stories forever."

Added Jamie McMurray, "You listen to the stories and you don't understand how that even could have happened with the way the sport is today."

As so many drivers with links to NASCAR's past begin to fade away—including Bill Elliott and Terry Labonte into semi-retirement, and Rusty Wallace and Mark Martin in their final seasons as Cup drivers this year—today's young drivers not only are witnessing the next chapter of NASCAR's tradition and history, they're the ones who are writing it for future racing generations.

"To go into the museums such as Daytona USA, the International Motorsports Hall of Fame in Talladega, Ala., it means a tremendous amount," Kurt Busch said. "It's up to us drivers presently to help reflect back on to the past and what those pioneers anchored for us. It's a privilege, an honor, a unique feeling."

# Where Should NASCAR Go Next, Globally?

Because of the global economic recession, NASCAR's expansion plans both nationally and internationally have essentially been shelved indefinitely. But like a good Boy Scout, NASCAR must always be prepared, in case the economy improves sufficiently to start entertaining expansion thoughts again.

Where does NASCAR go from here? When does it pull out of mediocre markets and tracks that are currently hosting Sprint Cup events and move to promising new markets in the United States and elsewhere?

Although NASCAR will likely expand first in the United States—a topic we've covered elsewhere in this book—let's now break down the most obvious international venues and see which ones have a chance and which don't:

**Canada.** You don't have to go very far to find what could be perhaps the most fertile international market for NASCAR racing, particularly the marquee Sprint Cup Series. Ever since NASCAR acquired CASCAR, its sanctioning-body counterpart north of the border, in 2006, there has been more and more movement into Canada. First came a new Nationwide Series road course event in Montreal in 2007, which was repeated in 2008 and 2009. NASCAR has had additional road course and even temporary street course races dangled in its face, not only in Montreal but also in Toronto and Vancouver. If and when NASCAR expands outside the United States for the Sprint Cup Series, Canada is numero uno on the map. I'm convinced that international expansion will happen eventually. The question is how long it will take, even though it's simply just a hop, skip, and a jump north of the border.

**Japan.** As strange as it may sound, a track actually has a decent chance of being built in Japan somewhere down the road. A select group of NASCAR drivers visited the Land of the Rising Sun for three consecutive years (1996–1998) for exhibition races. Unfortunately, much as in Mexico, attendance waned, and NASCAR did not renew its three-year contract. With the current economic woes of the world, it would take a lot for a Japanese promoter or company to court NASCAR again, unless a Japanese driver somehow found his way into the Cup Series. Still, I believe that NASCAR will eventually return to Japan in the next seven to ten years. And with the economic involvement of General Motors and Chrysler having been scaled way back in 2009, where else would we find eventual replacements? Japan, of course. Toyota is already a big player in the Sprint Cup, Nationwide, and Camping World series. As a result, we may see Honda (the most likely), Nissan, and perhaps even Korean automaker Kia join Toyota as foreign auto manufacturers in NASCAR. If that's the case, I guarantee that this would eventually lead to at least one manufacturer-sponsored, points-paying race. I can just see it now: the Toyota 500!

**Germany.** There was actually quite a bit of talk in 2005 and 2006 about taking NASCAR to Germany. The plan was to host as many as two exhibition races there, with the most likely venues being Berlin and Munich. Don't forget, there are many U.S. soldiers stationed in that country who are big NASCAR fans. Unfortunately, the recent economic woes nipped that possibility in the bud pretty quickly. But just as with Japan, if the economy gets back to where it once was, guys like Dale Earnhardt Jr. and Tony Stewart may want to take a quick Berlitz class in German.

**United Kingdom.** Britain—and London in particular—was considered around the same time that Germany was. There was talk about running two exhibition events in the British Isles, but that idea died far sooner than the idea of racing in Germany did. Even though the British are very similar to fervent race fans here in the United States, I'm not completely convinced that Queen Elizabeth, Prince Charles, and the rest of the royal family would necessarily be waiting with arms open wide. What could happen is ten current Cup teams putting on a one-race exhibition in the United Kingdom, but as far as the country being a potential site for expansion, as they say in England, that would be bonkers, old chap!

**Australia.** Costs, costs, costs. Although CART, Champ Car, and the Indy Racing League were welcomed for several years in Surfer's Paradise in Queensland, it's unlikely that Cup cars would run there any time soon or in venues like Sydney and Melbourne. Then again, Marcus Ambrose is from nearby New Zealand, and if he continues to explode upon the Cup scene and becomes a significant factor, I won't be surprised if someone steps forward to offer NASCAR a healthy amount of money to bring some of the best from the United States to the land down under.

**Brazil.** This is actually one of the most likely venues for NASCAR if it were ever to expand the Sprint Cup internationally. There's significant sponsorship money available, and the country has weathered the economic crisis of the past few years fairly well, which is part of the reason it was awarded the 2016 Summer Olympics. Since Juan Pablo Montoya comes from Colombia, I'm convinced that South Americans would turn out to see such a race, if only for the novelty factor. The problem for Brazil and most of the other international venues is where NASCAR would actually race. Face it, NASCAR-style speedways outside the United States are few and far between, and those that are currently in existence are several steps below NASCAR-quality racing. This means that NASCAR might have to consider more road courses similar to Watkins Glen and Infineon in Sonoma, or, God forbid, running on temporary street courses if it's to significantly increase its international reach.

**Mexico.** NASCAR's initial foray into Mexico with the Busch Series was a resounding success, but things didn't remain that way for the succeeding three events. By the fourth and final race in Mexico in 2008, the crowd went from about 140,000 in 2005 to roughly 60,000. Unless some very wealthy Mexican company or individual steps forward to promote and underwrite the cost, NASCAR is not likely to take the Sprint Cup south of the border any time soon—if ever.

# Why Has the Media Snubbed NASCAR in Recent Years?

NASCAR bills itself as the second largest spectator sport in the country—a claim that many would challenge—but you wouldn't know it by the dramatic decline in the media coverage of NASCAR in recent years. All motorsports media coverage has suffered a significant decline, but NASCAR seems to have suffered the most. It's not a good reflection of its status as the largest form of motorsports in the country and its self-proclaimed belief that it's the second-largest spectator sport in the country behind the NFL.

I have personally been affected by this issue, because I and my fellow NASCAR writer were laid off by Yahoo! Sports (Yahoo.com) at the end of 2008. The reason we were given was that the number of readers was not enough to justify the cost of two salaries as well as roughly $150,000 in combined travel expenses each season. Yahoo! chose to significantly reduce its NASCAR content and make deals with other content providers, primarily those that offer video, even though Yahoo! was the second most visited destination for NASCAR-related news in the world. Yahoo! constantly outdrew ESPN.com and FoxSports.com with its NASCAR coverage. Now it gets video and editorial copy from those content providers, and they bear all the out-of-pocket travel expenses.

Nor is this the only example. Respected newspapers like the *Atlanta Journal Constitution*, the *Fort Worth Star-Telegram*, the *Kansas City Star*, the *Miami Herald*, and the *Orlando Sentinel* jumped on the "get rid of NASCAR coverage" bandwagon, putting a lot of quality writers out of work. It's a lot cheaper for newspapers and Web sites to simply use coverage from the Associated Press (AP), which covers all the races.

There have also been certain newspaper sports editors who have adopted a "What's in it for me?" approach toward giving NASCAR ink. I know of one case in particular at one of the nation's largest newspapers, where the sports editor would not allow his reporter to write about certain drivers or teams unless their sponsors purchased ads in the paper. That reporter eventually decided to leave the paper because he couldn't work under those stifling and greedy conditions. When an editor doesn't like NASCAR, there's not really a lot you can do, much to the chagrin of the sanctioning body and, more important, the fans. And he wonders why his newspaper's circulation, like most other papers, has dropped significantly in recent years.

But NASCAR also has itself to blame somewhat for the media mess it finds itself in. It too often played favorites, giving exclusives to favored reporters—usually those at the largest newspapers or wire services. It also was often overly restrictive, putting limits on photographers and, to a lesser extent, writers. It also limited the prized issuance of "hard cards," which are media credentials that allowed a reporter to attend every NASCAR race in a season.

When NASCAR partnered with the *Sporting News* in 2006 to establish the *Sporting News* NASCAR Wire Service, the intent was to offer free, quality content to media outlets that didn't cover the sport on a regular basis or those that sought an alternative to the AP's usually dry and to-the-point-with-very-little-flair kind of coverage.

But as more and more newspapers began cutting back on coverage or laying off motorsports writers, the new wire service became more popular—even though its content far too often appeared to be pro-NASCAR, with nary a negative mention of the sport or some of the controversy that crept up in recent years: Mauricia Grant's sexual discrimination case (settled out of court), Jeremy Mayfield's suspension for alleged drug use, and similar situations.

In the next few years, the media landscape in NASCAR is going to change even more. With racetrack media centers and press rooms often less than half full, NASCAR is embarking on a path that has already been paved by other pro sports leagues: expanding its media reach from an internal rather than an external approach.

Much like baseball's MLB.com and football's NFL.com, which each has its own dedicated staff of "writers" and broadcasters whose salaries are paid for by their respective leagues, NASCAR is following suit by further expanding its in-house NASCAR Media Group.

During construction of the NASCAR Hall of Fame, the NASCAR Media Group made a multimillion-dollar investment in state-of-the-art facilities, including two TV studios that would rival those at ESPN or any other network. The media group has also sizably increased its staff in the last couple of years, with additional media offerings in TV, radio, print, Web sites, and other platforms reportedly in the works.

The biggest change that is likely is the rumored start of what is commonly being referred to as the NASCAR Network. Supposedly patterned after the professional baseball and football networks, the NASCAR Network is reportedly to start by 2012 as some type of pay-for-play enterprise. How that will work with NASCAR's current broadcasting contracts with Fox, Turner, ESPN, and ABC, which collectively do not expire until after 2014, remains to be seen.

There's also a planned expansion of in-house radio and Web products by both Motor Racing Network and RacingOne.com, which are both owned by NASCAR. The affiliated NASCAR.com, owned by Turner Networks (which owns CNN, Headline News, TBS, and TNT), also has expansion plans in place.

NASCAR has maintained a somewhat hands-off policy with NASCAR.com, allowing its writers full discretion in what they choose to write about. That's why most NASCAR.com stories, particularly columns, carry disclaimers like "the opinions expressed are solely those of the writer," much like NFL.com and MLB.com do with their writers' stories and columns.

Another significant change that began late in 2009 was NASCAR's acceptance and reaching out to what it calls "citizen journalists." That phrase encompasses professional and amateur bloggers, allowing them access to races and drivers and even providing hard cards for many.

NASCAR realizes that the media landscape has changed dramatically in the last few years and is trying to keep in step with it by embracing individuals and groups that only five years ago it might have snubbed or banished. But with so little media coverage, it has to find a way to reach out to those who have an interest in the sport.

"NASCAR has the hardest-working media in all of sports," NASCAR chairman and CEO Brian France said when the citizen corps was first announced in June 2009. "We will continue to rely on the traditional media to cover the sport on a day-to-day basis, but as the media world changes, so must NASCAR. It's fair to say that NASCAR fans are vocal about the sport and have something to say. We want to embrace that spirit and ensure they have the best access to better have their voices heard."

Will the changes be good for the sport? I think so, although I admit I do have some concerns that NASCAR's selection process will restrict coverage to Web sites or blogs that are deemed worthy of being included in the "NASCAR Citizen Journalists Media Corps." That selection process includes professionalism, reporting, commentary, and use of social networking tools such as MySpace, Facebook, and YouTube.

I fear that if a writer is routinely critical or writes negatively about the sport—even if the motive is to try to make the sport better—that his or her access will be pulled for what NASCAR deems as overly critical or negative reporting. This idea truly scares me; I have been one of NASCAR's biggest critics over the years, but only because I love the sport so much and want to see it regain its stature and popularity in the sports landscape.

"Many of these outlets have covered NASCAR from afar for many years," said Ramsay Poston, the managing director of NASCAR's communications (public relations) department, "but now they have the opportunity to cover the sport up close and personal. The 'citizen journalists' will have the very same access as the traditional media, including credentials to race events, access to media centers, press boxes, press conferences, teleconferences, news releases, video, audio, photos, stats, and graphics. We expect the 'citizen journalists' to maintain their journalistic independence and continue to provide unique points of view."

Just as long as they speak favorably about the sport, though, right?

## Should "The Double" Be Brought Back?

The greatest test of man and machine is not competing in either the Indianapolis 500 *or* the Coca-Cola 600, it's competing in both races on the same day. This is known in both the Indy Racing League and NASCAR (the sponsors of these races, respectively) as "The Double."

First a driver would compete in the Indianapolis 500 at noon on the Sunday of Memorial Day weekend, then he would catch a plane to Charlotte to compete in the Coca-Cola 600 at 5:45 p.m.

That's a total of 1,100 miles in eight to nine hours, at speeds of around 220 miles per hour in Indianapolis and 200 miles per hour in Charlotte.

Unfortunately, The Double no longer exists, much to the chagrin of race fans everywhere. When Indianapolis Motor Speedway officials, particularly former chairman Tony George, decided to move the start time of the 2005 Indianapolis 500 from noon to 1 p.m., it essentially ended any chance of drivers being able to compete in both races. Now a driver would need a supersonic jet to be able to make the second race.

One of the reasons the Indianapolis officials changed the time was that they didn't want a 500 winner rushing off right after the race. What would that do to the postrace celebration, which is an important ritual? These officials stubbornly refuse to move the start time back to noon in order to allow The Double to return—although, as of this writing, speculation was rife that the Indy 500 would indeed move up its start time to allow The Double to be viable once again in 2010. I see no logic in their refusal. What true racing fan wouldn't want to see guys like Tony Stewart, Robby Gordon, and John Andretti (who all attempted The Double several times from 1994 to 2004) race not only at Indy but also at Charlotte?

For the record, here are the highlights of The Double:

- John Andretti was the first driver to attempt The Double, finishing 10th at Indianapolis in 1994 and 36th in the 600 (due to a wreck on lap 220 of the 400-lap journey around the track).
- The best single-year performance in The Double was by Tony Stewart, who finished 6th in the 2001 Indianapolis 500, then finished 3rd in the Coca-Cola 600 that night. He also participated in The Double in 1999, finishing 9th in the 500 and 4th in the 600. (If any driver could win The Double, it would be Stewart, and that's probably what scared George into moving the time.)
- Robby Gordon was the last NASCAR regular to attempt The Double. In 2004, he finished 29th in the 500 (due to mechanical failure after 88 of the race's 200 laps) and 20th in the 600 that evening.

- The Double spawned a cottage industry of sorts in which well-heeled fans did their own Double, watching the 500 in Indy and then jetting down to Charlotte for the 600.

Sentiment has been building over the last couple of years because an increasing number of race fans want to see The Double return. The officials at Charlotte have even considered starting their race at 6:30 p.m. in order to once again give drivers enough time to fly from one race to the other. Unfortunately, starting a race that late—given the nature of the 600, its grueling length, and the number of time-consuming cautions due to crashes or debris on the racetrack—is just not logistically realistic. Even though the following day is both the official Memorial Day holiday and a Monday, which gives the fans time to travel home in time to go to work the next day, the idea of not getting out of Charlotte until after midnight is just not feasible.

If enough sponsors (in both series), team owners, and drivers joined together, they might be able to convince the Indianapolis officials that moving the 500 back to noon is for the betterment of all motorsports and for the sake of race fans everywhere. George, the biggest obstacle to date, was ousted in a power struggle in mid-2009. He was very stubborn and didn't share well: he refused to allow anything to detract from the running of the 500, and he did not want to share billing on any stage with the 600. If he had his druthers, things would revert back to the way they used to be: the 600 on Saturday night and the 500 on Sunday afternoon. We can only hope that with the reunification of the open-wheel Indy car series in 2008 and George's ouster in 2009, we'll see The Double return soon.

For the most part, NASCAR officials (with the exception of some team owners, who are concerned what would happen to one of their drivers if he were injured in the 500) welcome the idea of The Double's return. It would mean a thirty-three-car field that could potentially include not only guys like Stewart, Gordon, and Andretti but also former open-wheel drivers who now race in the Sprint Cup, like A. J. Allmendinger, Sam Hornish Jr., Juan Pablo Montoya, and Scott Speed. Why, even Jeff Gordon has expressed an interest in running in the Indianapolis 500 at least once before he retires as a race car driver.

Finally, if Dale Earnhardt Jr. and Danica Patrick could be convinced to try The Double, it would create perhaps the biggest day in motorsports history. TV ratings would go through the roof, both races would be big sellouts (even in a challenging economy), and Formula One, which also races that day, would be huddled in the corner, crying at the good fortune of NASCAR and the Indy Racing League. It's something to think about.

## Should the Sprint Cup Schedule Be Reduced?

I've already written about the Sprint Cup schedule potentially being increased, particularly if NASCAR decides to expand its reach into new geographic markets. So now I'll play devil's advocate and argue for subtracting races rather than adding them.

I'd like to see the schedule cut from thirty-six points-paying events to thirty-four, thirty-two, or even thirty races per year, if it would make the series stronger in the long run. By cutting two to six races from the current schedule, NASCAR could achieve a number of positives:

- Parity would increase, giving the race outcomes more meaning. The fewer races there are, the tighter the competition would be. The position of a driver at the end of each race would become more important, because he would know that he can't rely on extra races to try to right his sinking ship.
- More available race dates would open up, particularly if NASCAR does start expanding into new geographic markets. If one race date each was taken away from Pocono, Martinsville, and perhaps two other tracks, there would immediately be a pool of available dates. Eliminating the weakest races would only strengthen the competitive nature of the schedule, especially with the addition of new venues. Would you rather have a race in New York City with a 100,000 fans or a race in Pocono with 70,000 (on a good day)? To me, it's a no-brainer.

- It would also open the door to adding second races at existing tracks that currently host only one Cup event per season. (See "What Would I Change If I Ran NASCAR?" in the Black Flag section)
- Even though the number of races may increase again once the economy gets better, for now a cutback in race dates would result in cost savings and a less exhausting grind for drivers and other personnel who are currently on the road for thirty-five to forty weeks a year.

Some may not like giving up the extra frequent flyer and frequent hotel points they'd lose, but I'm willing to bet they'd be a lot fresher at the other races they attend.

## Is NASCAR Still a Redneck Sport?

"Born in the South and always a son of the South." That's one of many redneck battle cries, but is it still apropos in NASCAR today? For a sport that was conceived in the South, grew up in the South, and reached its maturity in the South, it's hard to forget those Southern roots even today when you talk about NASCAR.

The sport has expanded nationally, including having its annual awards banquet in New York City from 1981 until 2008, yet there remains a perception among many sports fans that NASCAR-style racing is still a bunch of bootleggers or their kin driving around in circles.

Granted, the story of bootleggers running from "revenuers" with cars full of illegal moonshine and hooch is a colorful one. I never tire of Junior Johnson telling some of his more colorful exploits of running from the cops in his early days before he got busted, sent to prison, and then came out "reformed" as a race car driver.

NASCAR has gone to great lengths in the last decade or so to distance itself from the redneck stereotype. Even though the sanctioning body's corporate headquarters remains in Daytona Beach, Florida, and its Hall of Fame and Museum is in Charlotte, North Carolina, chairman Brian France likes to brag about the sport's diversity.

France points to the fact that since 1990, only two season champions have been born and raised in the South: the late Dale Earnhardt and Dale Jarrett. The others (and where they hailed from) are the late Alan Kulwicki (Wisconsin), Jeff Gordon (California and Indiana), brothers Terry and Bobby Labonte (Texas), Tony Stewart (Indiana), Matt Kenseth (Wisconsin), Kurt Busch (Nevada), and Jimmie Johnson (California).

Yet the stereotype remains, partly due to the fact that many fans want to keep it alive. Go to places like Daytona, Atlanta, Richmond, Charlotte, and especially Talladega, and you'll be hard-pressed not to find at least a few Confederate flags (the symbol of choice for redneck NASCAR fans) flying either in the grounds or from the vehicles that stream in and out of the racetrack.

NASCAR has essentially let the Confederate flag situation rest the last couple of years. Even though France claims that he and the sanctioning body do not condone the display of the flag or what it means, they were highly criticized a few years ago when they tried to force fans who displayed the flag to take it down or remove it from public sight.

NASCAR's intentions are worthy: to distance itself from the vile and hateful symbolism of the Confederate flag (slavery, the Ku Klux Klan, lynchings, and segregation). And even though it might seem ironic that people who claim to be patriotic Americans still want to fly the flag of secessionism, the fact remains that its display is protected by the U.S. Constitution as freedom of speech.

Instead, NASCAR has backed off on fans who display the flag, hoping that they'll eventually be forced by their peers to remove them.

To answer my original question: NASCAR is still a redneck sport of sorts—not so much by the choice of the sanctioning body as by the design of fans who would like the Confederate flag to be our national flag and Lynyrd Skynyrd's "Sweet Home Alabama" our national anthem.

In recent years, Talladega has been the site of several protests by loosely organized groups rallying against the Confederate flag or advocating greater ethnic and racial diversity within the sport.

Unfortunately, these groups have been small, leading the media to dismiss them as just a few disgruntled critics.

Even rednecks laugh at comedian Jeff Foxworthy's "You Might Be a Redneck" jokes and thus at themselves. But it's no laughing matter that NASCAR will be considered a redneck sport by many until it completely distances itself from its redneck roots, redneck history, and lingering redneck sentiment.

# Which Driver Would Make a Good Politician After He Retires from Racing?

Without question, this is one of my favorite debates in this book. In a sport that is extremely political, both internally and externally, in which power brokers and sponsors (just like political lobbyists) often call the shots, it wouldn't surprise me if we eventually saw a well-known driver capitalize on his fame and convert it into votes at the ballot box.

Unfortunately, that aspiration didn't succeed when the sport's most famous driver, Richard Petty, earned the Republican nomination for North Carolina secretary of state in 1996. Many thought Petty would win handily in a state that is both ground zero for NASCAR and the longtime bastion of Republican leadership.

Guess again. Petty suffered arguably one of the worst defeats of his career, and it wasn't behind the wheel of a race car: Democratic nominee Elaine Marshall trounced the man in the trademark Charley One Horse hat. His handlers thought Petty was a slam-dunk win, given his name and his reputation. But what the voters judged him on was political experience, and his total lack of that was his downfall. In addition, Petty had campaigned only occasionally. Petty's biggest mistakes were listening to his handlers and assuming that he'd automatically win because of who he was.

This prompted him to utter one of the most famous lines ever in sports history when he conceded on election night: "If I had known I wasn't going to win, I wouldn't have run."

Not to be deterred, the Republican Party came after Petty to try his hand at another office, possibly state senator or even governor, but King Richard quickly declined, saying he'd prefer to remain stock car royalty and would stick to the empire he knew best.

Looking at today's crop of Sprint Cup drivers, with special emphasis on the older, more veteran types, several drivers come to mind as potential political candidates. But whether they actually would run for office once their racing career is over remains to be seen. Here's my list of the top five drivers who could one day be politicians:

5. **Jeff Gordon.** He is one of the most worldly and level-headed drivers in the garage, but he probably wouldn't want the headache of becoming a politician. I could see him in an executive or advisory role within the sanctioning body some day, but I don't think you'll ever see any commercials asking you to "Vote for Jeff!"

4. **Dale Earnhardt Jr.** Given his last name and his huge fan base, Earnhardt could potentially surprise people if he ever ran for office. Of course, let's not forget how overwhelmingly Petty was handed his hat to him by voters. Earnhardt may have been NASCAR's most popular driver for the last seven years and counting but that doesn't mean he knows anything about fiscal responsibility, social programs, education, or transportation in North Carolina, his home state.

3. **Michael Waltrip.** This may be a surprise pick, given that Waltrip likes to play the comedic foil role both as a driver and as a TV personality. But his outgoing ways and corny, down-home personality belie a very savvy, intelligent, and cunning businessman off the track. These attributes might be attractive enough to earn him a lot of votes. He'd keep whatever governing body he was elected to in stitches, that's for sure.

2. **Kyle Petty.** One of the most balanced, thought-provoking, opinionated drivers in the sport, Petty has a knack for seeing both sides of a story and, like most politicians, typically finds a middle ground from which to give his own views on the subject. He's very friendly, is a PR genius, has the Petty name going for him, and was the founder and chairman of Victory Junction Gang Camp, a

facility that helps ill and destitute children find medical treatment or become involved in social activities that otherwise might not be available to them. Despite his father's political defeat in 1996, Kyle is different enough in his views that he would probably make great sense to voters. If he catches a break or two, he could be one of the first ponytailed politicians in the world—that is, unless the voters demand that he cut it before he earns their votes.

1. **Jeff Burton.** He is already known as The Senator in the sport for his measured responses and his deep thinking on serious issues like unemployment, national security, medical coverage, and education. Ask Burton a question about anything, and you are guaranteed to get a very philosophical, intelligent, and well-thought-out answer. He's already said that he'd consider running for office in either North Carolina or his native Virginia. Given that he'll be forty-five years old in a couple of years and that his retired older brother Ward has increasingly become an environmental and animal-rights activist, don't be surprised if you see younger brother Jeff forming an ad hoc committee to gauge voter interest and determine whether he has a chance of winning an election. I don't know about you, but I'd vote for him, provided he was the best candidate available for the job. I kind of like the ring of, "The chair recognizes the fast-moving senator from the great state of Virginia [or North Carolina], former NASCAR driver Jeff Burton."

# Does NASCAR Really Need Road Course Races?

I'm really torn on this one. On the one hand, I love Infineon Raceway in Sonoma, California. Its wide expanse and incredible views make it one of the country's most scenic and challenging road courses in racing today. On the other hand, I am not a big fan of the serpentine road course on the Sprint Cup circuit, Watkins Glen International in upstate New York.

I understand why people who live near Sonoma or Watkins Glen would like to keep their respective Cup races. It's probably the only chance many of them get each year to see their favorite drivers up close. It also helps the local economy, because millions of dollars are spent at local hotels, restaurants, and other businesses.

But the whole road course concept goes so much against the grain of modern-day NASCAR. When stock car racing is mentioned, most people invariably think of places like Daytona, Bristol, or Texas—that is, oval or tri-oval superspeedways or short tracks.

I've never met anyone who said they first think of Infineon or Watkins Glen when asked about NASCAR. Granted, NASCAR's redneck roots required drivers to know how to navigate tight, twisting mountain or country roads. That's one of the reasons for road courses on the schedule. But does anyone get as excited about a road course race as a race on an oval track like Daytona, Bristol, Talladega, Las Vegas, or Texas?

Road courses will probably remain with us for at least the immediate future, because the two biggest companies in NASCAR each own one. International Speedway Corporation owns Watkins Glen, and Speedway Motorsports Inc. owns Infineon (formerly known, and still often referred to by many, as Sears Point Raceway).

In my opinion, racing on a road course is a gimmick-type race. There are lots of veggies and fruit but very little meat in those kinds of races. Passing is virtually nonexistent, the drivers have a tendency to want to get in and out of each place as quickly as possible (proving how much they despise road course racing), and you typically see only two or three turns at most from any one vantage point.

There's been talk of NASCAR finally giving in to the long-held hope by many fans for racing on a street course, much like Indy cars racing each spring on the streets of Long Beach, California. Perhaps this will happen by 2015, but there would have to be a gutsy mayor who would be willing to shut down a significant part of his city for close to a week (to include preparation) without ticking off his voting constituency. That's one reason the idea hasn't advanced very far.

So far, the only venues even remotely mentioned as potential street-course hosts for a Cup race are Toronto and Vancouver in Canada and Denver and Las Vegas in the United States. It has even been suggested to build a street circuit in New York City, perhaps around Times Square or in Central Park, but I just have to laugh. If New Yorkers went ballistic when Times Square was closed for several hours for the "Victory Lap" during the NASCAR Awards Week in 2005, 2006, and 2007, eventually bringing the event's cancellation in 2008, there's no way they're going to allow Broadway or Central Park West to be overtaken by forty-three loud, polluting vehicles.

There are also NASCAR fans who would like to see *more* road courses added to the schedule, including one during the ten-race Chase for the Sprint Cup. Various tracks have been suggested, including Mid-Ohio, Sebring (Florida), Lime Rock (Connecticut), Road America (Wisconsin) and Road Atlanta (Georgia).

I still don't get the allure that road course racing has, but I'm tolerant enough to let it continue as is, and I might even be amenable to adding one more track to the mix (my two picks would be Road America and Mid-Ohio). But that's it! No more after that, because if we start adding even more, and then start thinking about street courses, what's next? Races in big shopping mall parking lots? You have to draw the line somewhere, right?

## Should There Be a Second Stock Car Racing Organization to Compete with NASCAR?

Thanks to Kevin Schreur of Wyckoff, New Jersey, for this particular question. He suggests that a new stock car racing organization should be formed and named the American Stock Car Racing Association (ASCRA).

Ten years ago I would have said yes, because the time was right to form a competing sanctioning body. There was plenty of money to start a new organization, not to mention a seemingly endless supply of potential corporate sponsors. And much like the players who left the NFL to join the American Football League back in the 1960s or those who left the National Hockey League to join the rival World Hockey Association in the 1980s, several marquee drivers would have left NASCAR if the money had been right.

A competing organization might have had a chance at survival ten years ago, but it wouldn't today, particularly with the economy being the way it is. It would be nothing short of a sucker's bet if someone decided to start a rival organization today. A competing organization would attract some interest and attention from drivers, team owners, and sponsors, but in the long run, even if it did get off the ground, it would only serve to weaken stock car racing as we know it, both in NASCAR and in the ASCRA that Kevin proposes.

Octogenarian Bruton Smith, chairman of the board of Speedway Motorsports Inc. (SMI)—the chief rival to NASCAR's speedway arm, International Speedway Corporation (ISC)—threatened several times over the years to form a new organization built around SMI's tracks. But that was mainly talk and hyperbole so that Smith could ultimately get what he wanted from NASCAR whenever he threatened it.

Big threats often push NASCAR to act on something when it wouldn't do so otherwise. And given that both SMI and ISC are publicly traded companies, neither company would want to alienate its stockholders. ISC shareholders wouldn't want a rival stealing away "their" top talent and sponsors, thus devaluing their stock and its worth. Nor would SMI shareholders want to see hundreds of millions of dollars in company funds allocated to startup costs for a new sanctioning body that would have at best a fifty-fifty chance of succeeding in the long run.

So ISC and SMI have achieved a fairly peaceful coexistence. They've even become partners in several joint ventures, most notably Motorsports Authentics, the main producer and marketer of licensed fan souvenirs and collectibles such as diecast cars, clothing, baseball caps, and other items emblazoned with the name of a fan's favorite driver or team.

One other very important reason that SMI or any other ownership group never took on NASCAR head-to-head was the fallout in the open-wheel racing world in 1996 that resulted in the split between CART and the upstart Indy Racing League (IRL).

Tony George, then president of Indianapolis Motor Speedway and the IRL founder, predicted that his new organization would not only take its signature Indianapolis 500 to new heights, it would also quickly overtake CART in terms of popularity and attention. Unfortunately, neither happened. In fact, the 500 suffered through some of its most difficult years immediately after the split. Likewise for CART, which plummeted in popularity and attention like an out-of-control elevator dropping a hundred stories. CART needed the 500 but didn't have it, and the IRL needed CART but couldn't get it, either.

By the early part of the twenty-first century, some CART owners decided to cross the invisible picket line that had sprung up and rejoin the Indianapolis 500. After all, how can you own some of the most powerful and competitive teams in Indy car racing and not have them compete at the biggest race in the world?

Some holdouts remained, but as CART segued into the Champ Car Series, both it and the IRL continued to see deterioration to the point where a reunification of both groups wasn't just practical, it was downright necessary, lest open-wheel racing die a very painful death.

Bruton Smith, the late Bill France Jr., and subsequently Brian France, all saw what happened between CART and Indy and essentially agreed that they were better off with each other than going their separate ways. The union was born more out of necessity than desire, however.

It could still happen if the economy substantially picks up, if credit markets open up, and if someone with very deep pockets and enough ego and determination believes that he can outdo NASCAR with a rival group.

Then we would see what might have been a decade ago—and what has led to so many other start-ups falling by the wayside: bidding wars for talent, fights for sponsors, and a tug-of-war for fans. Sooner or later, someone is going to fall by the wayside—most likely the start-up, unless its original motive was to simply cause enough conflict and drama to bring about a merger that would line someone's pockets quite handsomely in the long run.

There are a lot of things right with NASCAR, but there are also enough things wrong that if someone really believes he can do things better, he is sure as hell going to try. But unless he can put a more compelling and more exciting product on the racetrack, the odds of survival are essentially slim to none. Otherwise, we would already be seeing four or five rivals to NASCAR operating today.

# If NASCAR Were to Host a Dirt Race, Which Cup Driver Would Be Best Suited for It?

The next question comes to us from Joe Neal of Ukiah, California:

> With the demise of the long schedules in the 1960s to the current 36-race season, one change NASCAR made was to eliminate dirt tracks from the schedule. If NASCAR brought back one race per season to run on dirt, which driver would be the best suited for dirt racing?

Oh, Joe, that's a tough question to answer, not because I can't, but because there are so many potential candidates to fill that role. Virtually every current Cup driver came up through the short-track racing ranks, but that's where the distinction ends, for many of them. Kevin Harvick, for instance, tore up asphalt racetracks before he made it to Cup stardom, but he had never raced on a dirt track until competing in Tony Stewart's Prelude to the Dream all-star race at Eldora (Ohio) Speedway in 2005.

Harvick was so hesitant about racing on dirt that he actually was tutored before the event that year and the next, then he went for remedial dirt-racing tutoring at North Georgia Speedway in Chatsworth on the morning of the 2006 Prelude before flying to Eldora. Stewart's high-profile exhibition race was postponed that night, however, when the track condition was ruled unraceable due to five hours of rain earlier in the day.

Alright, let's get to the meat of your question, Joe. There are any number of drivers that have considerable dirt under their fingernails . . . err,

I mean, experience racing on dirt tracks. The list of potential dirt track drivers is a virtual Who's Who of Sprint Cup racing: Jeff Gordon, Tony Stewart, Kasey Kahne, Greg Biffle, Carl Edwards, Denny Hamlin, Ryan Newman, Kurt Busch, Dave Blaney, Bill Elliott, and Clint Bowyer.

Before they became NASCAR superstars, Gordon and Stewart were superstars on dirt in sprint and midget cars; both won several national championships. Blaney also cut his racing teeth on sprint car racing on dirt tracks across the country before he jumped to NASCAR.

Kahne and Biffle both logged extensive time on dirt tracks in the greater Pacific Northwest. Newman, Edwards, and Bowyer were terrors on numerous dirt tracks in the Midwest. Kurt Busch grew up on the old Las Vegas Speedway "bull ring" dirt track (the predecessor to what is now Las Vegas Motor Speedway), and Hamlin competed in several dirt-track events up and down the eastern seaboard.

Because each of those drivers logged time on dirt in various parts of the country, it's hard to pick who would be the best on a winner-take-all dirt event (Tony Stewart's Prelude to the Dream notwithstanding), but I'll give it a try. Here's how I rank 'em, from tenth to best (along with one honorable mention):

HONORABLE MENTION: **Bill Elliott.** Awesome Bill from Dawsonville spent lots of time driving on the red dirt of his native Georgia early in his racing career before he became a Cup superstar and a champion in 1988. I would have included Elliott in the top ten, but given that he's racing on only a part-time schedule and is past fifty years old, I think many of us (including Bill himself) would agree that he's not quite the driver on dirt or paved racetracks that he was in his teens and early twenties. Still, I want to recognize him in this section because when he *was* racing on dirt, he was one of the best in the game.

10. **Kurt Busch.** The elder Busch brother cut many of his racing teeth on the old Las Vegas Speedway half-mile dirt "bull ring" before he went on to NASCAR stardom. Younger brother Kyle attended races there and eventually competed in some, but older sibling Kurt definitely has the edge here, probably the only edge he has over Kyle.

9. **Denny Hamlin.** Hamlin did a lot of dirt track racing early in his career, but it was primarily in a go-cart. However, he did do some dirt trackin' in regular race cars, as well.

8. **Dave Blaney.** Blaney left the sprint-car world at the height of his success and popularity to go NASCAR racing. Some thought that move was a mistake, because Blaney has never come close, driving a Sprint Cup race car, to the success he had on short tracks and on dirt in a sprint car.

7. **Carl Edwards.** Perhaps the most naturally talented driver on the Sprint Cup circuit, Edwards spent lots of time on dirt tracks in and around his Columbia, Missouri, home.

6. **Ryan Newman.** This Indiana native followed in the footsteps of his fellow Hoosiers, Jeff Gordon and Tony Stewart. It was his interest in the inner workings of a race car, especially on dirt, that led Newman to get a degree from Purdue University in vehicular structure engineering.

5. **Greg Biffle.** "The Biff" is much like Stewart: he'll readily race anything, anywhere, anytime. That includes dirt. Not only was he raised on dirt track racing around his Washington state home, he enjoys competing in several dirt track events during his limited time away from the grueling thirty-six-race Cup schedule.

4. **Kasey Kahne.** Like Biffle, Kahne is a native of Washington state and spent many a night racing on dirt tracks in the Pacific Northwest. Although he has achieved stardom in pavement racing, Kahne has said many times during his career that he's happiest racing on dirt tracks.

3. **Clint Bowyer.** This Emporia, Kansas, native was so good on dirt tracks that his former competitors were glad to see him go on to NASCAR stardom, because they were tired of him always beating them on dirt.

2. **Jeff Gordon.** I'll never forget Gordon's hesitation to return to the dirt when he finally agreed to accept Stewart's offer to race at Eldora in 2008. It had been sixteen years since Gordon had competed on dirt, but it took only a few short laps before he looked the way he did in his prime as a dirt track superstar. "It's just like riding a bike; you never forget it, I guess," Gordon told

me after that race. Unfortunately, when it came time for the main event that night, Gordon finished a dismal 14th out of twenty-five.

1. **Tony Stewart.** "Smoke," as Stewart is known, will race pretty much anything, from a forklift to an ATV to a sprint car and all the way up to a Sprint Cup car. What else would you expect from a guy who grew up on dirt tracks around his native Columbus, Indiana, owns several sprint-car and midget teams, and still competes in a number of dirt events during the year (including the annual January indoor dirt fest, the Chili Bowl, in Tulsa, Oklahoma)? Dollar for dollar and head-to-head, Stewart unquestionably is the best dirt track racer in NASCAR today, even if the circuit as a whole doesn't race on dirt.

# Will Anyone Ever Top Ricky Rudd's "Ironman" Record?

When it comes to NASCAR records being broken, I never say never—except maybe for Richard Petty's fairly untouchable mark of 200 career wins and 1,184 career starts. There's one other mark that I would also say is fairly untouchable, that of Ricky Rudd's "Ironman" mark of 788 consecutive race starts.

From the Winston Western 500 at Riverside, California, on January 11, 1981, through the Ford 400 at Homestead, Florida, on November 20, 2005, Rudd never missed a green starting flag in a Winston Cup or Nextel Cup race. That's a quarter of a century of not one missed start. (The prior "Ironman" mark was held by Terry Labonte, who started 655 consecutive races before there was a break in service.)

Rudd's incredible streak of endurance and perseverance ended not from illness or an injury-causing wreck—at least, not at first. Rather, in 2005 he simply walked away. Once the season was over, Rudd's career seemed to be over. He wanted to spend more time with his family and "do all the things I haven't been able to do since I got into racing in my teens," he said. He stopped of his own volition and on his own terms, leaving a legacy and setting a record that would be extremely difficult for anyone to equal, let alone surpass.

Actually, Rudd only "semiretired." At one point in 2006, Rudd was called on to stand by to replace an injured Tony Stewart in the driver's seat of the No. 20 Home Depot Chevrolet. Stewart had been mildly hurt in the Nextel All-Star Race in Charlotte in mid-May, then he reinjured his back and shoulder more seriously the following week in another crash at Charlotte during the Coca-Cola 600.

There was concern that Stewart could not run a full race with his injuries. With the next race at Dover, Rudd was asked—some say implored—by team owner Joe Gibbs to come out of his self-imposed retirement to sit on the sidelines and be ready to hop into Stewart's car, if necessary. It turned out that Rudd was never needed; Stewart persevered, albeit in tremendous pain.

Rudd then "unretired" to join his former boss, team owner Robert Yates, for one final season at Robert Yates Racing in 2007. Rudd started the first twenty-five races before he suffered shoulder, back, and rib injuries in a wreck at the California Speedway (now the Auto Club Speedway of Southern California).

NASCAR only recognizes consecutive starts from one season to the next. It does not allow a driver to take a year off and then resume the consecutive starts streak. So, even though Rudd's "official" streak ended at 788, he actually started 813 races before he retired; he just took time off before climbing into the car for the last 25 races.

It's possible that someone could beat Rudd's consecutive record of 788, but it's highly improbable. If NASCAR were to continue having a thirty-six-race schedule for the next twenty years, that would add up to 720 races, which is still 68 short of Rudd's mark. About the only full-time driver today who is still young enough to potentially come close to Rudd's record would be twenty-four-year-old Kyle Busch. The younger Busch brother comes into the 2010 season with 180 consecutive Sprint Cup starts.

For Busch to tie Rudd's record, he would have to extend his current streak by 608 starts. Based on NASCAR's current thirty-six-race schedule, this means that Busch would need to race for nearly seventeen more seasons, without missing a start, to draw even with Rudd. Busch would be forty-one years old at that time. Can he stay injury-free till then? Will he want to continue racing for another seventeen years?

Besides Busch, there are really very few drivers who are likely to catch Rudd. You could make a case for Busch's teammate Joey Logano, who won't even turn twenty-one until 2011, but he'd have to race nearly twenty-one more years to break the record.

Here's the current active "Ironman" list heading into 2010:

1. **Jeff Gordon.** At thirty-eight years old, with 581 consecutive starts coming into 2010, he would have to race nearly six more seasons to break Rudd's record. Gordon will likely retire before that, so as they say in New York, "Fuhgeddaboudit."
2. **Bobby Labonte.** At forty-five years old, with 580 consecutive starts entering 2010, he would also have to race nearly six more seasons to break Rudd's mark. It ain't gonna happen.
3. **Jeff Burton.** At forty-two years old, with 484 consecutive starts at the end of 2009, he would have to race nearly eight and a half more seasons to eclipse Rudd's mark. No way.
4. **Tony Stewart.** At thirty-nine years old, with 392 consecutive starts entering 2010, he would have to race another eleven seasons. Don't even think about it.
5. **Dale Earnhardt Jr.** At thirty-five years old, with 359 consecutive starts through 2009, he would have to race nearly another twelve years. Yeah, right.

Multiseason champion Jimmie Johnson came into the 2010 season with 288 consecutive starts (tied with Ryan Newman, who is thirty-two years old). At thirty-four years old, Johnson would have to start 500 more consecutive races, which would take him nearly fourteen seasons of thirty-six races to complete. He would be forty-eight years old by then.

It's probably not worth it for guys like Johnson to keep racing to that age just to break a record, even one as lofty and prestigious as Rudd's. So unless NASCAR suddenly decides to expand the schedule from thirty-six races to fifty or more races per season, it's a good bet that Rudd's mark is fairly safe for a long time.

# Who Should Have Been in the First NASCAR Hall of Fame Induction Class?

I'm giving a special acknowledgment to the editor of this book, Stephen Power, and to loyal reader Helen Newman of Dayton, Nevada  (but originally of Christchurch, New Zealand). Both had the NASCAR Hall of Fame on their minds. Stephen asked, "Who should have been the five inaugural members of the Hall of Fame?" His picks were Richard Petty, Dale Earnhardt, Bill France Sr., Cale Yarborough, and Benny Parsons. Helen stated, "The first 25 [nominees: are they] right or did the [selection committee] get it wrong? I am miffed Harry Gant isn't in there."

First, to Stephen: I agree with three of your picks. My top five picks for the first Hall of Fame induction class are NASCAR founder Bill France Sr., Bill France Jr., Richard Petty, Dale Earnhardt Sr., and David Pearson. I disagree about Benny Parsons.

Benny was a great racer and broadcaster, and, most important, he was a gentleman. But I'd be willing to bet that Benny himself would have said there were other more deserving nominees for the Hall of Fame's inaugural class. Pearson definitely deserved to be part of it, given all the success he had in his mostly part-time career in NASCAR. Unfortunately, Pearson didn't make it when the first class was announced in October 2009. I was correct on four of my picks, but Pearson was overtaken in the balloting by veteran driver and team owner Junior Johnson. That said, I expect Pearson to be selected for induction into the 2011 class.

Okay, Helen, now it's your turn. Here are the first twenty-five nominees:

- **Bobby Allison,** the 1983 NASCAR Winston Cup Series champion and the winner of 84 races
- **Buck Baker,** the first driver to win consecutive NASCAR Grand National championships

- **Red Byron**, the first NASCAR Grand National champion, in 1949
- **Richard Childress**, an eleven-time car owner champion in NASCAR's three national series
- **Dale Earnhardt Sr.**, who won a record-tying seven NASCAR Winston Cup championships
- **Richie Evans**, a nine-time NASCAR Modified champion
- **Tim Flock**, a two-time NASCAR Grand National champion
- **Bill France Jr.**, NASCAR's president, chairman, and CEO, 1972–2003
- **Bill France Sr.**, NASCAR's founder and first president, 1948–1972
- **Rick Hendrick**, an eleven-time car owner champion in NASCAR's three national series
- **Ned Jarrett**, a two-time NASCAR Grand National champion
- **Junior Johnson**, who had 50 wins as a driver, 132 wins as an owner, and six championships as an owner
- **Bud Moore**, who had 63 wins and two NASCAR Grand National titles as a car owner
- **Raymond Parks**, NASCAR's first champion car owner
- **Benny Parsons**, the 1973 NASCAR Winston Cup champion
- **David Pearson**, who had 105 victories and three NASCAR Grand National championships
- **Lee Petty**, the winner of the first Daytona 500 and the first three-time Grand National series champion
- **Richard Petty**, who had 200 wins and seven NASCAR Grand National (three Grand National, four Winston Cup) titles—both records
- **Fireball Roberts**, who won 33 NASCAR Grand National races, including the 1962 Daytona 500
- **Herb Thomas**, the first two-time NASCAR Grand National champion, in 1951 and 1953
- **Curtis Turner**, the first to win the Daytona 500, the Southern 500, and the Coca-Cola 600 in the same year
- **Darrell Waltrip**, the winner of 84 races and three NASCAR Winston Cup championships
- **Joe Weatherly**, a two-time NASCAR Grand National champion
- **Glen Wood**, who as a driver laid the foundation for the Wood Brothers' future success

- **Cale Yarborough**, the winner of three consecutive NASCAR Winston Cup titles, 1976–1978

This is, without question, the crème de la crème of NASCAR. As for Harry Gant, he was a great driver in his own right, but his accomplishments in his racing career were nowhere near those of the folks listed here. However, don't be surprised if Harry is eventually chosen for the Hall. It may not be for several years, but I think that you'll ultimately see him among the enshrined and honored.

# Acknowledgments

I'm a writer. I make my living with words. But right now, I'm at a great loss to come up with just the right thing to say to those who have meant so much to me in my life.

Simply saying thanks just doesn't seem to be enough to express the appreciation or pay back the patience, the giving, the understanding, and the love that those closest to me have shown for so many years—particularly during the difficult process of writing a book like *Trading Paint*.

I know it may sound like a cliché, but writing this book has truly been a labor of love: lots of labor that reflects my love for NASCAR and stock car racing. It has also been a lengthy—my editor will probably say *way* too lengthy—process.

I want to recognize a number of individuals who were either direct or indirect influences on and inspirations for my career, as well as those who offered invaluable help in the preparation and writing of this book.

This book couldn't have been written without the help, direction, and friendship I've received over the years—even if they didn't always agree with what I wrote—from NASCAR's public relations staff, particularly the incomparable Jim Hunter. Mike Forde was especially helpful with statistics and records.

Equally as valuable in the preparation of and inspiration for this book was a guy I like to call simply the Answer Man, official NASCAR historian Buz McKim of the NASCAR Hall of Fame and Museum.

Thanks to all the team, racetrack, and auto manufacturing public relations personnel, who have been great to work with throughout the years. Their assistance has been invaluable and has made a hard job a bit easier to do.

Special thanks to Jon Baum (my editor for eight years, first at ESPN .com and then at Yahoo.com), Sam Silverstein (who hired me at Yahoo!), John Marvel (the former executive editor of ESPN.com who hired me to cover NASCAR in 2001), Gene Policinski (former sports editor at *USA Today* and one of my mentors), Daniel Norwood and Steve Cohen of Sirius Radio, and Bob Carmichael (the man who gave a gangly, geeky fifteen-year-old his start in journalism more than thirty-seven years ago at the now defunct weekly *Calumet Index* in Chicago).

Last, but certainly not least—for if not for them, this book would never have come to fruition—my agent, Frank Scatoni, for his outstanding work (and Joblike patience with me); my editor at John Wiley & Sons, Stephen S. Power (you are the man!), who should get a medal and a big raise for his patience, fortitude, and professionalism in dealing with me; outstanding senior production editor Rachel Meyers, who made everything look great; and publisher Kitt Allen and her boyfriend, Jim Hill, both great NASCAR fans who not only were 110 percent behind this book but also offered some outstanding suggestions and ideas that made *Trading Paint* that much better in the long run.

Most important, thanks to all the readers and listeners who have read my columns and listened to me on the air throughout the years, as well as those who have given so freely of their time to send me e-mails or call in. I'm humbled that you've followed my work for so long, and I have come to consider many of you as so much more than just another reader or listener. You're like extensions of my family, and I'm honored to call you friends, whether or not I know you personally.

# A Final Note

I hope you've enjoyed *Trading Paint: 101 Great NASCAR Debates*.

I realize you have a lot of options in how to spend your money, particularly in the rough economic times that we've all gone through in the last couple of years. I'm not only grateful but also humbled that you chose to purchase and read this book.

And if you choose to disagree with some of my answers, I won't be offended. I truly appreciate other viewpoints. It'd be a pretty boring world if we all agreed on everything.

I welcome any feedback you may have about this book, as well as ideas and suggestions for a possible sequel. You can reach me at JerryBonkowski@gmail.com. Please don't hesitate to send me any ideas, even if you think they're too trivial or out in left field. You'd be surprised how many self-professed "bad" ideas have been offered to me throughout the years that have proven to be outstanding ideas in the long run.

Finally, though this book has now come to an end, I'll keep the debating going on my two Web sites: JerryBonkowski.com and Racing Debates.com. I look forward to continuing trading paint with you.

Thanks again, everyone. Catch you soon at the track!

# INDEX

Printed in the USA
CPSIA information can be obtained
at www.ICGtesting.com
JSHW012013140824
68134JS00025B/2399

9 780470 278758